TRADITION AND INNOVATION IN ENGLISH RETAILING, 1700 TO 1850

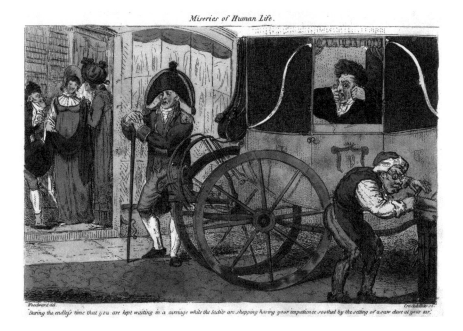

Miseries of Human Life, 'During the endless time that you are kept waiting in a carriage ... ', *c.* 1808

Source: Derbyshire Record Office: Woodward Collection of Prints and Drawings (D5459/3/20/6). Reproduced by permission of Derby Local Studies Library.

Tradition and Innovation in English Retailing, 1700 to 1850
Narratives of Consumption

IAN MITCHELL
University of Wolverhampton, UK

Routledge
Taylor & Francis Group

LONDON AND NEW YORK

First published 2014 by Ashgate Publishing

2 Park Square, Milton Park, Abingdon, Oxon OX14 4RN
711 Third Avenue, New York, NY 10017, USA

Routledge is an imprint of the Taylor & Francis Group, an informa business

First issued in paperback 2016

British Library Cataloguing in Publication Data
A catalogue record for this book is available from the British Library

The Library of Congress has cataloged the printed edition as follows:
Mitchell, S. Ian.
  Tradition and innovation in English retailing, 1700 to 1850 : narratives of consumption / by Ian Mitchell.
    pages cm. – (The history of retailing and consumption)
  Includes bibliographical references and index.
  ISBN 978-1-4094-4320-9 (hardcover)
1. Retail trade – Great Britain – History – 18th century. 2. Retail trade – Great Britain – History – 19th century. 3. Merchants – Great Britain – History. 4. Stores, Retail--Great Britain--History. I. Title.
  HF5429.6.G7M58 2013
  381'.10094209032--dc23

2013016004

ISBN 978-1-4094-4320-9 (hbk)
ISBN 978-1-138-24542-6 (pbk)

Contents

The History of Retailing and Consumption
General Editor's Preface

It is increasingly recognized that retail systems and changes in the patterns of consumption play crucial roles in the development and societal structure of economies. Such recognition has led to renewed interest in the changing nature of retail distribution and the rise of consumer society from a wide range of academic disciplines. The aim of this multidisciplinary series is to provide a forum of publications that explore the history of retailing and consumption.

Gareth Shaw, University of Exeter, UK

List of Figures

List of Tables

List of Abbreviations

BPP	British Parliamentary Papers
CALS	Cheshire Archives and Local Studies, Chester
DRO	Derbyshire Record Office, Matlock
NA	National Archives, Kew
SRO	Staffordshire Record Office, Stafford
WYAS	West Yorkshire Archive Service

Preface

This book has been some 40 years in the making. I first became interested in retail history when researching for my DPhil in the 1970s. It soon became apparent that not only was this then a neglected topic, but that eighteenth-century shops were both more widespread and more sophisticated than had usually been supposed. Opportunities for further serious research and writing were curtailed by a career firstly in the Civil Service and then as a Church of England minister. During those years historians paid increasing attention to shops, though less so to markets; and the history of consumption became a fashionable area of study. In the last decade, my involvement with the Centre for the History of Retailing and Distribution (CHORD) at Wolverhampton University has both provided the incentive to pursue my long-standing fascination with retail and consumption history and the practical resources needed to do so.

Chapters 8 and 9 include parts of two articles that have already appeared in print: 'Innovation in Non-Food Retailing in the Early Nineteenth Century: The Curious Case of the Bazaar', *Business History*, 52/6 (2010): 875–91 which is reprinted by permission of Taylor & Francis Ltd (http://www.tandf.co.uk/journals); and 'Supplying the Masses: Retailing and Town Governance in Macclesfield, Stockport and Birkenhead, 1780–1860', *Urban History*, 38/2 (2011): 256–75, copyright © Cambridge University Press and reprinted with permission. The Appendix includes material from the Mass Observation Archive which is reproduced with permission of Curtis Brown Group Ltd, London on behalf of the Trustees of the Mass Observation Archive and is copyright © The Trustees of the Mass Observation Archive.

Archival research for the sections on Browns of Chester (Appendix) and Proto Department Stores (Chapter 7) was made possible by a grant from the Pasold Research Fund for which I am very grateful.

Many people have made this book possible. Archivists and librarians at the numerous places listed in the bibliography have been unfailingly helpful. I have benefited from informal discussions with University of Wolverhampton colleagues as well as from participation in CHORD conferences and workshops. John Benson and Laura Ugolini convinced me to consider writing a book. Nancy Cox has offered many wise words in conversations over several years as well as offering very helpful comments and suggestions on the initial draft of this book. Jon Stobart at Northampton University has encouraged me to stay in touch with the academic community both inside and beyond the UK and kindly read this book in draft. Suggestions from Gareth Shaw helped me to provide a clearer focus to the argument I put forward here. My wife, Mary, has put up with my obsession with retailing and consumption for the whole of our married life and tolerated with good humour the hours spent in record offices or at the computer keyboard. This book would not have been written without her support.

Introduction

In September 1833, the *Bury and Norwich Post, and East Anglian* invited those planning to attend the musical festival in Norwich also to visit the Royal Norfolk and Norwich Bazaar. As well as being able to purchase a variety of textiles, they would find books, jewellery, hardware and many other items on sale in the gallery, together with an exhibition of pictures for sale.[1] The Bazaar, which opened in 1831, was operated on similar principles to those which had become so popular in London since the mid 1810s: shops and counters were let to traders who had to demonstrate their respectability and abide by strict rules.[2] Bazaars were fashionable, though not always very successful, in the first half of the nineteenth century. But should they be regarded as innovative, helping to pave the way for department stores? Or were they simply a variant on a very traditional method of retailing – the market – occupied, as one detractor said, by a motley group of 'here today, gone tomorrow' sellers?[3] Both views contained an element of truth. Early nineteenth-century bazaars illustrate the difficulty of fitting the actual practice of retailing in all its various shapes and sizes into a coherent theoretical model of retail development, or indeed into a tidy chronological pattern. Old and new existed side by side, not just in the same town or same street, but even in the same retail establishment.

It is hardly surprising therefore that historians have come to very different conclusions about retailing in England before 1850. Nearly 60 years ago in his pioneering study of the era of multiple shops, cooperatives and department stores, J.B. Jefferys argued that eighteenth- and early nineteenth-century retailing was relatively unsophisticated. He claimed that window displays were practically unknown except in a few shops in larger towns, that goods were often purchased in large quantities and on long credit and that haggling over price remained the norm. He also emphasized the importance of markets and itinerant retailers for working-class consumers, both in towns and the countryside. In his view developments during the period were mainly of degree, modification and shift of emphasis, not significant structural change.[4] Some 30 years later, Michael Winstanley, also writing from an essentially nineteenth-century perspective, suggested that while there was general agreement that the foundations of an increasingly complex

---

[1]   *Bury and Norwich Post, and East Anglian*, 11 September 1833.

[2]   Norfolk Record Office, Norfolk and Norwich Bazaar, SO 18/20, 29.

[3]   *An Appeal to the Public on the Subject of Bazaars* (London, 1816). See Chapter 7 for a fuller discussion of the significance of bazaars.

[4]   James B. Jefferys, *Retail Trading in Britain 1850–1950* (Cambridge: Cambridge University Press, 1954), pp. 4–5.

distributive sector were laid before the end of the eighteenth century, it remained an open question whether this should be viewed as a retail revolution or quite leisurely change.[5] Other historians have been bolder in their conclusions. Dorothy Davis writing in the 1960s argued that the seventeenth century was the decisive period when shops emerged as the normal places for consumers to spend large parts of their money.[6] The Muis had little doubt that fixed shops, including village shops, had by about the end of the eighteenth century effectively replaced more traditional modes of retailing such as markets and fairs.[7] Jon Stobart, in a series of books and articles, has provided substantial evidence for the expansion and transformation of fixed shop retailing in eighteenth century, particularly in the context of polite society. Luxury and semi-luxury retailing was widespread by the end of the century with shopkeepers making sophisticated use of display and advertising techniques.[8] Nancy Cox has explored just how retailers traded and related to their customers and to each other in the early modern period, revealing a high degree of sophistication in retailing.[9] But Stobart has also warned that 'It is all too easy to take a Whiggish view of the shop as modern and progressive, developing to inevitably eclipse traditional forms of retailing such as markets, fairs and pedlars'.[10] This warning needs to be heeded.

Visual representations of the outside of shops and of shopping streets are not all that common for the early modern period. Markets, fairs and itinerant traders were more often depicted.[11] The street scenes of Chester etched by George Batenham in the 1810s are therefore of particular interest. Some depict what were clearly high-class shops with bow windows and elaborate window displays. On the other hand, on Northgate Street a run of respectable-looking drapers, tea dealers and grocers terminates in a butcher's shop depicted with joints of meat shown hanging in open window spaces.

---

[5] Michael J. Winstanley, *The Shopkeeper's World 1830–1914* (Manchester: Manchester University Press, 1983), p. 2.

[6] Dorothy Davis, *A History of Shopping* (London: Routledge & Kegan Paul, 1966), p. 181.

[7] Hoh-Cheung Mui and Lorna H. Mui, *Shops and Shopkeeping in Eighteenth-Century England* (London: Routledge, 1989).

[8] Key works include Jon Stobart and Andrew Hann, 'Retailing Revolution in the Eighteenth Century? Evidence from North-West England', *Business History*, 46/2 (2004): 171–94; Jon Stobart, Andrew Hann and Victoria Morgan, *Spaces of Consumption: Leisure and Shopping in the English Town, c.1680–1830* (London: Routledge, 2007); Jon Stobart, *Spend, Spend, Spend: A History of Shopping* (Stroud: Tempus, 2008).

[9] Nancy Cox, *The Complete Tradesman: A Study of Retailing in Early Modern England* (Aldershot: Ashgate, 2000). See also Nancy Cox and Karin Dannehl, *Perceptions of Retailing in Early Modern England* (Aldershot: Ashgate, 2007).

[10] Stobart, Hann and Morgan, *Spaces of Consumption*, p. 15.

[11] Cox and Dannehl, *Perceptions*, ch. 2.

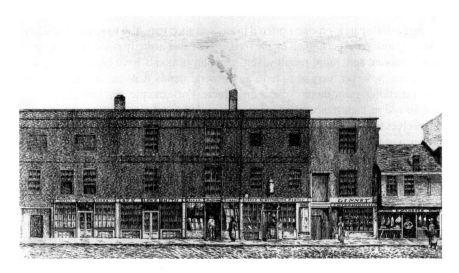

Figure I.1   Part of the east side of Northgate Street, Chester

Source: *Ancient Chester: A Series of Illustrations of the Streets of this Old City Drawn by G. and W. Batenham and J Musgrove. With descriptions by T. Hughes* (London and Manchester: H. Sotheran and Co., 1880). Reproduced by permission of Manchester Libraries, Information and Archives, Manchester City Council.

Similarly in the market place women are selling from baskets outside the premises of one of the city's leading booksellers.[12] None of this is surprising. But it should at least serve as a reminder that shopping in the early nineteenth century was not only a polite activity accompanied by gossip and flirtation in a mercer's or draper's shop, but was also about supplying basic needs in much less salubrious surroundings. Old and new were in close proximity and there was more life in the old ways than historians have sometimes suggested.

Does this mean, therefore, that it is impossible to offer any models or theories of retail change and development? With regard to change over the long term, the answer is surely no. The simple and elegant model proposed by Wild and Shaw remains a very useful tool. Retail systems have tended to evolve from periodic markets and fairs through craftsmen/retailers to retail specialization and finally large scale retail institutions, though no era has been totally dominated by any of these.[13] Put more generally, it can be said that transient forms of retailing have tended over time to give way to those situated in fixed locations; that the mix of production, processing and selling once typical of many shops has been replaced by a focus on retailing even if

---

[12]   George Batenham, *Panoramic Delineations of the Four Principal Streets of the City of Chester* (Chester: John Fletcher, 1816).

[13]   Gareth Shaw, 'The Study of Retail Development', in John Benson and Gareth Shaw (eds), *The Evolution of Retail Systems, c.1800–1914* (Leicester: Leicester University Press, 1992), pp. 1–14.

the range of disparate products offered in any one shop may also have increased; and that functions once performed by the retailer have increasingly passed to customers as self-service and, more recently, self-scanning of goods have become common. These are, however, very long term and general trends that can conceal changes that sometimes seem more cyclical than linear. For example, markets have ebbed and flowed in importance over the centuries and have had a tendency to reinvent themselves to cope with changing circumstances. The shift from long credit to ready money and fixed-price selling in the eighteenth century has generally been seen as an indicator of more modern forms of selling. Yet so also has been the extension of credit to more working-class consumers in the late nineteenth century and early twentieth.[14] Is the trade in second-hand goods to be viewed as essentially an element of traditional retailing liable to diminish in importance as consumers become more wealthy and able to purchase new goods? If so, then what of the growth of niche second-hand trades such as antiques in the nineteenth century or 'retro' items more recently?[15] General models of change need to be complemented by a careful reading of actual changes in specific places and at specific historical periods.

All of this raises questions about what initiates and drives changes in retailing and consumption. Specifically in the case of retailing, is change mainly driven by internal pressures or by changes in the external environment? One model of internally driven change is of low-cost, cut-price, narrow-margin retail forms trading up through improved customer service, enhanced display and better locations so that they become vulnerable to new cut-price entrants into the market. In due course these new entrants will tend to follow the same pathway. This 'wheel of retailing' has rarely been tested in the literature on retail history and it is at least arguable that it offers a partial explanation of some aspects of retail evolution in the eighteenth and nineteenth centuries. For example, bazaars tended to become more exclusive and high class over time and eventually struggled to compete against new entrants to retailing like department and multiple stores. In general, however, changes in the external environment are likely to have been much more important.[16] These include changes in levels of income and expenditure; changes in transport technology; changes in product technology; and growth in both total, and perhaps more importantly, urban population. In addition, retailing is influenced

---

[14]   On changing attitudes and access to credit see in particular Margot Finn, *The Character of Credit: Personal Debt in English Culture, 1740–1914* (Cambridge: Cambridge University Press, 2003).

[15]   Nicky Gregson and Louise Crewe, *Second-Hand Cultures* (Oxford: Berg, 2003) explores the meanings of second-hand consumption while Jon Stobart and Ilja van Damme (eds), *Modernity and the Second-Hand Trade: European Consumption Cultures and Practices, 1700–1900* (Basingstoke: Palgrave Macmillan, 2010) offers historical perspective.

[16]   Andrew Alexander and Simon Phillips, '"Fair Play for the Small Man": Perspectives on the Contribution of the Independent Shopkeeper 1939 – c.1945', *Business History*, 48/1 (2006): 69–89, concludes that external factors were of prime importance in explaining changes in twentieth century small retailing.

by the broad social, political and cultural context. Existing retailers may seek to use political influence or legal process to impede change.[17] On the other hand, changing attitudes to the possession and use of goods can stimulate growth and change in the retail sector even against a background of economic stagnation.[18]

What then were the key factors influencing retail change in England in the period 1700–1850? Some of these are quite easy to identify. The population of England and Wales grew steadily in the first half of the eighteenth century from around 5.3 million to 6 million and then more rapidly reaching around 9 million by the end of the century and 16 million by the middle of the nineteenth century.[19] The distribution of population also changed. England's urban population was around 13 to 16 per cent of the total in 1700, rising slowly to 22 to 24 per cent in 1800 and then rapidly to 45 per cent in 1850.[20] Some towns grew in a spectacular fashion such as Birmingham from a population of 8,000 in 1700 to 183,000 in 1841, Leeds from 7,000 to 152,000, Liverpool from perhaps 6,000 to 286,000 and Manchester from 8,000 to 311,000.[21] Other industrializing towns like Derby, Nottingham, Leicester, Sheffield, Stockport, Preston and many more experienced similarly rapid growth. Not only were there many more people who needed to use markets and shops, but because more of them lived in towns and worked in factories they were increasingly dependent on buying, rather than growing or making, most of the items they needed to feed, clothe and house themselves. Even if nothing else had changed, these demographics were bound to have a major impact on retailing.

Other things had of course changed. Historians may be less cavalier than they were a generation or so ago about speaking of an 'industrial revolution' that transformed Britain's economy in the late eighteenth century and early nineteenth. But even if growth rates were not spectacular by modern standards and the most dramatic changes were concentrated in cotton textiles, many contemporaries still sensed that they were living in unusual times. There were changes to the landscape like the factories of the Derwent Valley, the forges of Coalbrookdale, the great manufacturing enterprises such as Matthew Boulton's in Birmingham or the canals being cut in many parts of the north and midlands. There were new products, particularly in ceramics, metalware and printed textiles, whether imported from Asia or increasingly home produced. There was the fascination with science and

[17]   Shaw, 'Study of Retail Development', pp. 6–9.

[18]   B. Blondé and I. van Damme, 'Retail Growth and Consumer Changes in a Declining Urban Economy: Antwerp (1650–1750)', *Economic History Review*, 63/3 (2010): 638–63, challenges the link between economic growth, urbanization and retail development and highlights the importance of changing material culture patterns in promoting retail growth at a time of economic decline.

[19]   Joel Mokyr, *The Enlightened Economy: Britain and the Industrial Revolution 1700–1850* (London: Penguin, 2009), p. 281.

[20]   Joyce M. Ellis, *The Georgian Town 1680–1840* (Basingstoke: Palgrave, 2001), p. 26. A town is defined as having over 5,000 inhabitants.

[21]   Ibid., pp. 148–9.

technology depicted by artists like Joseph Wright of Derby and exemplified in the Lunar Society. Faster road transport and the rapid growth of the provincial press meant that people were living in a country that perhaps seemed to be shrinking. Less visible but also important were advances in management and marketing. All of these tended to extend the market for goods and services with implications for retailing and for material culture. Equally more efficient retail systems could have a positive feedback into the economy as a whole.[22]

It is important, however, not to get too carried away. While it was true that qualitative change, incremental advances in technology and product innovation had an impact on the economy as a whole through transferable skills and the widening of markets, and that it would be wrong to draw too firm a distinction between 'innovative' and 'traditional' sectors of the economy, it was also the case that large parts of the economy were relatively unaffected by the changes sweeping through the textile and iron industries. Handicraft production remained important in the making of clothes and domestic furnishings. There were few changes in the construction industries. Moreover, the majority of the population experienced no significant improvement in real wages or living standards until towards the end of the period covered by this book. Working-class consumption per head seems not to have increased during the period generally regarded as the 'industrial revolution', though it may have done so in the first three-quarters of the eighteenth century. Middle-class consumption did, however, increase and there was probably growing income inequality in at least the earlier part of the industrial revolution.[23] But there is something of a puzzle here. There is ample qualitative evidence of a rapidly expanding world of goods from at least the late seventeenth century with widespread participation in material culture running ahead of the quantitative evidence on economic growth and real wages. Jan de Vries has offered a persuasive explanation of this. He suggests that north-west Europe and British North America experienced an 'industrious revolution' in the long eighteenth century (1660–1820) in which growing numbers of households reallocated their productive resources, most notably the way family members used their time. In particular households increased both their supply of market-oriented, money-earning activities and their demand for goods offered in the market. Individuals worked longer hours as wage-earners, had less time and scope for household self-provisioning and so spent more

---

[22]   The most comprehensive recent survey of British economic growth and the industrial revolution is Mokyr, *Enlightened Economy*. On new consumer goods and how they were made see Maxine Berg, *Luxury and Pleasure in Eighteenth-Century Britain* (Oxford: Oxford University Press, 2005). Jenny Uglow, *The Lunar Men: The Friends Who Made the Future 1730–1810* (London: Faber, 2002) looks at links between science, art and commerce. John Smail, *Merchants, Markets and Manufacture: The English Wool Textile Industry in the Eighteenth Century* (Basingstoke: Macmillan, 1999) is an important study of innovation in a more 'traditional' industry.

[23]   Mokyr, *Enlightened Economy*, ch. 18.

money in shops and markets.[24] There is evidence of increases in working hours in the long eighteenth century, even if sometimes as in the case of farm workers this had more to do with maintaining a basic standard of living than providing the means to purchase new consumer goods.[25] There may still be questions around the timing and extent of the 'industrious revolution' but its existence is consistent with the sort of changes in consumer behaviour and the growth of retailing from the mid seventeenth century that are now well established.

If it is hard to offer a generally agreed reading of economic change in England in the eighteenth century and first half of the nineteenth and of how this impacted on retailing and consumption, it is even harder to do so with regard to English society as a whole. Should, perhaps, 'enlightenment' be seen as the predominant narrative? It is certainly possible to argue a case for this. To do so means emphasizing features like rationality, Lockeian political philosophy, the popularization of science and technology, a growing interest in the motivations and behaviour of self-aware individuals and the declining influence of orthodox Christianity in the face of attacks from Deists and free-thinkers. All of these were in evidence in the period. But has such a reading focused too much on surface features, particularly in the middling and upper echelons of society, and ignored the realities of eighteenth-century life as experienced by most people? More conservative-minded historians have argued that England continued at least until the second quarter of the nineteenth century to be an essentially aristocratic and hierarchical society in which most people knew their place and were bound to each other in a network of obligation. They have stressed the danger of reading history backwards and thus placing too much emphasis on those aspects of politics and society that appear 'modern' to the contemporary reader. Such historians have also argued for the continued importance of traditional religious beliefs and practices, with rational religion seen as essentially a minority interest. There is substantial evidence that the beliefs and practices of the Church of England as well as those of a myriad of dissenting bodies (and to a lesser extent Roman Catholicism) affected many aspects of daily life. The rest of the conservative argument regarding eighteenth-century England is more controversial but still needs to be heard.[26]

---

[24] Jan de Vries, *The Industrious Revolution: Consumer Behaviour and the Household Economy, 1650 to the Present* (Cambridge: Cambridge University Press, 2008).

[25] R.C. Allen and J.L. Weisdorf, 'Was there an "Industrious Revolution" before the Industrial Revolution? An Empirical Exercise for England, *c.*1300–1830', *Economic History Review*, 64/3 (2011): 715–29.

[26] On enlightenment and rationality see Roy Porter, *Enlightenment: Britain and the Creation of the Modern World* (London: Allen Lane, 2001) and Roy Porter, *Flesh in the Age of Reason* (London: Allen Lane, 2003). The classic conservative work is J.C.D. Clark, *English Society 1688–1832* (Cambridge: Cambridge University Press 1985). On the need to take religion seriously see Jeremy Gregory, 'Transforming the "Age of Reason" into "An Age of Faiths"; or, Putting Religions and Beliefs (Back) into the Eighteenth Century', *Journal for Eighteenth-Century Studies*, 32/3 (2009): 287–305, and Carolyn Steedman,

The contradictions in English society in the period covered by this book were not confined to the realm of ideas but were also manifested in behaviour. Should it perhaps be characterized as an age of politeness and respectability? It is not difficult to find evidence for this in, for example, urban improvements, the creation of assembly rooms, walks and other places for polite company to gather; in the sociability of the coffee house and club; in learned societies and book clubs; in modes of domestic behaviour focused on the tea table; and in the blurring of the boundaries between leisure and shopping. On the other hand it was also an age in which the urban mob could make its presence felt both in political demonstrations and at times of food shortage and high prices. Such lower-class political activism did not just disturb the surface of polite society but increasingly through working-class associations offered a radical challenge to the political status quo. The French Revolution both encouraged some of these radical activists and provoked a patriotic backlash. There was a firm and even repressive response from the state, particularly in the late eighteenth century and early nineteenth. More generally, the growth of the fiscal-military state in the long period of intermittent warfare that characterized much of the period, and more especially in the era of the French Revolutionary and Napoleonic wars, had an impact on everyday life if only through the introduction of new taxes and the increased visibility of civil and military power.[27]

What, however, does all this have to do with retailing and consumption? A significant part of the answer lies in our understanding of material culture and the world of goods. Objects not only provide important clues to how societies and individuals understand themselves but also help shape their behaviour. Polite society expressed itself through items like ceramics, domestic furniture and books. Using objects appropriately was a declaration of social and cultural status. Using objects in a novel or risky way could change codes of behaviour and make a statement of individuality. Things were used to express political opinions, or to convey coded messages within a subversive grouping. The period covered by this book saw a very considerable increase in the number and variety of objects available, particularly to consumers of at least middling wealth and status. Interpreting these objects and the way they were used cannot be separated from

---

Master and Servant: Love and Labour in the English Industrial Age (Cambridge: Cambridge University Press, 2007). Clive D. Field, 'Counting Religion in England and Wales: The Long Eighteenth Century, *c.*1680–1840', *Journal of Ecclesiastical History*, 63/4 (2012): 693–720, is a bold attempt at quantifying religious affiliation.

[27]   Useful works here include Peter Borsay, *The English Urban Renaissance: Culture and Society in the Provincial Town 1660–1770* (Oxford: Oxford University Press, 1989); Peter Borsay, *A History of Leisure* (Basingstoke: Palgrave Macmillan, 2006); Helen Berry, 'Polite Consumption: Shopping in Eighteenth-Century England', *Transactions of the Royal Historical Society*, 12 (2002): 375–94; Woodruff D. Smith, *Consumption and the Making of Respectability 1600–1800* (London: Routledge, 2002); E.P. Thompson, *The Making of the English Working Class* (Harmondsworth: Penguin, 1968); and Martin Daunton, *State and Market in Victorian Britain: War, Welfare and Capitalism* (Woodbridge: Boydell Press, 2008).

some attempt to grapple with wider currents in society and culture. Moreover, objects were increasingly acquired through the market, even if inheritance and gifting remained important.[28] All this had implications for the growth of retailing and the need for more sophisticated promotional and sales techniques alongside more traditional shops and markets. A further part of the answer relates to the ways in which government, both central and local, could affect retailing. These included regulations around, for example, food-marketing and taxation policy.

Is it then possible to regard consumption and material culture as controlling narratives for the eighteenth century and first half of the nineteenth? Despite the best efforts of some historians,[29] the answer is surely no. The period was simply too complex and too full of contradictions to be characterized as the 'age of reason', the 'age of elegance' or anything else. Moreover, it is arguable that any such 'grand narrative' is liable to conceal and mislead as much as it explains and clarifies. But if a grand narrative is ruled out, then narrative(s) may still be a helpful way of proceeding. Historians tell stories and the best stories tend to be open-ended. They permit a variety of voices to be heard and recognize that there is a gap between what can be told (or indeed known) and an unreachable final explanation. The ends do not have to be tied up in a neat fashion.[30] There are clues here regarding how best to approach the world of buying and selling, acquiring and using in the eighteenth century and the first half of the nineteenth. There is no one story. Rather there the stories of, among others, the market traders, the producer-retailers, the smart shopkeepers and the backstreet provisions dealers, each with their own customers and each negotiating a world populated by local magistrates, tax collectors, local government officers and others who might help or hinder the business of buying and selling. The result is closer to *bricolage* than to a comprehensive model of retail evolution, but perhaps also closer to reality.

This is not to say that there are no firm foundations on which to start building. Recent research into the history of retailing and consumption has cleared a great deal of the ground and provided some generally agreed starting points. The first of these concerns the world of goods. While it may be anachronistic to speak of a 'consumer society' in the eighteenth century, and while it is true that both the

---

[28] General works here include Grant McCracken, *Culture and Consumption: New Approaches to the Symbolic Character of Consumer Goods and Activities* (Bloomington: Indiana University Press, 1988); Tim Dant, *Material Culture in the Social World* (Maidenhead: Open University Press, 2005); and Peter N. Stearns, *Consumerism in World History: The Global Transformation of Desire* (London: Routledge, 2001). On eighteenth-century consumption see John Brewer and Roy Porter (eds), *Consumption and the World of Goods* (London: Routledge, 1993) and Berg, *Luxury and Pleasure*.

[29] N. McKendick, J. Brewer and J.H. Plumb, *The Birth of a Consumer Society* (London: Hutchinson, 1982) remains a bold attempt at this.

[30] Stephen Prickett, *Narrative, Religion and Science: Fundamentalism versus Irony, 1700–1999* (Cambridge: Cambridge University Press, 2002) is helpful on narrative and post-modernism with its embrace of pluralism and suspicion of grand narratives.

sixteenth century and the late nineteenth can claim a 'consumer revolution', there is no doubt that both more consumer goods, and a much wider variety of them, were available to a wider range of people in the early nineteenth century than at the beginning of the eighteenth.[31] Secondly, there was a substantial increase in the total number of shops, in the number of places that had shops and in the variety of shops in all but the smallest towns in the period covered by this book. There were also bigger shops. Thirdly, retailers displayed an increasingly wide range of sophisticated techniques to attract customers. These included advertisements, trade cards and how goods were displayed within the shop. They were also able to target different parts of the potential market by focusing on, for example, price, credit availability, quality or customer service.[32] Finally, shopping was a skilled activity involving complex decision-making and a good understanding of prices and qualities. Being a skilled shopper had been an important attribute for the mistress of a household since at least the mid seventeenth century.[33]

All of the above is true, but it is not necessarily the whole story. The central argument of this book is that the evolution of retailing in the century and a half before 1850 was a more fractured and fragmented process than might be assumed from some of the literature. Buying and selling should be set in the context of tradition and deference, including institutions like local government and retail guilds, as well as novelty, rationality and politeness. Any discussion of the genesis of modern retailing also runs into terminological issues. In the eighteenth century 'modern' might simply mean contemporary, or indeed be used to convey an unfavourable comparison with what went before. It was not until the nineteenth century that it tended mean improved or efficient.[34] In this book features such as fixed prices, ready money sales, the use of advertising and window displays, the ability of customers to browse and a less deferential relationship between customer and retailer are regarded as distinguishing 'modern' from more 'traditional' retailing. 'Modernity' is another contested term. It is used in this book to refer to post-enlightenment society characterized by rationality, secularism and a strong emphasis on individual autonomy. I also draw a distinction between adaptation and evolutionary change on the one hand and more radical innovation implying

---

[31]   McCracken, *Culture and Consumption*, ch. 1, discusses these three pivotal eras in the history of consumption.

[32]   Stobart and Hann, 'Retailing Revolution in the Eighteenth Century', offers a useful summary of the evidence. On advertising see Jon Stobart, 'Selling (through) Politeness: Advertising Provincial Shops in Eighteenth-Century England', *Cultural and Social History*, 5/3 (2008): 309–28.

[33]   Claire Walsh, 'Shopping at First Hand? Mistresses, Servants and Shopping for the Household in Early Modern England', in David Hussey and Margaret Ponsonby (eds), *Buying for the Home: Shopping for the Domestic from the Seventeenth Century to the Present* (Aldershot: Ashgate, 2008), pp. 13–26.

[34]   Raymond Williams, *Keywords: A Vocabulary of Culture and Society* (London: Croom Helm, 1976), p. 174.

a significant break with past practices on the other, even if this distinction is not always entirely clear cut.

The argument is developed in the book's three parts. Part I explores what might be regarded as the world of traditional retailing including markets (Chapter 1); urban retailers and producer-retailers (Chapter 2); and the more dispersed and marginal retailers such as hawkers and village shopkeepers (Chapter 3). Much of this retailing was sophisticated, some was clearly modern and almost all was capable of adaptation and evolutionary change. Radical innovation was rarer, but not unknown especially among leading town centre shopkeepers. Part II focuses on some of the key developments in ideas and practices that were a disruptive influence on this broadly traditional world. These included changing attitudes to material goods (Chapter 4); the growing importance of fashion, novelty and shopping for pleasure as well as for necessities (Chapter 5); and the way in which some of the more extreme manifestations of consumption, including obsessive collecting, heralded a new emphasis on individuality (Chapter 6). Part III takes the story forward into the 1820–50 period and, without arguing for a retail revolution in these decades, has a stronger focus on radical innovation including new retail spaces such as bazaars and proto-department stores (Chapter 7) and large and spectacular covered market halls (Chapter 8). These complemented rather than replaced more traditional retail practices. The concluding chapter considers changing attitudes to consumption, including homemaking, taste and the way in which appropriate consumption could raise standards of culture and morality, before offering some closing reflections on consumption as one of the key narratives of modernity.

To some extent, therefore, the central thrust of this book's argument is to reinstate the middle decades of the nineteenth century as a key watershed in the history of retailing. This is not because earlier retailing was in any way primitive. Eighteenth-century shops were frequently sophisticated both in their appearance and their business methods. Urban retailers were keenly aware of changing fashions and made a point of keeping up with them. Some were genuinely innovative in their use of display and advertising. More traditional forms of retailing like markets were fully able to adapt to changing needs and circumstances. Yet dynamic and often modern as eighteenth-century retailing was, it was essentially structured to meet the needs of a commercial rather than an industrial society. It was suited to the world of Adam Smith rather than that of Friedrich Engels. In the decades immediately prior to 1850 there were some significant signs of structural change and radical innovation affecting the scale of individual retail businesses and the way in which they were organized. Consumer attitudes were also changing. The really radical developments, like the spread of multiple and department stores, the increasing importance of branding and the emergence of a mass consumer market were, however, essentially a feature of the second half of the nineteenth century. This book tells the story of English provincial retailing in the period immediately up to the retail revolution of the later nineteenth century and the contemporaneous appearance of the first real mass consumer society. It explores the background to these momentous changes; discussing the changes themselves would require another volume.

PART I
Traditional and Dynamic:
Retailing *c.* 1700–1820

Chapter 1
Basic Goods at a Fair Price:
The Morality of the Market

In the summer of 1713 a Derbyshire jury was summoned to consider the implications for the small market town of Tideswell of proposals to establish markets and fairs in the neighbouring villages of Hope and Castleton. The jury concluded that a market at Castleton would damage that at Tideswell, but was split on the proposal for Hope. Those against allowing a market there subsequently complained that they had been pressurized into agreeing to it.[1] Early in the following year John Balguy of Hope petitioned the Crown for a Saturday market and four annual fairs there.[2] He obtained his grant, although by the middle of the eighteenth century only two of the fairs seem to have survived.[3]

There was nothing particularly unusual about these legal proceedings even in the eighteenth century. Markets and fairs remained important for the sale of foodstuffs, livestock and a range of durable goods. They could be profitable to the person who owned the right to hold them and to collect toll on goods sold in them. They might stimulate trade in the place where they were located and the surrounding area, or they might threaten an existing market. It was worthwhile for a local landowner or local authority to spend time and money on obtaining a formal grant of a market and fairs in order to establish and protect their rights and potential income. Even though traditional markets and the regulations surrounding them were increasingly challenged by changing attitudes and alternative modes of selling, and examples can be found both of individual markets that were decaying as well as those that were thriving, there is no strong evidence to suggest that markets in general were declining in importance until at least the second third of the nineteenth century.[4]

This chapter explores how traditional markets in growing towns operated in practice. It discusses the legal framework within which markets were situated and the changing effectiveness of regulation. The extent to which it was appropriate for the market authorities to attempt to control trade in the market, and to prevent

---

[1]   Sheffield Archives, Bagshawe Collection, Bag C/779/66.

[2]   National Archives (NA), State Papers Domestic, Petition of John Balguy, SP 34/37/101.

[3]   W. Owen, *An Authentic Account Published by the King's Authority of All the Fairs in England and Wales* (London, 1756), p. 21.

[4]   Martin Phillips, 'The Evolution of Markets and Shops in Britain', in Benson and Shaw (eds), *The Evolution of Retail Systems*, pp. 53–75.

it overflowing into unregulated spaces was a particular concern in times of scarcity. There were those who called for more rigorous enforcement of the laws surrounding market trading; and those who argued for greater freedom. Although the latter view prevailed, the contest was a real one and at times closely fought. Urban improvement also impacted on markets. By the late eighteenth century there was pressure in many towns for markets to be tidied up and removed from main thoroughfares. The final section of this chapter discusses several instances of market improvement and expansion in some growing industrial towns.

The Traditional Market

Although the number of market towns in England and Wales decreased after the mid seventeenth century, there were still over 600 such towns in 1720 and 728 were listed by Owen in 1792.[5] Not all of these markets were of any real significance and some may have existed more in name than in reality. In the 1670s Richard Blome described the market at Tarvin in Cheshire as 'inconsiderable', that at Sandbach as 'not very considerable', and that at Knutsford as 'indifferent', while that at Ashbourne in Derbyshire was 'much decayed' of late and that at Chapel-en-le-Frith 'now disused'.[6] Some towns disappeared from the lists during the eighteenth century to be replaced by new entrants, which may themselves have struggled. For example, in Cheshire the inhabitants of the small Wirral town of Neston made fruitless attempts in the sixteenth and seventeenth centuries to establish a market and fairs in the face of opposition from Chester. A market and three fairs were finally granted to Sir Roger Mostyn in 1728. These never flourished, however, and were on a very small scale. Income from the market in its first year was a mere £1 14s 9d with expenditure of 11s 1½d plus the initial outlay on dishes and scales.[7] Neston was not listed as a market town in the 1796 edition of Owen, but did have a small market for meat and potatoes according to the 1800 crop return.[8]

The relative insignificance of some market towns, and the decline of other markets in the eighteenth century, particularly as small centres were eclipsed by larger ones, was only part of the picture. Other new markets flourished. The townspeople of Penistone in south Yorkshire faced opposition from Barnsley and Huddersfield when they tried to establish a market at the end of the seventeenth century. Rather than give up, however, they sought the support of the inhabitants of towns on both sides of the Pennines from Salford in the west to Doncaster in

---

[5]   John Chartres, 'The Marketing of Agricultural Produce, 1640–1750', in John Chartres (ed.), *Chapters from the Agrarian History of England and Wales, 1500–1750: Agricultural Markets and Trade 1500–1750* (Cambridge: Cambridge University Press, 1990), pp. 160–2.

[6]   Richard Blome, *Britannia* (London, 1673), pp. 56–7, 77–8.

[7]   Geoffrey Place, 'The Quest for a Market Charter', *Cheshire History*, 5 (1980): 11–21.

[8]   NA, Home Office Papers, HO 42/54/152.

the east and Wakefield in the north to Hope in the south. Over 2,000 people signed their petition and in 1699 Penistone held its first Thursday market. Both town and market prospered in the eighteenth century.[9] The markets of middling and larger towns often attracted favourable comments from travellers. Celia Fiennes noted that the market in Chesterfield was 'very large; it was Saturday which is their market day and there was a great Market like some little faire'.[10] Daniel Defoe wrote of the market at Shrewsbury that it was 'the greatest market, the greatest plenty of good provisions, and the cheapest that is to be met with in all the western part of England'; of Nottingham that 'there is a very good market, with a vast quantity of provisions, and those of the best sort, few towns in England exceeding it'; and of Leeds that 'the ordinary market for provisions … is the greatest of its kind in all the north of England, except Halifax'.[11] Leeds also had a very important cloth market.

It seems likely that in the seventeenth century the markets in around two in five English towns specialized in some product or group of products, as well as providing a focal point for the sale of provisions and other basic goods.[12] The latter may not have been glamorous, but was important. It was also picturesque, an acceptable subject for illustrators and artists.[13] Moreover, market day was often the busiest day for town shopkeepers, particularly those in prime locations around the market place.[14] Disputes between some traders and the Corporation in the Cheshire silk town of Macclesfield in the mid eighteenth century suggest a flourishing market with shopkeepers taking advantage of those who came to the town on market days. For example, toll was demanded in 1759 of Mark Furnall who sold goods such as breeches and stays from outside his market place shop on market days. Furnall refused, but offered to pay a smaller amount. The Corporation claimed that other traders, including a shoemaker, had agreed to pay toll in similar circumstances.[15] A freeman butcher, Nicholas Chapman, was also in dispute with the Corporation over his refusal to pay stallage for a second stall in the market, needed because of the increase of his business.[16] Lists of tolls chargeable in the 1750s show the town authorities making provision for charging not just those selling provisions

---

[9]   David Hey, *Packmen, Carriers and Packhorse Roads: Trade and Communications in North Derbyshire and South Yorkshire* (Leicester: Leicester University Press, 1980), pp. 164–6.

[10]   Celia Fiennes, *The Journeys of Celia Fiennes*, ed. and with an Introduction by Christopher Morris (London: Cresset Press, 1947), p. 96.

[11]   Daniel Defoe, *A Tour through the Whole Island of Great Britain*, (2 vols, Everyman edn, London: J.M. Dent, 1962), vol. 2, pp. 76, 145, 204.

[12]   Alan Everitt, 'The Marketing of Agricultural Produce, 1500–1640', in Chartres (ed.), *Chapters from the Agrarian History of England and Wales*, p. 39.

[13]   Cox and Dannehl, *Perceptions*, pp. 45–6.

[14]   Cox, *Complete Tradesman*, p. 85, referring in particular to William Stout of Lancaster in the late seventeenth century.

[15]   Cheshire Archives and Local Studies (CALS), Earwaker Collection, CR63/2/341.

[16]   Wirral Archives, John Stafford (Macclesfield) Collection, MA/B/II/17.

(including lemons and oranges) but also breeches makers, glovers, shoemakers, hatters, handkerchief and lace sellers, potters, glaziers, coopers, and sellers of maps and pictures.[17] This is not, of course, evidence that such a wide range of goods was regularly on sale in the market, and some of these items may have been more common at fairs, but at least implies that Macclesfield market amounted to a lot more than just a few provisions stalls. The market tolls were generally leased by the Corporation to a toll collector and trade in the market seems to have been increasing significantly in the second half of the eighteenth century. Jonathan Downes agreed to pay £65 a year in 1752; by 1794 George Oldfield was paying £120 a year.[18]

At the other end of Cheshire the markets in the ancient city of Chester, which experienced much slower population growth in the eighteenth century but which was a prosperous service and leisure centre, also remained important. Chester lacked a large central market place with the result that markets were spread around the city. In the 1780s Northgate Street was the principal market area, with butchers' shambles and a daily market for fish and vegetables (Figure 1.1).

Figure 1.1   Chester market place, Northgate Street

Source: *Ancient Chester*. Reproduced by permission of Manchester Libraries, Information and Archives, Manchester City Council.

Poultry, butter and cheese were sold in Eastgate Street, the most prestigious of the city's shopping streets. The markets were described as well supplied and cheap.[19] Not all shoppers agreed. There were complaints in the 1770s of the high prices of turkeys and of fish as well as of their quality: 'Great plenty of salmon ... I

---

[17]   CALS, Earwaker Collection, CR 63/2/341.

[18]   CALS, Macclesfield Assembly Minute Books, 1734–68 and 1769–1822, LBM/1/3–4.

[19]   [Peter Broster], *The Chester Guide* (Chester, 1781), pp. 21–2, 31–3.

saw no other fish, except a few small, stinking mackerel at ten pence each'.[20] These dispersed markets had never been wholly satisfactory and could easily cause congestion. There was also little scope for expansion, at least until major improvement schemes were set in hand in the early nineteenth century. Profits from the butchers' markets fell from around £100 a year in the 1730s to £70–£80 in the 1770s before rising again to reach £120–£130 by 1800. Income from the fish market was much less, rising from around £7 to around £12 in this period.[21] These were not markets that attracted much attention from visitors or writers of guide books to the city, but they were indispensable to the city's inhabitants.

Part of the reason why markets mattered was that they operated within a framework of law and regulation. Acquiring the right to found a new market or alter an existing one might involve complex and potentially costly procedures, including legal advice and representation. The extent to which market rights were enforceable could lead to legal proceedings, or at least the preparation of a case for counsel's opinion. Disputes between owners and users of markets could easily end up in one of the courts of equity. The fact that it tends to be legal records that have survived probably gives a somewhat distorted view of the volume of disputes regarding market rights. Markets that worked smoothly have left less historical evidence. Yet even allowing for this, it is clear that some, particularly private, owners of markets rights in the eighteenth century and early nineteenth behaved very much as rent-seeking monopolists with only limited interest in the public utility of their markets.

Sir George Warren in Stockport was a good example. In the second half of the eighteenth century he endeavoured to maintain or revive all his traditional manorial rights, including those from the town's markets.[22] Tolls on the sale of cheese were a particularly contentious issue. Stockport was a significant cheese market and increasingly cheesemongers would rent premises in or near the market place on market day in order to sell cheese. Warren wanted them to pay toll; they refused on the grounds that they did not use his scales or sell in the market itself. Warren sought legal advice on whether ancient grants of market rights could be used to bolster his income and protect his position.[23] Stockport was already an important hat-making town with a rapidly developing cotton industry, and the intransigence of Warren and his successors significantly hindered attempts by the people of Stockport to improve and extend their markets.[24] Warren was not

---

[20]   Flintshire Record Office, Nerquis Hall Mss, Letters of Bagot Read to Kitty Boland, 2 April 1774, 24 June 1775, D/NH/1070.

[21]   CALS, City of Chester, Treasurers' Account Books, 1734–1822, ZTAB/5–9.

[22]   Robert Glen, *Urban Workers in the Early Industrial Revolution* (London: Croom Helm, 1983), p. 48.

[23]   Stockport Local Heritage Library, Warren Papers, HX 182 and 229.

[24]   Ian Mitchell, 'Supplying the Masses: Retailing and Town Governance in Macclesfield, Stockport and Birkenhead, 1780–1860, *Urban History*, 38/2 (2011): 256–75 (266–7).

unusual in his behaviour. At the beginning of the eighteenth century the Booth family who owned the manorial rights of Warrington were trying to compel the town's butchers to trade only in their market hall on market days. Booth argued that this would be to their benefit, but was no doubt also concerned to protect his income.[25] In 1743 Viscount Chetwynd sought legal advice about attempts by some traders at Uttoxeter market to avoid paying toll by claiming to be burgesses or to live in the town. He was also concerned about sales by sample or outside the market.[26] In 1771 Chesterfield inhabitants petitioned the Duke of Portland about the behaviour of the lessee of the market tolls, complaining that he demanded excessive tolls and behaved in a violent and oppressive manner.[27] Many of these disputes can seem petty and arcane, but they serve as a reminder that the eighteenth-century market was often a focus for conflict. The legal status of the market probably made such conflict more likely and less easy to resolve, particularly when lawyers and courts became involved.

If the legal framework within which markets operated could be exploited by their owners, it could also offer protection for buyers and sellers. Some manorial courts continued to appoint officers to regulate the market well into the nineteenth century. This was the case in Stockport in the 1830s where the Court Leet dealt with a steady trickle of offenders accused of selling unwholesome meat or fish, of using defective or unstamped weights in the market place and in one instance of selling nine loads of potatoes short of weight. The original £5 fine in this last case was remitted because the potatoes were seized and used in the workhouse.[28] The Manchester Court Leet was actively dealing with marketing offences throughout the eighteenth century. As in Stockport most were for selling unmarketable beef, veal or mutton, or for selling produce like butter short of the proper weight. Other offenders included John Chorlton, a Stockport butcher, who was amerced in 1736 for not keeping his board clean; four Cheshire butchers in 1758 for not cleaning their stalls in the shambles; Richard Hobson, a Cheshire butcher, in 1770 for selling meat in the market after 11.00 p.m.; and Thomas Paynter, an apple dealer of Northwich in Cheshire, in 1787 for selling a Manchester fruiterer called Catherine Unsworth two pots of apples containing only three instead of four pecks. The tenacity with which marketing offences were pursued seems to have depended on the enthusiasm of the individuals holding office in any particular year. The number of repeat offenders or those referred to as 'an old offender' also suggests that the Court was not always very effective or well respected. Moreover, by the last decades of the eighteenth century the emphasis shifted away from market traders to shopkeepers amerced for false weights. Even with all these reservations,

---

[25]   Greater Manchester Record Office, Legh Family of Lyme Hall, E17/89/33/1–6.

[26]   Staffordshire Record Office (SRO), Cowlishaw and Mountford Collection, D1504/6/14/1.

[27]   Nottinghamshire Archives, Portland Mss, Chesterfield Market, DD/P 60/25–7.

[28]   CALS, Vernon and Warren Family, Stockport Court Papers, Court Leet Proceedings 1834–50, DVE 9/7.

a manorial court like that in Manchester could ensure some degree of quality control and consumer protection in the market and help create a sense of fairness for those trading there.[29]

Preventing the sale of bad meat and ensuring that proper weights were used was much less contentious than enforcing the laws around forestalling, regrating and engrossing.[30] For example in 1764 the Chesterfield Court Leet set penalties of 3s 4d for bringing corn to be sold but not bringing it to the market; for forestalling butter; and for selling hides and skins before coming to the place where they should be sold.[31] Trying to prevent trade from escaping the regulated market into unregulated locations had long been a problem. There were unlicensed markets beyond the control of urban authorities from at least the fourteenth century and the laws against forestalling had always tended to catch minor dealers rather than major ones.[32] Complaints about markets being affected by traders operating outside them were hardly novel in the eighteenth century, though they may have become more prevalent with regard to smaller and more vulnerable market towns. The historian of Faversham in Kent writing in the 1770s bemoaned the fact that the markets and fairs of the towns were mere skeletons of what they had once been. He blamed the small dealers in items like poultry, butter and eggs who 'go all the country over, purchasing the above named articles of farmers at their houses, giving them as good prices as can be got by sending the same to our market'.[33]

There is no doubt that markets became less important for some types of trade during the eighteenth century. The practice of selling grain by sample or at the farm gate was well established and tended to attract the attention of the authorities at times of scarcity. For example, in 1757 several Cheshire dealers and farmers were examined at the Quarter Sessions about unauthorized 'meetings' for the sale of corn and about deals being struck in inns or private houses. It was clear from what they said that such practices were common and had been in existence

---

[29]   *The Court Leet Records of the Manor of Manchester from 1552 to 1686, and from 1731 to 1846* (12 vols, Manchester: Henry Blacklock, 1884–90), vols 7–10.

[30]   A sixteenth century statute defined forestalling as buying goods before they reached the market or dissuading potential sellers from bringing their goods to a market; regrating as buying goods in a market in order to sell them again in the same or a nearby market; and engrossing as buying or contracting to buy quantities of corn, butter or cheese in order to sell them again. Such practices were still widely regarded as unfair in the eighteenth century, particularly in times of scarcity. See pages pp. 23–7 for a more detailed treatment of this topic.

[31]   Derbyshire Record Office (DRO), Heathcote Collection, Chesterfield Court Leet, 1763–1841, D267, Box 20.

[32]   Richard Britnell, 'Urban Economic Regulation and Economic Morality in Medieval England', pp. 5–7, in Richard Britnell, *Markets, Trade and Economic Development in England and Europe, 1050–1550* (Farnham: Ashgate Variorum, 2009).

[33]   Edward Jacob, *The History of the Town and Port of Faversham, in the County of Kent* (London, 1774), p. 63.

since at least the beginning of the century.[34] Trading that had once taken place in the market was increasingly shifting to a town's inns. Chester had between 15 and 20 significant inns with important trading functions, including the Hop Pole where there were warehouses for the storage of long-distance goods, hop sheds, the workshop of a cabinet maker and the offices of the *Chester Chronicle* newspaper.[35] Changes of this nature may seem to have had little relevance to the role of markets in retailing meat, fish or fresh produce. This may have been true to some extent, but there was always a danger that as farmers and others drifted away from the market, market days became less busy, other potential customers looked elsewhere and what remained was less and less sustainable, particularly in a prime town-centre location.

Properly established markets were also threatened by unregulated ones such as that at Gloverstone in Chester. This was a street that ran for about 100 yards up to Chester Castle, was outside the jurisdiction of the city authorities and was owned by a Mrs Mary Daffy who lived in London. Mrs Daffy's sister, Elizabeth Brereton, lived in Chester and in February 1758 advertised in the local newspaper that there would be a toll-free market in Gloverstone on Wednesdays and Saturdays. The Mayor and Corporation of Chester were not happy. Trade, particularly in corn, was drifting from the city's official markets to Gloverstone with potentially serious consequences for toll receipts. The city authorities were advised to take legal action against Daffy requiring her to show by what right she held the market. They could not, however, act against those using the market as people trading there had no obligation to find out whether or not it was legal. The evidence gathered was probably not entirely to the city's liking. At least some witnesses were prepared to say that a general provisions market had flourished in Gloverstone some 30 or 40 years previously with goods like meat, bread, flour, fish, eggs, butter, milk and cheese being on sale at standings set up on both sides of the street. The market had then declined, but some country butchers and bakers continued to trade there, the former because they had not been apprenticed and dare not sell in the shambles. The city authorities decided to prosecute Daffy and Brereton in the Court of King's Bench but dropped the prosecution in September 1758 because Daffy had died.[36] It is probably significant that the legality of Gloverstone came to a head at a time of corn scarcity when the city authorities were trying to ensure that the public markets were well stocked and conducted according to the traditional regulations. But it also illustrates the relative ease with which loopholes could be exploited to offer alternative, and popular, trading facilities.

---

[34]   CALS, Quarter Sessions Files, 10 January 1758, QJF 186/1/116–22.

[35]   E.M. Willshaw, 'The Inns of Chester, 1775–1832: The Functions of Provincial Inns and their Importance to the Local Community', unpublished MA thesis, University of Leicester, 1979, pp. 9–14.

[36]   CALS, Chester City Council, Lawsuits, *Rex v. Daffy and Brereton*, 1758, ZCL/118; Chester Assembly Minutes 11 September 1758, ZA/B/4.

Changing Attitudes to Markets and Market Regulation

The traditional market remained important in the eighteenth century, offering benefits to buyers and sellers and a source of income to whoever owned it. Most sellers probably came from within about 10 miles of the market while buyers were predominately inhabitants of the market town, supplemented by those from its hinterland.[37] Opportunities to trade outside the market were not new but were increasing while attitudes were also changing. Was the regulated market the best way of meeting growing demand for food and other basic goods? Were perceived ideas of 'fairness' discouraging enterprise and so restricting the supply of goods coming to market? Would freer trade lead to increased supply and cheaper prices? Or might there perhaps be a need for different rules in times of scarcity than in more normal times? Also changing was how at least some people perceived their urban environment. Perhaps markets were not so much picturesque as untidy and dirty and ought therefore to be moved away from the town centre.

Questions of this nature exercised contemporaries at both a theoretical and a practical level. With the benefit of historical perspective it is possible to see their pamphleteering about the corn laws and about market regulation as part of a wider debate about the fundamental principles of the economy. Was Smithian rationality with its accompanying doctrines of free trade and laissez-faire in the ascendant? It is certainly possible to argue that the eighteenth century and early nineteenth saw curbs on ancient privileges and monopolies so that by the 1830s rent-seeking was almost extinct and laissez-faire had triumphed.[38] Yet in many ways this seems like an over-simplification. Older conceptions of morality and the importance of obligation and trust persisted throughout the eighteenth century, even if some of the traditional regulatory mechanisms were rarely used except at times of crisis.[39] Economic questions remained important for Westminster politicians even if the state was generally reactive in the first half of the century. Local magistrates retained a regulatory role around economic behaviour and lawyers like Lord Mansfield masterminded a re-codification of commercial law in the middle of the century.[40] At the end of the century Lord Kenyon made it clear that forestalling was still an offence at common law despite the repeal of the statutes in 1772 and was concerned that law should protect the interests of all those affected by how markets operated, including the poor.[41]

---

[37] Everitt, *Marketing of Agricultural Produce*, pp. 45–51.

[38] Mokyr, *Enlightened Economy*, pp. 7–9.

[39] Craig Muldrew, 'Interpreting the Market: The Ethics of Credit and Community Relations in Early Modern England', *Social History*, 18/2 (1993): 167–83.

[40] Perry Gauci, 'Introduction', in Perry Gauci (ed.), *Regulating the British Economy, 1660–1850* (Farnham: Ashgate, 2011), pp. 8–15.

[41] Douglas Hay, 'The State and the Market in 1800: Lord Kenyon and Mr Waddington', *Past and Present*, 162 (1999): 101–63.

Opinion on how markets should operate was sharply divided throughout the eighteenth century. There were many who continued to blame forestallers and regraters for a multitude of ills. They harmed honest traders like butchers and bakers by pushing up the price they paid to suppliers; they damaged retailers by driving trade out of market towns; and they hurt consumers by increasing the price of basic commodities.[42] Other pamphlets in the 1750s and 1760s blamed the high price of provisions on sale by sample and the profits made by millers who had taken to dealing in as well as grinding corn.[43] There were demands as late as 1800 for the prohibition of sale by sample, the enforcement of the traditional laws against forestallers and for all the necessary articles of life to be sold only in the open market.[44] On the other side of the argument were those who believed that free trade would tend to increase the supply of grain and so lower the price of provisions. They tended to blame both the traditional laws and the activity of rioters for high prices, arguing that these discouraged farmers from bringing produce to the market. According to one writer in the 1750s, 'It is these wicked licentious Mobs who cause the seeming Scarcity; and to guard against so great an Evil hereafter, shew them less Lenity'.[45] John Arbuthnot was a particularly firm proponent of free trade, arguing that 'every restraint in the sale of a commodity, is a check on the trade, and must necessarily enhance the price of the commodity'.[46]

The Essex corn miller and magistrate Charles Smith took a slightly more pragmatic view. He was convinced that scarcity was primarily due to poor harvests, not market manipulation, and believed that the legitimate activities of farmers and middlemen were the best defence against dearth. He opposed the use of the laws on forestalling but not regulation as such. He saw no need to strengthen any of the existing laws and argued that selling and buying by sample was not the same as forestalling. Instead sale by sample was an efficient way of using a market town as the focal point for the supply of corn to a whole region without the need to bring all the corn to that town. The laws against regrating should not be strictly enforced. On the other hand, the authorities had a duty to ensure that prices were at a level that allowed the poor to buy bread and the farmer to make a living. To

---

[42]   *An Essay to Prove that Regarators, Engrossers, Forestallers, Hawkers and Jobbers of Corn, Cattle and Other Marketable Goods, Provisions and Merchandises are Destructive of Trade, Oppressors to the Poor, and a Common Nuisance to the Kingdom in General* (London, 1718).

[43]   Eusebius Silvester, *The Causes of the Present High Price of Corn and Grain* (London, 1757); Nathaniel Forster, *An Enquiry into the Causes of the Present High Price of Provisions* (London, 1767).

[44]   J.S. Girdler, *Observations on the Pernicious Consequences of Forestalling, Regrating, and Ingrossing* (London, 1800), pp. 141–6.

[45]   *Sentiments of a Corn-Factor, on the Present Situation of the Corn Trade* (London, 1758).

[46]   J. Arbuthnot, *An Inquiry into the Correlation between the Present Price of Provisions, and the Size of Farms* (London, 1773), p. 110.

this end magistrates should carefully exercise their power of setting the assize of bread to prevent excessive price fluctuations but not to buck market trends.[47] The views of practical men like Charles Smith increasingly prevailed, at least in terms of explaining the principles on which the corn trade might best be conducted. They were perhaps less influential when local magistrates were confronted with the activities of an angry and hungry mob.

There is substantial evidence to suggest that, in practice, the laws against forestalling and regrating were far from defunct in the second half of the eighteenth century. This was particularly the case at times of scarcity and high prices when they were perceived as beneficial not just by those who were hungry but by the civic authorities. In Chester, the authorities were vigilant in attempting to enforce the traditional regulations in the 1750s and 1760s. In 1765 the Assembly proposed that the Corporation appoint a person with an adequate salary to be diligent in discovering forestallers, regraters and engrossers[48] so that they could be prosecuted with the utmost rigour of the law.[49] The city authorities seem to have been convinced that scarcity and high prices were caused by the activities of greedy farmers, middlemen and bakers who purchased outside the market. The Town Clerk was a strong advocate of traditional open markets, arguing that 'when the Farmer can Sell in no other manner, the Buyer must come, the Publick must be Supplied and the farmer is Sure of Parting with his Corn and being paid for it at the honest Price, *the Times really require*'.[50] It was not just corn dealers who might fall foul of the law. In 1794 it was alleged that hucksters (probably small shopkeepers) bought fowls, cheese, butter and other items in the city before they were on open sale in the markets. The Mayor was determined to punish them with the utmost severity. City butchers also were accused of buying carcasses from country butchers for resale before the meat reached the market; the country butchers were ordered to cut up the meat as soon as they brought it to market and only sell it by retail to the city's inhabitants.[51]

Enforcement of these traditional laws could seem to bear particularly heavily on those trading on a relatively small scale. One Sarah Burgess of Heaton Norris, a township just across the Mersey from Stockport, fell foul of the law in 1755 for buying butter and eggs in Stockport market with the intention of selling them again, possibly in a small shop. At her examination before the magistrates in Chester, it was said that on 14 February she bought 15 lbs of butter and at least 17

---

[47]   Richard Sheldon, 'Practical Economics in Eighteenth-Century England: Charles Smith on the Grain Trade and the Corn Laws 1756–72', *Historical Research*, 81/214 (2008): 636–62; Charles Smith, *Three Tracts on the Corn Trade* (London, 1767).

[48]   See n.30 above for definitions of these terms.

[49]   CALS, Chester Assembly Minutes, ZA/B/4, 4 September 1765.

[50]   House of Lords Record Office, Committee on the Dearness of Provisions, 1765, Thomas Brock of Chester.

[51]   *Chester Courant*, 23 December 1794; 5 June 1794.

eggs and on 21 February 11 lbs of butter and 80 eggs.[52] In 1800 George Ridgeway, a Stockport huckster, was prosecuted for regrating – again perhaps to supply his shop at a time of high prices.[53] As well as making life difficult for enterprising small traders, trying to control trade in this way almost certainly did not help to ensure a consistent supply of foodstuffs by urban shopkeepers or stallholders or benefit the final consumer.

Enforcement, however, was as much about making a statement as about trying to influence the realities of market trading. At times of food shortage and high prices the market place could become a stage on which the hungry, the authorities and the food dealers performed a range of rituals – but rituals that could easily turn violent if any of the participants departed from the script. Those who were struggling to buy food at affordable prices, or indeed to buy food at all, needed to put pressure on the authorities to take action to secure local food supplies and prevent what they perceived as hoarding and profiteering. They might also have wanted to vent their anger on any particularly notorious corn dealers or millers. It is arguable as to how far crowds were motivated by ideology. They and many of those in authority, like local gentry, probably had a shared understanding of the importance of fairness and just dealing rather than simple profit maximization. Demanding the use of the traditional laws against forestalling could be a useful way of forging an alliance with more traditionally minded members of the governing classes. But this may have been a tactical move rather than an ideologically motivated assault on laissez-faire. The authorities needed to secure public order and were unlikely to have wanted to see the poor starve. They organized practical relief where it was possible to do so. Using, or threatening to use, the traditional laws could be a more dangerous game which might prevent riots if the people trusted that local magistrates could secure food supplies at reasonable prices or might legitimize and energize mob action. The use of force against a rioting mob was a last resort. Not only might it antagonize those sympathetic to the plight of the poor but it could backfire if the troops took the side of the people not the dealers. Farmers and dealers needed to make a living and could take advantage of shortage years to increase their profits. But it was not in their interests to be left to the mercy of the mob and have their premises attacked or looted or indeed to have provisions seized from their market stall and sold at a reduced price, with the proceeds going to those who seized them. There was a fine line between bargaining by riot, or threatened riot, and a breakdown in order that benefited no one.[54]

---

[52]   CALS, Quarter Sessions File, 8 April 1755, QJF/183/2.

[53]   CALS, Quarter Sessions Book, 1798–1804, QJB 3/18, pp. 163, 166.

[54]   John Bohstedt, *The Politics of Provisions: Food Riots, Moral Economy and Market Transition in England, c. 1550–1850* (Farnham: Ashgate, 2010) is the most recent and most comprehensive study of this topic. Bohstedt acknowledges the importance of E.P. Thompson's argument about the 'moral economy' (E.P. Thompson, 'The Moral Economy of the English Crowd in the Eighteenth Century', *Past and Present*, 50 (1971): 76–136) but offers a valuable and persuasive critique of this.

Enabling ordinary people to obtain basic provisions at a fair price could be a common goal which might be achieved by direct intervention in the market. It was reported from Congleton in Cheshire in 1796 that five gentlemen had subscribed considerable sums of money to purchase different sorts of grain, bacon and cheese and sell them again at very near to cost price. This was justified because, 'this town has been very much oppressed with Hucksters & Jobbers'.[55] In the previous year the civic authorities in Chester organized the supply of fixed amounts of barley flour at nine shillings a pound to the city's poorer families.[56] Farmers might be encouraged to bring corn to the market, or threatened if they did not do so. The Earl of Warrington placed a notice in the *Manchester Magazine* in 1757 'recommending' his farmers and tenants to 'thrash up their Corn, supply the Wants of their poor Neighbours, and afterwards bring what they have to spare to be sold in the public Markets on REASONABLE TERMS'. He hoped this would put an end to disturbances and warned that any who disobliged him would not receive future favours.[57] Fear of trouble might influence the authorities. An anonymous letter to the Mayor of Chester in 1767 threatened that his house would be burnt down and all the Corporation murdered if forestallers were not punished and the markets looked after properly.[58] Two years earlier the Corporation had made threatening noises about forestallers. Was the anonymous letter essentially intended to prod the authorities into serious action?

Collusion between the magistrates and the mob was sometimes suspected. A Manchester magistrate reported a food riot in Stockport at the Friday market on 1 February 1799. The riot took the usual form of attacks on farmers' carts, the forced sale of provisions, or their distribution free to the poor, and some looting of shops. He added that the mob had seen the town's magistrates and told them what they were planning. The magistrates had responded by giving them letters to farmers and holders of grain requesting them to bring supplies to the market and sell at moderate prices. Perhaps because this did not defuse the situation, the magistrates became more assertive. A public notice was posted on 3 February assuring farmers that 'a sufficient Power will at all times be ready to afford them effectual Protection and Security'. Rioters would be punished with the utmost rigour of the law.[59] Troops might put down a riot or might contain the situation. It was reported from Wells in April 1795 that troops had entered the market place and compelled those who had purchased large quantities of butter at 9½d a pound to sell it at 8d. They also fixed the price of potatoes. The authorities regarded this as a better outcome than having a mob seize foodstuffs and remove them without any recompense to the seller.[60] Troops were much more in evidence in

---

55   NA, Privy Council, Papers Concerning the Scarcity of Grain, PC 1/33/88.

56   *Chester Courant*, 8 December 1795.

57   *Manchester Magazine*, 29 November 1757.

58   *London Gazette*, 14–18 April 1767.

59   NA, Privy Council Miscellaneous Unbound Papers, PC 1/43/151.

60   NA, Home Office, Domestic Correspondence, George III, HO 42/34 fols 348–9.

the final wave of disturbances in the market places of Cheshire towns in 1812 and punishment of perceived ringleaders was swift and severe.[61]

Traditional expectations about how markets should operate and be regulated could persist well into the nineteenth century. The Mayor and Corporation of Macclesfield took action against a butcher in the 1830s for selling meat at his own shop in the town on market days, claiming that all meat sold in the town on market days should be sold in the public market.[62] The town's historian writing in the 1810s argued forcibly for strict regulation of the markets not just to protect consumers from poor quality meat and produce but to prevent the 'extortion' practised by petty shopkeepers who bought goods in the market or directly from farmers for sale in their shops.[63] These sorts of demands were, however, increasingly unrealistic and out of touch with prevailing views about freedom to trade. Competition rather than regulation was perhaps the best way to ensure a regular supply of basic goods at a fair price.

Attitudes towards what should be allowed to happen in the market place were also changing. In early modern England it had been an important location for popular recreations, including bull baiting and festival bonfires. Urban improvement tended to mean that open spaces in the centre of towns were increasingly closed to public recreation and plebeian sports and were set aside for commerce and trading.[64] This was not just a feature of leisure towns. There were several convictions in Uttoxeter in 1822 for setting dogs at a bull that had been tied to the stake in the town's market place.[65] Market space could be contested by several possible users. Corn dealers trading in the Chester markets petitioned the Assembly in 1807 with a request to be allowed to move from their present location in the open street to the underpart of the Exchange. They claimed that most of the bakers who traded there had shops in the city and did not need the market space. Hucksters had already been moved from there to provide space for citizens to walk in. Despite this the corn dealers were given permission to meet under the Exchange on Saturdays after two o'clock in the afternoon.[66]

Markets might be picturesque but they could also be a nuisance. So there was pressure to tidy up markets and remove them where possible from the main thoroughfares of a town. Examples of this include the borough authorities in Macclesfield in 1765 ordering the removal of some stalls from the market place and

---

[61] S.I. Mitchell, 'Food Shortages and Public Order in Cheshire, 1757–1812', *Transactions of the Lancashire and Cheshire Antiquarian Society*, 81 (1982): 42–66.

[62] Mitchell, 'Supplying the Masses', p. 264.

[63] John Corry, *The History of Macclesfield* (London: J. Ferguson, 1817), pp. 48–50.

[64] Emma Griffin, 'Sports and Celebrations in English Market Towns, 1660–1750', *Historical Research*, 75 (2002): 188–208; A. Hann, 'Modernity and the Marketplace', in S. Pinches, M. Whalley and D. Postles (eds), *The Market Place and the Place of the Market* (Leicester: Friends of the Centre for English Local History, 2004), pp. 67–88.

[65] SRO, Quarter Sessions, Q/SB 1822M/3/6–9.

[66] CALS, Chester Assembly Minutes 1785–1825, ZA/A/B/5 fol. 127.

giving very specific directions about where stalls should be placed because several turnpike roads had recently been made through the town.[67] A new town hall was completed in Newark in 1773 including butchers' shambles so that they could be removed from the market place. The butchers were not keen and it took 25 years to persuade them to move.[68] In 1818 several inhabitants of Upper Northgate Street in Chester complained about the weekly cattle market taking place in their street which was part of the route from Liverpool to Chester and therefore heavily used by coaches. They offered to relocate it at their own expense to a piece of waste ground belonging to the Corporation. This was agreed.[69] Following the Mansfield Improvement Act of 1823, the Commissioners there ordered the removal of penthouses and sheds and permitted greengrocers' and fishmongers' stalls in the streets on the condition that they did not cause an obstruction.[70] The intensity of feeling that nuisances (in this case from fairs) could provoke is well illustrated by a letter of 1827 to the *Derby Mercury*: 'It is absolutely intolerable, that the finest street in Derby [Friargate] should be so very unnecessarily converted into a nuisance, ten times greater than the filthiest cow-yard in the neighbourhood of the Metropolis'.[71] What was the future for town markets and fairs?[72]

New and Improved Markets

In the face of changing attitudes both towards how goods were marketed and towns provisioned themselves, and towards the acceptability of an open market in an improved town centre suitable for polite pursuits like leisure shopping, it might have been expected that markets would be pushed to the margins of retailing and retail space from the late eighteenth century onwards. This, however, was not necessarily the case. There are many instances of market improvement and expansion in the late eighteenth century and early nineteenth. In some cases entirely new markets were established. The initiative might come from the inhabitants of a town or from the owner of the market rights. Some owners were keen to cooperate with local schemes for market improvement. Others were more obstructive, being more interested in defending their existing rights than in improving facilities for townspeople. This could lead to pressure for public authorities to purchase market rights. Markets may increasingly have been contained within a bounded space, but they were certainly not marginalized.

---

[67]   CALS, Macclesfield Assembly Minute Book, 1735–68, LBM/1/3, 22 November 1765.

[68]   Catherine Smith, 'Urban Improvement in the Nottinghamshire Market Town, 1770–1840', *Midland History*, 25 (2000): 90–114.

[69]   Chester Assembly Minutes, ZAB/5 fol. 207.

[70]   Nottinghamshire Archives, Mansfield Municipal Borough, Improvement Commissioners Minutes, 1823–33, DC/M/1/2/1, pp. 9–15.

[71]   *Derby Mercury*, 13 June 1827.

[72]   For a brief discussion of retailing at fairs see Chapter 3, p. 65.

There could be considerable support for the establishment of a market in a growing town. It could also, however, be hard to achieve anything. A petition from the clergy, gentlemen, manufacturers and other residents of Salford in the 1760s stated that it was a populous and increasing town where no market was held on Wednesdays for the sale of provisions or other necessities. The nearest Wednesday market was at Warrington. They asked for a royal grant of a Wednesday market in Salford. The implication that the inhabitants of Salford were seriously deprived of public markets was somewhat disingenuous. Warrington was indeed around 15 miles away, but there were markets in Manchester on at least three days in the week and even if these were described as being for meat it seems unlikely that they were so restricted. Perhaps the petitioners hoped that the authorities in London would have only a limited knowledge of the geography of the Manchester area. If so they were to be disappointed. There was opposition from John Mosley who owned the rights to the Manchester markets and from traders in Manchester who feared that they would lose trade to Salford. The proposal eventually foundered and Salford did not acquire a market until the 1820s.[73] On the other side of Manchester, the inhabitants of Stockport petitioned the House of Commons in 1785 complaining that, 'the Place assigned for the Market weekly held in the said Town is, from the great Increase of Provisions and other Articles brought to Market, become insufficient for that Purpose'. An improved market place was needed. But as so often in eighteenth-century Stockport, Sir George Warren was not inclined to cooperate and nothing was done.[74] Sometimes local initiative could be defeated by the complexities of manorial law. The inhabitants of Blackburn ran into unresolved legal arguments about who if anyone held the manorial rights of the town when they attempted in 1792 to improve and extend its market facilities[75]

Some townspeople were more successful in their endeavours. The market in the West Riding town of Halifax had traditionally been held in the streets. As so often in a growing town this was increasingly perceived as causing obstructions that were inconvenient or even dangerous. In 1788 some of the town's leading inhabitants organized a subscription to purchase a large piece of ground to be used as a market. Shambles and a slaughter house were built and provision made for stalls and standings for the sale of fish, poultry and other provisions. Over £3,000 was subscribed in 1788 and 1789 and by the mid 1790s over £6,000 had been spent. The original subscribers hoped to make a profit out of the market but had not done so by 1796. Butchers had been charged £3 13s 0d a year for their shops but after an additional slaughterhouse was built it was proposed that this should be increased to five guineas. This was not popular and the subscribers sought advice on how best to evict those who refused to pay. Many seem then to have accepted

---

[73]   NA, Duchy of Lancaster, Petition etc. Concerning Salford Market, DL 9/50/1.

[74]   British Parliamentary Papers (BPP), *Journals of the House of Commons*, vol. 40, p. 583, 4 March 1785.

[75]   Lancashire Archives, Shuttleworth, Dallas & Crombleholme, Solicitors of Preston, Manor & Rectory of Blackburn, DDCM/2/165.

the new charges and by 1810 at least 50 of the shops were letting for £7 a year. By then the market was profitable, paying a dividend of 5 per cent. Income came from rents, not tolls. It was also substantial, comprising around 70 shops, mainly for butchers, 34 covered stalls and 100 standings.

The success of the market meant that there was a need for legislation to enable money to be raised for further improvements and to regulate the market more effectively outlawing nuisances such as slaughtering in the open market place. Bye-laws were published in October 1810. The market was to be confined to the new market place and locations were specified for a range of different types of trader, including shoemakers, breeches makers, hardwaremen, gardeners, sellers of sweets and eatables and hawkers and peddlers. Not everyone was happy. The gardeners, hucksters and others complained in November 1810 that because of where they were situated in the large area of the new market they suffered much from want of shelter from the weather. The butchers attempted to set conditions before they would agree to a 30 shillings increase in their annual rental. They wanted, for example, manure to be removed weekly from the slaughter house yard; the privy to be removed to a more private situation, claiming that the smell from it was so bad that customers sometimes thought their meat was bad; and stalls removed from the front of their shops so that they would have room to sell hides and skins. Despite these and other complaints the market can be regarded as a successful example of local initiative.[76]

There were more ways than one of trying to create or improve markets in growing towns. The approach at Cromford in Derbyshire, home of Arkwright's cotton mill, was somewhat unconventional. A notice in the *Derby Mercury* in May 1790 referred to the large manufactures and growing population of the village and stated that there was a need to form a plan whereby the people of the neighbourhood might be encouraged to come there every Saturday to sell the necessaries of life. A 'meeting' would therefore be held at the Greyhound Inn with prizes for those who sold the most. Among the prizes would be a mahogany eight-day clock valued at £9 for the person selling the most beef and veal; a 30-hour clock valued at four guineas for the most bread; and an oak square dining table valued at 18 shillings for the most cheese.[77] Very large quantities of goods were said to have been sold at the first meeting at which there was also a procession with several bands.[78]

The owner of the market rights at Middleton north of Manchester acted in a more conventional way. Middleton was also a rapidly growing manufacturing town where the number of houses was said to have increased from around 20 in the 1760s to between 400 and 500 in the 1790s.[79] Lord Suffield, who owned the

---

[76]   West Yorkshire Archive Service (WYAS), Calderdale, Halifax New Market Papers, MISC 111/11.

[77]   *Derby Mercury*, 13–20 May 1790.

[78]   Ibid., 10–17 June 1790.

[79]   John Aikin, *A Description of the Country from Thirty to Forty Miles round Manchester* (London: John Stockdale, 1795), p. 243.

manorial rights, petitioned the Crown in 1791 for the grant of a Friday market and three fairs in the town. The subsequent enquiry found that since there was no market within five miles of Middleton the inhabitants would benefit and no other town would suffer if a grant was made. Suffield got his market and was allowed to collect tolls on a wide range of items including fruit, vegetables, cheese and earthenware as well as corn, livestock, meat and fish.[80] Obtaining a formal grant of a market was not cheap. Suffield paid out £140 18s 10d in legal and other expenses, including £11 17s 6d for dinner, wine and entertainment for the jury that deliberated on his proposal.[81] That was only the start of his expenditure as Suffield had grand designs. He commissioned the fashionable architect George Steuart, responsible for Attingham Hall in Shropshire, to design the market buildings. They were intended to make a statement with a large domed building and an imposing facade.[82] Aikin described the market house as 'elegant' and 'well supplied with butchers' meat and other provisions'.[83]

Ideally townspeople and market owners would work together to secure the best marketing facilities for the town. Sheffield provides a good, and quite rare, example of this.[84] The preamble to the 1784 Market Act recited the usual reasons for improvement: the town was large and populous, the market place was too small, the streets around it were frequently obstructed and the slaughter houses were in the wrong place.[85] The Earl of Surrey (later Duke of Norfolk) as owner of the market rights took the initiative in Parliament, but the townspeople made sure their views were taken into account. They set up a committee and commissioned reports about the state of the market, the likely increase in population and how best to meet the needs of the town's butchers. In their proposals to the Earl of Surrey they also recognized the need for him to make a profit from the market by building shops that would let for a high rent.[86] The 1784 Act authorized a group of market Commissioners, drawn from Sheffield's leading citizens and townspeople, to buy up property in order to extend the market area. The butchers' trade was divided between a live cattle market, a killing shambles on the river bank and the

---

[80]   Greater Manchester Record Office, Papers of the Assheton Family of Middleton, Middleton Market, E7/5/1/50/12–17.

[81]   Ibid., E7/5/1/51.

[82]   Ibid., Volume of Architectural Drawings, E7/28/2.

[83]   Aikin, *A Description of the Country from Thirty to Forty Miles round Manchester*, p. 243.

[84]   Janet Blackman, 'The Food Supply of an Industrial Town: A Study of Sheffield's Public Markets 1780–1900', *Business History*, 5/2 (1963): 83–98. Manchester's experience with the Mosley family was generally less happy (see Roger Scola, *Feeding the Industrial City: The Food Supply of Manchester 1770–1870* (Manchester: Manchester University Press, 1992), pp. 150–1).

[85]   *An Act for Enlarging the Market Place, and Regulating the Markets, within the Town of Sheffield ... 27 Geo III c. 5.*

[86]   Sheffield Archives, Arundel Castle Manuscripts, Sheffield Market, ACM/S/476/1c.

retail trade in the new market buildings.[87] Rules for those occupying the shambles in the new market were drawn up in 1787. Tenants were forbidden to alter their premises without consent, to sharpen knives on the stone pillars of the market, to play games or gamble or to encourage any dog to come into the market. Urinating against the walls or in the passages was also banned. Tenants who broke the rules could be evicted.[88]

The new market was extensive, including 53 butchers' shops and 41 butchers' stalls with yearly rents ranging from 12 guineas for the best shop to 3 guineas for some stalls. There were 54 outside shops occupied by a wide range of different types of trader such as shoemakers, breeches makers, clockmakers, staymakers, hucksters, hardwaremen, a bookbinder and a cabinet maker. Among those occupying stalls in the semicircle were 17 shoemakers, 8 breeches makers, 5 fishmongers and 5 fruiterers. The cellars provided space for a grocer and brandy merchant.[89] Although there were some empty stalls in the 1800s, the market still seems to have been very successful with rental income of nearly £1,400 a year.[90] There could be some tension between shopkeepers and those who traded in the market. In 1818 the master shoemakers who occupied standings in the market petitioned the Duke of Norfolk with a request to be allowed to remain where they were. They argued that their activities were not injurious to shoe shops near the market. The shoes sold in the market were more suitable for the lower order of society than the 'fancy articles' sold in the shops.[91]

Further changes to the market were being considered in the 1810s. In 1816 the Duke of Norfolk's agent saw advantages in replacing the existing butchers' and gardeners' stalls inside the market with 40 good butchers' stalls at an annual rental of 12 guineas. This would almost double the Duke's income. He also listed the location of butchers' shops elsewhere in Sheffield, noting that some were illegal because they were detached buildings. A growing town needed more butchers, but the market owners could benefit if more of them were contained within the market. The Duke bought more land in the late 1810s[92] to extend the existing market but by the late 1820s the markets were widely recognized as being inadequate. In 1826 Michael Ellison, the Duke's zealous Sheffield agent, drew up a comprehensive scheme for radically improved and extended markets, and a new Act of Parliament was obtained in 1827.[93] From this point onwards the story of Sheffield's markets is best understood in the context of the building of market halls in many major towns in the second quarter of the nineteenth century.[94]

---

[87] Blackman, 'The Food Supply of an Industrial Town', pp. 85–6.

[88] Sheffield Archives, ACM/S/334.

[89] Ibid., Market Rentals 1790, ACM/S/343/1.

[90] Ibid., Market Rentals 1806, ACM/S/343/7.

[91] Ibid., Market Petitions, ACM/S/344/6.

[92] Ibid., New Market, ACM/S/346/1.

[93] Ibid., ACM/S/346/3.

[94] See Chapter 8, pp. 156–8.

Sheffield was fortunate in having a market owner who took a real interest in the affairs of the town, while of course looking after his own interests. This did, however, mean that there was no great incentive for the town authorities to try to acquire the market rights and this did not happen until 1899.[95] In other places, acquiring or trying to acquire the market rights was one way in which markets might be made more responsive to local needs and bring in some income for the town council. It could, however, be expensive and might therefore significantly affect what the new owners could spend on the markets themselves. The £200,000 paid by Manchester to Sir Oswald Mosley in the late 1840s was thought by many, in retrospect, to have been excessive.[96] Uncertainty about the future ownership of market rights could also deter investment. A committee was appointed in the small Shropshire market town of Oswestry in 1811 to organize a subscription for the purchase of the market tolls from the devisees of the late Earl of Powis. Although the committee was enthusiastic, it appears to have had limited success in collecting any money and the initiative came to nothing.[97] It was not until the 1840s that the town authorities were able to make significant improvements to the market. There was a long-running dispute in Congleton between the Shakerley family who owned the market rights and the borough authorities. The borough could not afford to buy the market rights but wanted to lease them. Shakerley agreed to this at a nominal rent provided the borough secured his right to the tolls through an Act of Parliament. This was not done and the issue was not finally resolved until 1858 when Shakerley agreed to give up his rights provided the Corporation operated a toll-free market.[98]

Conclusions

John Balguy, with whom this chapter began, failed to establish Hope as a market town. This was almost certainly because Hope was too small and because there were other markets not too far away. His attempt probably proved quite costly, at least in legal fees, but was not necessarily foolish. There was still a place for new markets in the eighteenth century even if these were more likely to prosper in growing manufacturing towns than in a moorland village. There was also merit in going through the proper channels and obtaining a formal grant with its associated legal powers. Some 130 years later a wine merchant of the Piazza in Covent Garden and of Herne Bay in Kent sought a licence for a daily market on a plot of land in the Kent seaside town. A formal enquiry held at the Pier Hotel on 14 June

---

[95]   Blackman, 'The Food Supply of an Industrial Town', p. 84.

[96]   Scola, *Feeding the Industrial City*, p. 161.

[97]   Oswestry Town Council, Records Relating to Tolls, Corn Markets and Fairs, A52–A57.

[98]   CALS, Shakerley Family of Hulme and Somerford, Congleton Tolls, DSS 3991/369/1–3.

1841 found that such a market would not damage any neighbouring ones. Belshaw had used the same legal process as Balguy and got his market.[99] The sort of trading that went on there would, however, have been rather different from that in a Peak District village in the early eighteenth century: probably miscellaneous household goods rather than horses, sheep and cattle.

All markets were to some extent different and local context was paramount. It was not just that the nature and development of a market was influenced by changes in the town where it was located. The relationship of one market to another within the hierarchy of local or regional market centres was also important. Local studies of clusters of market towns are crucial to a proper understanding of markets in early modern England. But there is also a place for the sort of general survey represented by this chapter. Generalization might be dangerous but is not impossible. Markets were important throughout the eighteenth century and early nineteenth even if the fortunes of individual markets could ebb and flow. While it is impossible to quantify how much of any type of commodity was sold in markets rather than shops, it is clear that markets were especially important for meat, fish, poultry, dairy products and vegetables. There may even have been an increasing tendency towards the end of the eighteenth century to contain meat and fish sales within markets. This did not mean that only these goods were sold in markets. Bread, shoes, some clothing, some household goods and even items like books were also retailed through markets. This is apparent from the Sheffield evidence while Chester, for example, had a mug market. The legal status of markets mattered. It provided a clear framework within which they operated and offered mechanisms for pursuing, and very occasionally resolving, disputes. It was linked to the perception of fairness and economic justice that was associated with markets. There was adaptation and evolutionary change during the period. By the early nineteenth century the traditional laws around forestalling were effectively disused and competition was perhaps seen as a more effective safeguard for fair play. Markets were also being pushed out of fashionable shopping streets into their own spaces. They were not, however, marginalized and continued to complement both fixed shop retailing and to a lesser extent itinerant trading. Radical innovation was essentially a feature of the period after 1820 when spectacular and highly regulated market halls were built in many industrial towns (see Chapter 8).

---

[99]   NA, Chancery, Petty Bag Office, Writ Files, C 202/230/29.

Chapter 2
Pillars of the Community: 'Traditional' Urban Retailers

Had he lived two hundred years later Peter Broster might well have been known by the local media as 'Mr Chester'. Born in 1741, he was apprenticed in 1759 to John Lawton, a Chester bookseller and stationer, became free of the city in 1766, Sheriff in 1776 and Mayor in 1791. He rented a shop in the Exchange in Northgate Street in 1764 and remained there for 50 years, trading as a bookseller and printer. He published the first edition of his *Chester Guide*, also containing a directory, in 1781 and continued to bring out new editions until 1797. He was interested in Cheshire history and topography and corresponded with other antiquaries on these subjects.[1] It is almost possible to imagine Broster in his shop conversing with members of the Chester elite about antiquarian books while a few yards away in the market place country women were encouraging the working people of the city to buy their poultry and eggs. Broster and traders like him represented one pole of traditional urban retailing: respectable, respected and involved in city political and cultural life. The market traders were perhaps the opposite pole at least in terms of wealth and status, though also often perceiving themselves as respectable. Both, however, were important to the economy and daily life of towns and cities. Broster was also typical of many retailers in that his business included manufacturing (printing and publishing) as well as selling.

This chapter focuses on fixed shop retailing in the eighteenth century and first part of the nineteenth. It looks at retailers both in long-established service centres like county towns which saw relatively little change in the period and in market towns that grew rapidly to become centres of industry. It is mainly concerned with the sort of shop retailer who traded from premises near the town centre and who would have regarded him or herself as having a role to play in the economy and society of the town. The chapter considers both the role of these shopkeepers in the wider urban community and their business methods. Some shopkeepers were quick to adopt new ways of trading including fixed prices, impressive window displays and regular newspaper advertising; others continued to trade in ways that would have been the norm in the late seventeenth century. A few were capable of real innovation in how they traded, particularly those who explored novel ways of displaying fashionable goods. The chapter begins, however, by looking

---

[1]   Ian Mitchell, 'The Book Trades in Cheshire 1680–1830', *Transactions of the Lancashire and Cheshire Antiquarian Society*, 95 (1999): 23–38 (35).

at producer-retailers who made up a substantial proportion of the urban trading community throughout the eighteenth century and beyond.

Producer-Retailers

It is an obvious point, but nevertheless worth emphasizing, that very many eighteenth-century retailers were also the producers, or at least processors, of the goods they sold. The exceptions tended to be the elite textile traders like mercers, drapers and haberdashers; those who sold newly fashionable items such as glass, china, toys and trinkets; and those at the lower end of the spectrum such as second-hand dealers and hucksters. A recent analysis of trade directories for the 1770s and 1780s has shown that grocers, shoemakers, tailors and drapers were among the seven most common occupations in the places studied.[2] Of these, many tailors and shoemakers may have been principally manufacturers who also engaged in retailing; grocers still needed important processing as well as marketing skills; and only drapers were pure retailers with skills focused on product knowledge and effective marketing. The *Universal British Directory* reveals a similar pattern for some key retailing occupations in a sample of manufacturing towns and service centres (Table 2.1). Although the comprehensiveness of the directory clearly varies from town to town, particularly with regard to craft and similar occupations (the contrast between Manchester and Birmingham is very apparent), the overall pattern is clear.[3] Grocers, tailors and shoemakers were more numerous than drapers and much more numerous than booksellers. Producer-retailers were a familiar sight on the main streets of fashionable and not so fashionable towns and are a good starting point for any survey of retailing in the eighteenth century.

Producer-retailers were not only found in the clothing and footwear trades. They also included bakers; household furnishers such as upholsterers and cabinet makers; and specialists like silversmiths and watchmakers. They both made and repaired goods. Some items were made to order, but many producer-retailers

---

[2]   Penelope J. Corfield, 'Business Leaders and Town Gentry in Early Industrial Britain: Specialist Occupations and Shared Urbanism', *Urban History*, 39/1 (2012): 20–50.

[3]   The deficiencies of eighteenth-century directories including the *Universal British* are well known. There was unattributed copying from town directories (see C.W. Chilton, '"The Universal British Directory" – A Warning', *Local Historian*, 15/3 (1982): 144–6 on Hull); trade classifications were inconsistent; and coverage was almost always better for higher-class and town-centre trades than for more marginal ones in peripheral areas (see David Foster, 'Albion's Sisters: A Study of Trade Directories and Female Economic Participation in the Mid-Nineteenth Century', unpublished PhD thesis, University of Exeter, 2002, and Gareth Shaw, *British Directories as Sources in Historical Geography*, Historical Geography Research Series, No. 8 (Norwich, 1982). Table 2.1 can be no more than indicative of the broad picture: it is inconceivable, for example, that there were no linen drapers in Derby in the 1790s, yet to assume that they were included among the 11 mercers would simply be a guess.

Table 2.1   Retail occupations 1790s

Town	Baker	Grocer	Tailor	Shoe-maker	Linen draper	Book-seller
Manchester	61	63	146	110	45	16
Birmingham	70	62	37	53	28	12
Newcastle	15	42	33	31	15	8
Bolton	6	44	25	23	12	4
Nottingham	24	36	18	19	23	6
Wolverhampton	13	29	19	25	12	2
Derby	14	28	12	15	0	3
Chester	29	27	25	24	10	6
Stockport	17	24	15	23	14	1

Source: P. Barfoot and J. Wilkes, *Universal British Directory* (4 vols, London, no date [1792–96]).

also made speculatively and some would buy in goods for resale. These were not back-street trades. In Chester, for example, there were clearly defined fashionable shopping streets by the mid eighteenth century if not earlier.[4] This did not, however, preclude producer-retailers from occupying premises on such streets, often next to more prestigious shopkeepers. A sketch map drawn in the 1750s of the shops in Eastgate Street, the city's most desirable retail location, shows that butchers' shops were common at street level along with a bakehouse; and that even at row level there were shoemakers and an upholsterer among the drapers and mercers who particularly held sway there.[5] According to the *Universal British Directory* of the 1790s, bakers, tailors and shoemakers were all still to be found in Eastgate Street, Bridge Street and the city's other main thoroughfares as well as in the lanes leading off them.[6] Such traders were more widely distributed throughout the city and less concentrated in the centre than the most prestigious shopkeepers, but they were not excluded from prime locations.

Turning to some specific trades, bakers operated in a semi-regulated environment, reflecting traditional perceptions of their role as servants of the public. They were still expected to provide baking facilities for their customers as well as to bake bread for sale. Even though the assize of bread, regulating either the weight or price of a loaf, was increasingly disused in the eighteenth century, it was still put into effect in

---

[4]   Jon Stobart, 'Shopping Streets as Social Space: Consumerism, Improvement and Leisure in an Eighteenth-Century County Town', *Urban History* 25/1 (1998): 3–21.

[5]   CALS, Earwaker Collection, Sketches and Letters by Peter Broster, ZCR 63/2/133. The 'Rows' were, and continue to be, a feature of each of Chester's main streets. They consist of covered passageways with shops at the rear running above the street level shops. Shops at row level were generally more prestigious than those at street level.

[6]   P. Barfoot and J. Wilkes, *Universal British Directory* (4 vols, London, no date [1792–96]), vol. 2, pp. 712–22.

years of scarcity.[7] J.S. Girdler, the strong proponent of traditional regulation, argued in 1800 that in preference to baking bread for sale, bakers should be obliged to bake any loaf or loaves brought to them by the inhabitants of the parish where they resided and should have to heat their ovens daily for the express purpose of doing this. He also suggested how much bakers should be paid.[8] Other restrictions faced by bakers included attempts by urban authorities or individuals to enforce monopolies. For example, action was taken in Macclesfield in 1765 against one Edward Shaw for setting up a large oven and bakehouse in the town in breach of the existing monopoly.[9] Not surprisingly, in nearby Stockport Sir George Warren attempted to maintain his bakehouse monopoly, claiming to have built two new bakehouses to meet the needs of the growing town.[10]

In practice it was almost impossible to maintain such restrictions in the face of growing urban demand. Even so, bakers were still complaining in the early nineteenth century that the amounts they were allowed by the magistrates for baking household bread were so low that they could make no profit. The bakers in Derby threatened to close their ovens unless the allowance was increased. Yet this sort of baking was increasingly only a small part of the trade of many of them. It was said that of the 26 bakers in Derby, only 5 or 6 lived by baking while the rest had chandlers' shops or other businesses.[11] Focusing on baking bread for sale and even running a small bread distribution business was not new. John Chapman in Chester faced opposition from the Bakers' Company in the 1730s for selling brown bread to the hucksters in Handbridge, across the River Dee from the city, who then supplied the poor labouring people of the area.[12] Bakers needed relatively little equipment. The bakehouse and shop of Joseph Vies of Heaton Norris near Stockport contained two tables, two shelves, two kneading troughs, a tub, a weighbeam and 16 pounds of weights, a cross-cut saw and two loads of flour. He was owed £16 in trade debts.[13] Personal wealth inevitably varied greatly, but could reach £300 in Chester.[14]

---

[7] Sidney and Beatrice Webb, 'The Assize of Bread', *Economic Journal*, 14 (1904): 196–218. The assize was in use in Chester in the scarcity years of 1767–68 (CALS, Mayor of Chester, Assize of Bread, 1767–8, ZMBB).

[8] Girdler, *Observations on the Pernicious Consequences of Forestalling*, p. 109.

[9] CALS, Earwaker Collection, Case on Macclesfield Bakehouse, ZCR 63/2/341.

[10] Stockport Local Heritage Library, Case of Sir George Warren respecting the Bakehouse, 1767, HX 181.

[11] BPP, *Minutes of Evidence Taken before the Committee to Alter and Amend Two Acts ... as far as Relates to the Price and Assize of Bread*, 1812–13, III (259), pp. 452–3.

[12] NA, Palatinate of Chester, Exchequer Pleadings (Paper), CHES 16/125.

[13] Lancashire Archives, Will and Inventory of Joseph View of Heaton Norris, Baker, 1768.

[14] Indications of personal wealth are derived from a sample of probate records in Cheshire Archives and Local Studies covering the period 1730–1815.

Much more visible among the producer-retailers operating along main shopping streets were clothing and footwear traders, particularly tailors and shoemakers. Tailors spanned the worlds of workshop production and the retailing of high fashion. Traditionally their role was to make up clothes in accordance with their customers' wishes, either in their workshops or in the houses of their customers. Their work was not confined to male garments but included women's gowns and cloaks, even if they were increasingly challenged by mantua makers in the eighteenth century. Many tailors also kept some stock of ready-made and second-hand clothing, although this was probably more common in the south than in the north of England. Nor is it always clear whether inventory descriptions refer to pieces of cloth from which garments were to be made or to the finished garment.[15] Robert Mansbridge who worked in north Hampshire in the early nineteenth century had around 220 different customers between 1811 and 1815 drawn from a catchment area of some 60 square miles. At first the bulk of his work consisted of repairing worn or damaged clothes, but increasingly the sale of ready-made garments came to predominate, accounting for two-thirds of his sales. Mansbridge does not appear to have sold second-hand clothes.[16]

Urban tailors could operate on a significant scale. In 1814 George Birkin in Stockport wanted a 'number of Journeymen Tailors ... good Workmen will meet with constant Employment at the advanced wages'. He had just returned from London with examples of the latest fashions.[17] The importance of the spring fashion season could render master tailors vulnerable to the demands of their journeymen without whom they would not have been able to make up fashionable clothes quickly enough. The Chester journeymen tailors went on strike in April 1788 after seeking an increase in wages from 12 to 14 shillings a week. Ten master tailors threatened them with prosecution at the next Quarter Sessions and announced that they would not employ any journeymen who were found guilty of combination.[18] The journeymen seem not to have obtained their demands since four years later they were back on strike asking for 13 shillings a week. Having initially refused this, 14 master tailors announced on 5 June that the 'hurry of business' and their desire to accommodate their customers had forced them to agree to a temporary increase in wages. One master had broken this agreement and all were therefore now forced to pay the higher wage to avoid loss of business.[19]

---

[15]   John Styles, *The Dress of the People: Everyday Fashion in Eighteenth-Century England* (New Haven and London: Yale University Press, 2007), pp. 153–6; Miles Lambert, 'Bespoke versus Ready-Made: The Work of the Tailor in Eighteenth-Century Britain', *Costume*, 44 (2010): 56–65.

[16]   Christina Fowler, 'Robert Mansbridge: A Rural Tailor and His Customers 1811–1815', *Textile History*, 28/1 (1997): 29–38.

[17]   *Macclesfield Courier*, 23 April 1814.

[18]   *The Cheshire Sheaf*, 3, 1883–6 (Chester, 1891) citing the *Chester Courant* for 10 and 17 April 1788.

[19]   *Chester Courant*, 5 June 1792.

The world of fashion, which will be considered in more detail in Chapter 5, was not wholly disconnected from the world of skilled workers trying to improve or even maintain their standard of living. Fashion had long been important to tailors. Richard Orme in Chester's Foregate Street just outside the city walls advertised in 1746 that he made jackets and riding habits after the 'best and neatest manner, as in London'.[20] Having a connection with London could be important for marketing. Samuel Browne, who made a point of describing himself as 'Freeman and Citizen', referred to his 24 years of practice in London, particularly at Mr Lynch's in Pall Mall where he was finisher for 12 years.[21] Henry Hancock tried to go one better. He had established a correspondence with the tailors to the Prince of Wales and would regularly receive 'the true, genuine, and most prevailing Fashions, worn at Court' and which he would be able to execute with neatness and punctuality.[22] Speed of execution could also be a selling point. George Birkin, the Stockport tailor, advertised 'Gentlemen's Clothes, Ladies Habits, Pelisses, and Servants Liveries at a few hours' notice'.[23] A successful tailor needed traditional craft skills and eye for fashion.

Much the same might be said of boot and shoemakers. Shoemaking was an important industry in the eighteenth century, consuming between 60 and 70 per cent of all leather. Almost everyone wore shoes, with average consumption running at two pairs a year. Men possibly owned more shoes than women and men's shoes were more expensive. Craft skills remained important with bespoke shoes generally being viewed as superior to ready-made.[24] Workshop production was the norm, although this could take place in a subcontractor's workshop far distant from the London or provincial shop where the shoes would be sold. For example, John Edwards of Wrexham supplied London shoemakers with 900–1,800 pairs of shoes each year in the 1750s. He produced a restricted range of types of shoe essentially for the London ready-to-wear market.[25] The shops where these sorts of goods were sold might carry very large stocks but did not need to be particularly sophisticated in terms of fixtures and fittings.[26] Shoe warehouses with large stocks of ready-made shoes became increasingly common from the mid eighteenth century. In Bath, for example, a Cheshire Shoe Warehouse was opened in 1766 as an outlet for the Nantwich footwear industry.[27]

---

[20]   *Adam's Chester Courant*, 6 December 1746.

[21]   Ibid., 31 May 1774.

[22]   Ibid., 6 July 1784.

[23]   *Macclesfield Courier*, 29 April 1815.

[24]   Giorgio Riello, *A Foot in the Past: Consumers, Producers and Footwear in the Long Eighteenth Century* (Oxford: Oxford University Press, 2006), ch. 2.

[25]   Ibid., pp. 179–81.

[26]   Ibid., (p. 117) cites the example of Rowland Rugeley from just outside London who had stock worth over £400 at his death in 1738, but shop fittings valued at only £2 10s.

[27]   Trevor Fawcett, *Bath Commercialis'd: Shops, Trades and Market at the 18th-Century Spa* (Bath: Ruton, 2002), p. 94.

An emphasis on cheapness and cash sales did not, however, preclude the need to be aware of and promote fashion. Samuel Davis of Stockport inserted a lengthy advertisement in the *Manchester Mercury* in 1764. He had just opened a wholesale and retail shoe and leather warehouse in the town. His advertisement included a price list for men's boots, shoes and pumps and for women's shoes and pumps. Men's best boots retailed at 20 shillings and women's best silk and satin shoes at 8 shillings. As well as ready-to-wear stock he would 'wait on any Person who chuses to have them bespoke' and he assured his customers that 'The newest Form and Fashion he will receive constantly from London'.[28] A decade earlier William Brown in Chester offered to serve the ladies with 'Silk and Stuff Shoes, as neat as in London'.[29] The shoe warehouses of the early nineteenth century may have made a point of discounting prices, but still offered bespoke shoes that would be suitably elegant.[30] Moreover those entering the trade fully recognized the need to take pains to learn their craft. Thomas Dunning, who was born in Chester in 1813, told of how after his father's death his mother married a Nantwich shoe manufacturer. Dunning did not want to limit his knowledge to the making of strong shoes for the working classes but rather wished to master the best class of ladies boots and shoes and sought out those who could teach him.[31] The Banbury shoemaker George Herbert similarly prided himself on his skill and on being able to satisfy the demands of noble and professional customers in the 1830s and 1840s, even if he failed to make much money.[32] The producer-retailer model of shoemaking prevailed until the second half of the nineteenth century.

House furnishing similarly combined craft and retail skills. The traditional occupations were those of upholsterer and cabinet maker. They were not all that numerous: the 1747 Chester poll book lists 9 upholsterers and 14 cabinet makers, compared with 153 cordwainers, 56 tailors and 36 bakers.[33] Directory evidence from the early nineteenth century suggests an increase in the number of cabinet makers, not only in Chester but also in towns like Stockport and Macclesfield,

---

[28]   *Manchester Mercury*, 17 July 1764.

[29]   *Adam's Weekly Courant*, 22–29 April 1755.

[30]   For example, J. Whitebrook in Watergate Street, Chester (*Chester Courant*, 16 October 1804).

[31]   David Vincent (ed.), *Testaments of Radicalism: Memoirs of Working Class Politicians 1790–1885* (London: Europa, 1977), pp. 119–24.

[32]   George Herbert, *Shoemaker's Window: Recollections of a Midland Town before the Railway Age*, ed. Christiana S. Cheney (Oxford: B.H. Blackwell, 1948), pp. 7–22.

[33]   *An Alphabetical List of the Names of All the Freemen of the City of Chester who Polled at the General Election ...* [in]*1747* (Chester, no date). The comprehensiveness of poll books clearly depends on how many of those eligible to vote voted, and on how many in any trade were free. Craft occupations seem to be better represented than purely retail ones and they include significant numbers of producer-retailers who either escaped the notice of directory compliers or who were employees not masters. The 1784 Chester poll book lists 24 cabinet makers compared to 6 in Broster's 1783 directory.

while the number of upholsterers remained in single figures.[34] Upholsterers were, however, important traders. From at least the late sixteenth century they had supplied and fitted all the textile furnishings in the home and increasingly became advisers on and arbiters of taste.[35] Abner Scholes of Chester, whose inventory was taken in 1736, was a very substantial businessman. He appears to have had a series of showrooms laid out as the rooms of a house.[36] These contained a mixture of a bed, chairs, looking glasses, prints and other items of furniture. Room number four, for example, consisted of a canopy bed, a screen, a yellow easy chair, a crimson easy chair, six chairs with leather bottoms and a looking glass. There were 10 such rooms. Scholes also had a shop full of fabrics, quilts, blankets, rugs and some miscellaneous furniture. His shop goods, including the new furniture in the showrooms, were valued at £420 and he was owed over £1,000 by customers, including other upholsterers, from the Chester area and parts of north Wales.[37] Scholes was almost certainly exceptional in the scale of his business and genuinely innovative in the way in which he displayed his goods. More typical was a Shrewsbury upholsterer whose goods were appraised in 1729 and who had fabric, blankets, rugs, a bed, a table and some chairs in his shop valued at £65. In Chester, John Brook's shop goods were valued at £43 in 1749 and similarly comprised fabric, quilts and carpets.[38]

Cabinet makers needed craft skills but could also be numbered among fashionable producer-retailers. John Cook announced in 1770 that he had moved to a shop in Eastgate Street Row in Chester next to Mr Griffith, silk mercer, and that he made and sold all sorts of cabinet work and chairs.[39] This was one of the most upmarket addresses in Chester. By 1785 he had moved to John Street slightly away from the fashionable heart of the city, but also had a warehouse in St Werburgh's Lane. Did he perhaps need more space or were producer-retailers like Cook being squeezed out by mercers and drapers? Whatever the reason, he was now selling a large variety of ready-made furniture, including mahogany wardrobes, desks, bookcases with glass doors, pier glasses and clocks.[40] The distinction between a high-class cabinet maker (as opposed to a cheap furniture shop) and an upholsterer was increasingly blurred by the early nineteenth century. In Macclesfield T. Smallwood described himself as a 'Cabinet-Maker, Upholsterer,

---

[34]   For example, *The Commercial Directory for 1816–17* (Manchester, 1816).

[35]   Clive Edwards, *Turning Houses into Homes: A History of the Retailing and Consumption of Domestic Furnishings* (Aldershot: Ashgate, 2005), pp. 27–9.

[36]   Andrew Hann and Jon Stobart, 'Sites of Consumption: The Display of Goods in Provincial Shops in Eighteenth-Century England', *Cultural and Social History*, 2/2 (2005): 165–87 (177).

[37]   CALS, Admon. and Inventory of Abner Scholes, 1736.

[38]   Lichfield Record Office, Inventory of Thomas Dickin of Shrewsbury, Upholsterer, 1729, B/C/5/1729/75; CALS, Sheriffs of Chester, Files, 1749–50, ZSF/182.

[39]   *Adam's Chester Courant*, 3 July 1770.

[40]   *Adam's Weekly Courant*, 4 October 1785.

Paper Hanger, Carver and Gilder' when he advertised 'a large assortment of Paper Hangings and Borders, which are the Newest Patterns from some of the principal Houses in London'.[41] In the middle of the nineteenth century the Barnsley cabinet maker William Tomlin was operating as a general house furnisher making, repairing, selling and altering furniture and upholstery items. In the course of 1845 he sold one Mr Elmhurst two fire screens and two picture frames, repaired some of his chairs, altered two mattresses and had one of his men repair a table. Other customers, like W. Newman, Esq. who paid a bill for £225 in 1843, received a complete house furnishing service.[42]

Watch and clock makers, goldsmiths and silversmiths were to be found in most towns of any size. Their businesses included selling new goods bought from London, or possibly Sheffield and Birmingham, making some items for sale, repairing customers' goods and buying old items for cash or in part exchange. George Lowe of Chester provides a good example. Lowe became free of the city in 1791, trading initially in Watergate Street as a silversmith and jeweller before moving to a more prestigious location in Bridge Street Row in 1804. Lowe's advertisement for that year expressed the hope that his stock was comparable to any outside London.[43] Lowe's customers were drawn from much of Cheshire and north Wales. They included Chester watchmakers, the Macclesfield ironmonger and jeweller William Royston and local gentry and professional men.[44] Traders like Lowe represented one end of the spectrum of producer-retailers, with back-street shoemakers at the other end. All, however, needed craft skills, the ability to sell goods to discerning consumers and in many instances an awareness of fashion. They might also have had a strong sense of belonging to some sort of organization or network that protected the interests of those who had invested time and perhaps money in learning their craft.

Belonging and Status

The Nantwich shoemaker Thomas Dunning took part in a procession of almost 500 members of his craft in 1833. He described how King Crispin rode on horseback in royal regalia with train bearers and how the officers carried beautiful specimens of boots and shoes. A sermon was then preached by the Unitarian minister, the Anglican Rector having declined to do so.[45] Although this can be read as a show of strength by a nascent trade union, it was not far removed in appearance from the traditional displays of the artisan craft guilds in, for example, a celebration like that

---

[41]   *Macclesfield Courier*, 1 April 1815.

[42]   Barnsley Archives, William Tomlin Ledger, 575/B1/1 (examples from pp. 188 and 106).

[43]   *Chester Courant*, 24 April 1804.

[44]   Lowe's of Chester, Day Books, 1792–5, 1810–11. In the possession of the firm.

[45]   Vincent (ed.), *Testaments of Radicalism*, pp. 125–6.

of the Preston guilds in 1802 when there was a week of processions and exhibitions involving all sections of the community.[46] It is important not to be too hasty in writing off guilds. In a place like Chester, leading citizens and important traders were likely not just to be members of a guild but also to take an active part in running it. Abner Scholes, the very enterprising upholsterer of the 1730s, was for many years a member of the Painters, Glaziers, Embroiderers and Stationers Company. Peter Broster, the bookseller and antiquarian, was steward of the Company on at least five occasions and had been a member for nearly 50 years when prolonged ill health led to him resigning his office in 1813. Other leading Chester booksellers and printers like John Poole and George Bulkeley were also members.[47]

It would be very difficult, particularly in the light of Sheilagh Ogilvie's magisterial survey, to argue that guilds brought general benefits to the wider economy of a region or nation. Guilds tended to be rent-seeking monopolies that sought to restrict their membership, limit competition and intimidate non-members. Their activities distorted the market and pushed up prices. They may have generated social capital but it is questionable whether any benefits from this outweighed the disadvantages of trade restrictions.[48] By the eighteenth century most urban craft guilds in England, and indeed in north-west Europe, were much less powerful institutions than they had been in the later middle ages, but they could still be important as part of the context within which business networks were created and sociability expressed.[49] One aspect of this was representing the interests of a particular trade when these appeared to be threatened by, for example, greater liberalization. In March 1779 the York Bakers' Company received a letter from the London Bakers' Company alerting them to the Bill that had been brought into the House of Commons to allow anyone to exercise the trade of butcher or baker without having been apprenticed. They were asked to petition their Member of Parliament and ask him to oppose the Bill on the grounds that bakers needed the protection of the apprenticeship laws, which controlled entry to the trade, because the assize of bread meant that their profits were restricted. The York bakers also argued that, because many in the city baked their own bread, there was little scope for increasing the numbers in the trade and that encouraging this would drive some of their members out of business. There was clearly a strong element of special pleading here and the MP, Charles Turner, initially argued that enforcing the apprenticeship laws harmed trade: 'Almost in every Town in England where Trade flourishes greatly they never ask whether a Man has served his Apprenticeship'; and that cheaper bread would boost population and economic

---

[46]   Thompson, *The Making of the English Working Class*, pp. 464–67.

[47]   CALS, City of Chester, Painters, Glaziers, Embroiderers and Stationers Company, Minute and Account Book, 1700–1906, ZG 17/4.

[48]   Sheilagh Ogilvie, *Institutions and European Trade: Merchant Guilds, 1000–1800* (Cambridge: Cambridge University Press, 2011).

[49]   Bert de Munck, 'One Counter and Your Own Account: Redefining Illicit Labour in Early Modern Antwerp', *Urban History*, 37/1 (2010): 26–44 provides an interesting case study of the declining but by no means extinguished power of the guilds in the Low Countries.

activity. Correspondence from the Bakers' Company seems to have softened his view and after the Bill was thrown out he told the Company that he had obtained a promise that any legislation would protect the ancient rights of the citizens of York.[50]

Guilds also took an interest in the welfare of their members, and indeed of others who practised their craft. In the Netherlands some guilds offered benefits such as sick pay, pensions, widows' pensions and burial assistance to both masters and journeymen, operating as a sort of middle-class welfare provider.[51] English guilds made payments to 'travelling brothers' who were presumably seeking work. Such payments were frequently made by the York bakers' in the first half of the eighteenth century, while among those made by the Chester Painters were 2s 6d to a travelling bookbinder and 1s to a travelling glazier in 1712.[52] The Lichfield Butchers' Company made loans of up to about £5 to its members and charged 5 per cent interest.[53] Other welfare provision more often fell to friendly societies that might in some ways look rather like guilds. The Barnsley Cordwainers' Society, founded in 1747, claimed to be the oldest such society in England. Although originating in the shoe and leather trades, its membership quickly expanded to include a wide range of occupations. The Society agreed in 1764 to make a £3 payment on the death of anyone who had been a member for seven years. Members forfeited sixpence for non-attendance at the Easter feast. Two years later it was ordered that each member should pay sixpence on the death of a member and that the Society's officers should attend members' funerals. There was also provision for sick pay, limited by an 1802 order to not more than 13 weeks in a year for any one complaint.[54]

Belonging to a guild or similar society brought benefits, including the sociability and networking of annual feasts. Being unable or unwilling to join could lead to exclusion from a town's trading community, or pressure to pay a fee for the right to trade. The ability of guilds to control entry to a trade varied from place to place and time to time, but in general it diminished during the eighteenth century and threats to non-members could more easily be ignored. Indeed it was said that in Chester some guilds chose to discourage membership in order to limit the numbers entitled to a share in the Owen Jones charity.[55] Individuals did, however, at times fall foul of the guilds. For example, in Chester the Bakers' Company took action in 1736 against John Northover, a pastrycook and confectioner, for exercising the

---

[50]   British Library, Ordinary of the Company of Bakers in the city of York, Add. Ms 34605, fols 12–17.

[51]   Marco H.D. van Leeuvan, 'Guilds and Middle-Class Welfare, 1550–1800: Provision for Burial, Sickness, Old Age and Widowhood', *Economic History Review*, 65/1 (2012): 61–90.

[52]   British Library, Add. Ms 34605; CALS, ZG 17/4.

[53]   Lichfield Record Office, Butchers' Company Minute Book, 1631–1865, D77/4/3.

[54]   Barnsley Archives, Barnsley Cordwainers' Society, General Ledger, 1747–1867, A/2065/G/2/1.

[55]   BPP, *Report from Commissioners on Municipal Corporations in England and Wales, North-Western Circuit*, 1835, vol. XXVI (116), p. 497 (pp. 2633–7 of Report).

trade of a baker without being free of the Company. Northover argued that he was not a baker and had been apprenticed to a confectioner.[56] The Mercers' Company employed an attorney to take action against Thomas Bulkeley in 1740 for retailing goods without being free and in 1775 attempted to compel eight traders into the Company on payment of a £10 fine.[57] In Derby, action was taken against John Booth for employing a 'foreigner' John Gould as a mercer in order to make him a burgess. Booth was told that he no longer had the right to keep shop in Derby and that he was to shut up his shop window. As in Chester a suitable payment could purchase the right to trade as Dorothy Gratton discovered in 1710 when she paid the Mercers' Company £30 to have a milliner's business.[58] As late as 1820 the Lichfield Guilds took legal advice on their right to compel those following a range of retail and other trades in the city to pay £10 for membership of the appropriate company or face penalties. They were told they had such a right.[59] In Chester and elsewhere the civic authorities also took action on several occasions throughout the eighteenth century to compel traders to become free of the city. In the second half of the eighteenth century over 100 Chester traders were accused of trading without being free, and around half of these took up their freedom.[60]

Negotiating the regulations around trading in a city like Chester with its many guilds might have been regarded as an irritant, and minor cost, by retailers; or it might have been viewed as a route into useful networks, information and even status. Other ways into these included confessional networks, particularly membership of nonconformist churches, and involvement in local government.[61] Quaker families, such as the Fothergills and the Chorleys, were significant in Warrington in the eighteenth century, trading as ironmongers and linen drapers. Samuel Fothergill, a linen draper, had trained with Henry Arderne, a Quaker shopkeeper in Stockport where there were also a number of Quaker grocers.[62] In Derby, there was an influential grouping of Unitarians focused on the Strutt family and including the banker Samuel Crompton, the printer and bookseller John

---

[56]   NA, Palatinate of Chester, Exchequer Pleadings (Paper), CHES 16/127/1.

[57]   CALS, Mercers, Ironmongers, Grocers and Apothecaries Company, Account and Minute Books, 1668–1762 and 1751–1923, ZG/16/6582/3 and /16.

[58]   Derby Local Studies Library, Derby Company of Mercers, Apothecaries, Grocers, Ironmongers, Upholsterers and Milliners, Minute Book and Other Records, 1674–1740, Parcel 200/26–30.

[59]   Lichfield Record Office, Smiths' Company, Counsel's Opinion, D 77/4/6/4.

[60]   CALS, City of Chester, Assembly Minutes, ZA/B/4–5.

[61]   Robert Lee, 'Commerce and Culture: A Critical Assessment of the Role of Cultural Factors in Commerce and Trade from *c.*1750 to the Early Twentieth Century' in Robert Lee (ed.), *Commerce and Culture: Nineteenth-Century Business Elites* (Farnham, Ashgate, 2011), pp. 1–35.

[62]   Charles F. Foster, *Capital and Innovation: How Britain Became the First Industrial Nation* (Northwich: Arley Hall Press, 2004), pp. 245–54.

Drewry and some prominent retailers.[63] Despite his Roman Catholicism, the York upholsterer George Reynoldson had a range of contacts in civic and county life and played a major part in furnishing the Mansion House and Assembly Rooms in the city.[64] The Kendal mercer, Joseph Symson, was wealthy and influential with a wide network of business contacts and twice served as mayor of his town.[65] Peter Broster's role in Chester's civic life has already been mentioned. He was typical of those who served the city as sheriff and mayor. Between 1730 and 1815 grocers, wine merchants, druggists, drapers, apothecaries, hatters, mercers, stationers and printers featured strongly among the occupations of sheriffs.[66] Chester's more important shopkeepers made up its ruling elite.

Looking ahead into the mid nineteenth century, the Cornish shopkeeper Henry Grylls Thomas seemed almost to belong to a different and bygone age. The shop that he and his brother John ran in St Just sold drapery, haberdashery, groceries, ironmongery and other goods. Like many linen drapers and haberdashers had done in the eighteenth century, Henry visited London in the spring and autumn to purchase stock and to do some shopping for his wife and daughters. He was heavily involved in the life of his local community, including being on the committee of the Literary and Philosophical Institute, a member of the Board of Guardians and actively involved in the local Wesleyan Chapel. In August 1843 he entertained the local preachers and their wives for tea and supper as a sort of farewell to the preacher at St Just. John was an Anglican and was chosen as churchwarden in April 1843.[67] Henry must have been typical of many shopkeepers in small and medium-sized towns who had long been pillars of their local community. This sort of participation in local life was not only motivated by a desire to serve the community. Building networks and securing a reputation for trustworthiness was also crucial to running a successful business, particularly in a society where face to face relationships were crucial.

Networking and Trust

When Defoe's Moll Flanders entrusted £100 to a goldsmith and subsequently lost £70 of it, she commented that his 'credit, it seems, was upon the ebb before, but I, that had no knowledge of things and nobody to consult with, knew nothing of

---

[63]   Derbyshire Record Office, Friargate Unitarian Church, Minute Book, 1697–1819, D1312/A1.

[64]   Christopher Hutchinson, 'George Reynoldson, Upholsterer of York, fl. 1716–1764', *Furniture History*, 12 (1976): 29–33.

[65]   S.D. Smith (ed.), *'An Exact and Industrious Tradesman': The Letter Book of Joseph Symson of Kendal 1711–1720* (Oxford: Oxford University Press, 2002), Introduction.

[66]   I.M.B. Pigot, *History of the City of Chester* (Chester, 1815), pp. 250–9.

[67]   Richard G. Grylls (ed.), *A Cornish Shopkeeper's Diary 1843: The Diary of Henry Grylls Thomas, Draper and Grocer of St Just-in-Penwith, Cornwall* (Truro: Dyllansow Truran, 1997).

it, and so lost my money'. The moral she drew from this was that 'to be friendless is the worst condition, next to being in want that a woman can be reduced to'.[68] The implication was that men were more likely to have access to those networks that provided information or gossip about who could or could not be trusted and about the current state of business. Leaving aside for the moment the question of whether women were particularly disadvantaged in this way, there is no doubting the importance of networks. These included the web of commercial and transport links centred on key towns, business networks based around particular trades and those made up of family and friends. In north-west England a town like Blackburn could act as the gateway to north-east Lancashire, linking the textile towns there to Manchester and to major transport routes. Chester was the hub of a network extending across much of north Wales. Warrington, situated at the meeting point of north–south and east–west routes was more important than might have been expected given its size. Personal networks, as evidenced by probate records, tended to be quite local, with most linkages existing within a 20-mile radius. Most Chester apprentices came from towns and villages up to 12 miles away, though some originated in Manchester, Staffordshire and north Wales.[69]

Being part of a trading community was important to retailers. William Stout of Lancaster associated with his former apprentice companions and his close neighbours but also needed connections in London, Sheffield, Preston and elsewhere in order to stock his shop. The Sussex village shopkeeper Thomas Turner also had many links with London, settling accounts with nearly 30 suppliers on one trip there in 1759.[70] Joseph Symson bought his shop stock from a wide area, although links with London merchants in the Ludgate and Billingsgate area were again important. He used John Marsden at the Chester sugar house to receive payments for him and provide him with price information.[71] The Worcester grocer, Thomas Dickenson, was well acquainted with suppliers in London, Bristol and Liverpool. The London grocer and tea dealer Philip Cook not only supplied tea and coffee but also provided information about quality and the prices achieved at tea sales.[72] The best way of learning a trade was often by associating with others. It was said of the early nineteenth-century Stockport bookseller Thomas Claye that he haunted the bookshops in St Paul's Churchyard and learnt his business while employed by Robert Scholey of Paternoster Row for whom he undertook several business journeys.[73]

---

[68]   Daniel Defoe, *The Fortunes and Misfortunes of the Famous Moll Flanders* (1721; Oxford World's Classics edn, Oxford: Oxford University Press, 2011), pp. 107–8.

[69]   Jon Stobart, *The First Industrial Region: North-West England c.1700–60* (Manchester: Manchester University Press, 2004), ch. 7.

[70]   Cox, *Complete Tradesman*, pp. 179–85.

[71]   Smith, *Exact and Industrious Tradesman*, pp. cxxiii – cxxiv.

[72]   SRO, Thomas Dickenson, Purchasing Book, 1740–51, D 1798/HM/29/5.

[73]   Stockport Reference Library, *The Diary of Thomas Claye, 1803–1810* (photocopy).

It is easy to assume that this world of business association was almost exclusively male. This was, however, not necessarily the case. Women were by no means absent from retailing and their role was occasionally recognized by institutions such as guilds. In 1726 the Lichfield Butchers' Company admitted Mary Hollis, a widow, to the guild following her apprenticeship to Elizabeth Breward, the widow of another butcher.[74] The York Bakers' Company admitted Ann Hudson, widow of Thomas and who had married a butcher, as a free sister in August 1785.[75] The rise of male-oriented associations in the later eighteenth century may have pushed women out of economic power networks, but they continued to have a significant presence on the high street and not just in stereotypically feminine trades[76] In Manchester, for example, Mary Berry was a grocer in the market place in the 1770s while Elizabeth Baron was running her late husband's cabinet and upholstery business in 1804. Women supplying Dunham Massey in the 1820s and 1830s provided goods like clothing, bedding, chimney pots and leather.[77] Women shopkeepers were found in some of the best locations, such as Miss Lighthazle's millinery shop in St Anne's Square in Manchester in 1788, or Mary Dearlove, musical instrument manufacturer and Ann Broster, confectioner in Boar Lane, Leeds in 1826. Nor were they excluded from cultural networks: in 1816 the librarian of the Manchester Circulating Library was a Miss Blinkhorn.[78] As Hannah Barker says, 'lower middling women remained firmly enmeshed in the commercial lives of their towns well into the nineteenth century'.[79]

Participation in business and other networks, whether formal or informal, may have brought social or cultural pleasure, but one of its key commercial purposes was to establish who could be trusted either as a supplier or a customer. At the heart of this was the question of credit. The term still had moral as well as commercial connotations, at least in the earlier part of the eighteenth century, being associated with honour, reputation and trust. In the early modern period the market not only provided a structure for the exchange of goods but also for the communication of social trust.[80] To be credit-worthy implied not only financial solidity but also social respectability. The terms on which credit was offered helped to position the debtor within the social hierarchy. The extending of credit, like the bestowing

---

[74]   Lichfield Record Officer, Butchers' Company Minute Book 1631–1865, D 77/4/3.

[75]   British Library, Add. Ms. 34605, fol. 17.

[76]   Margaret R. Hunt, *The Middling Sort: Commerce, Gender, and the Family in England, 1680–1780* (Berkeley and London: University of California Press, 1996), pp. 129–33.

[77]   Hannah Barker and Karen Harvey, 'Women Entrepreneurs and Urban Expansion: Manchester 1760–1820', in Rosemary Sweet and Penelope Lane (eds), *Women and Urban Life in Eighteenth-Century England* (Aldershot: Ashgate, 2002), pp. 111–29.

[78]   Hannah Barker, *The Business of Women: Female Enterprise and Urban Development in Northern England 1760–1830* (Oxford: Oxford University Press, 2006), pp. 90–102.

[79]   Ibid., p. 104.

[80]   Craig Muldrew, *The Economy of Obligation: The Culture of Credit and Social Relations in Early Modern England* (Basingstoke: Macmillan, 1998), pp. 3–5.

of gifts, required proper acknowledgement and was situated in a web of mutual obligations. This was beginning to change as the century progressed, particularly with the growth of consumer culture. Much eighteenth-century fiction was situated in this changing world, and in some cases helped the reader to learn the skills necessary to probe character and, by implication, credit-worthiness. Both literary and economic texts had a role to play in creating a society in which credit relations were the norm and were becoming increasingly divorced from some of the earlier notions of hierarchy and obligation.[81]

Credit was fundamental to retailing. According to Defoe, 'Credit, next to real stock, is the foundation, the life and soul of business in a private Tradesman; it is his prosperity; 'tis his support in the substance of his whole trade'.[82] According to the writer of the *Tradesman's Director* most country dealers obtained an average of 12 months' credit from their London suppliers. He gave the sound, but not particularly helpful, advice that 'every Man from a Knowledge of his Customers, forms to himself particular Rules and Maxims in his Business, and manages it according to the Experience of the Persons he deals with'.[83] There is evidence of retailers extending credit to customers from at least the sixteenth century and book debts often represented 10 to 20 per cent of their moveable wealth. Individual debts were frequently for less than £1 and many retailers received regular but partial payments from their customers.[84] Higher class customers might expect to settle the bulk of their account annually and could resent being chased for payment. Parson Woodforde was outraged when in 1799 his draper and tailor sent him unsolicited bills for goods and resolved to use different traders in future.[85] Some customers took unreasonable (at least in the eyes of the retailer) advantage of these conventions. Writing in 1752 to Edward Sulyard at Haughley Park near Stowmarket, John Stannard who had supplied him with wine and brandy said that he was always willing to extend eight months credit but no more. He complained that if he paid his creditors in the same way that Sulyard paid him he would not be trusted for a farthing and added, 'I wish Gentlemen wou[l]d Consider ye Hardship Tradesmen Labour under w[he]n such Credit is taken'.[86] Sulyard was also reminded by one of his correspondents when informing him that the plumber

---

[81]   Finn, *Character of Credit*, especially Introduction and ch. 1. Mary Poovey, *Genres of the Credit Economy: Mediating Value in Eighteenth and Nineteenth-Century Britain* (Chicago: University of Chicago Press, 2008) is a thought-provoking account of the separation of literary and economic genres and of their role in mediating value and helping people to understand the new credit economy and market model of value.

[82]   Daniel Defoe, *The Complete English Tradesman* (London, 1727), p. 336.

[83]   *The Tradesman's Director, or the London and Country Shopkeeper's Useful Companion* (London, 1756), p. 54.

[84]   Cox, *Complete Tradesman*, pp. 147–57.

[85]   Finn, *Character of Credit*, p. 96.

[86]   SRO, Sulyard Family, Edward Sulyard (1707–1785) of Haughley Park, Correspondence, D 641/4/J/14/2/7.

was in need of payment that 'no one thing is more Dishonour to a Gentleman than non paym[en]t when a workman Brings his Bill'.

Not all customers had this sense of honour. Most retailers had some bad debts and all were likely to have had customers who delayed paying bills for as long as possible. In the nineteenth century bad debts may have amounted to 50 per cent of the total number of debts, but perhaps only 4 per cent of turnover.[87] Traders had to be persistent in chasing some customers. The London tailors Say and Pierce wrote to Dr Wighton at Wetherby in June 1758 about his son's outstanding bill for £16 11s 9d. They asked for payment and refused to make clothes for the son's man without the father's orders. They were still chasing the bill in March 1760.[88] Failing to control credit properly could lead to a retailer becoming insolvent. Many found themselves subject to the legislation concerning insolvent debtors. William Tatnall, mercer and grocer of Eccleshall in Staffordshire, was not untypical. His schedule of debts taken in 1781 implies that he was trading on a significant scale and numbered many local traders among his customers. Debts for goods sold and delivered ranged from £46 to a few pence. Most were for amounts of under £1. It seems likely that, however popular Tatnall's sugar, tobacco, starch, stockings, gloves, handkerchiefs and other goods were with his customers, he had not taken proper care to secure prompt payment.[89]

Trust was an essential ingredient in eighteenth-century retailing. Abuse of trust could have serious consequences. Such abuse could take many forms. There might be misunderstandings about how bills were to be paid. In the 1710s Thomas and Elizabeth Bowers of Poulton in Cheshire regularly bought meat on credit from Randle Pickmore, a Chester butcher. When Thomas died in 1720 it was claimed that he owed £29 10s 9½d to Pickmore. His widow then ran up further debts. After Pickmore's death his executors tried to collect the money only to be met with a counterclaim from Elizabeth Bowers that she and her late husband had supplied the butcher with cattle to a value largely equal to that of the meat purchased.[90] Retailers had to trust those who entered their shops not to attempt to steal goods or defraud them. Shoplifting was sufficiently common for London retailers to take preventive measures such as improved lighting, internal partitions and mirrors behind counters. Some had alarms or traps in their windows.[91] Shopkeepers who allowed themselves to be distracted could become victims of theft. Thomas Roberts of Bilston in Staffordshire sold a shawl to a customer in September 1812. He then turned to reach an umbrella from his shop window and noticed that the

---

[87]   David Alexander, *Retailing in England during the Industrial Revolution* (London: Athlone Press, 1970), pp. 180–1.

[88]   NA, Chancery: Master Farrer's Exhibits, Say and Pierce Letter Book, 1756–63, C 108/30 fols 308 and 323.

[89]   SRO, Quarter Sessions Files, Q/SB/1781 M/217.

[90]   NA, Palatinate of Chester, Exchequer Pleadings (Paper), Chester 16/123(2).

[91]   Shelley Tickell, 'The Prevention of Shoplifting in Eighteenth-Century London', *Journal of Historical Research in Marketing*, 2/3 (2010): 300–13.

shawl had gone. His customer offered to be searched but he refused to do this as he suspected another person who had just left his shop. He stopped this person, one Ann Baugh, in the street and found the shawl in her pocket with his mark on it, thus disproving her claim to have bought it at Wellington.[92] A Chester grocer was the victim of fraud in 1764. A person claiming to be a carrier and to have come from Thomas Hughes of Mochdre in north Wales entered Thomas Griffith's shop with a letter and ordered goods including 12 pounds of tobacco. The goods and a bill were delivered to Hughes. Soon afterwards Griffith's clerk William Edwards saw Hughes and asked if he had received the goods. Hughes said he had neither ordered nor received them. Edwards subsequently discovered that other retailers had received counterfeit letters, all in the same handwriting, ordering goods.[93]

Not every retailer was wholly trustworthy. Even Defoe accepted that some slightly sharp practices were acceptable: no shopkeeper who said that he could not abate the price asked should be taken literally.[94] Sometimes, however, it was the quality of the goods that were in question. Joseph Parker, a Chester upholsterer, frequently sold beds to Richard Wickstead, a gentleman, in the 1730s and 1740s. Between 1733 and 1736 Wickstead ran up a bill for £21 17s 7d for goods including a blue standing bed costing £10 4s 12 chairs costing 2s 6d each, and feathers and blankets. He subsequently disputed part of the bill, claiming that the blue bed was second-hand and not worth above £5; that the feathers of the feather bed were so dirty that they could not be used until they were dressed again and that when this was done 40 pounds of dirt and old feathers were taken out; that a quilt had been burnt during printing; and that the chairs were only worth 18 to 20 pence each.[95] As so often in such cases the outcome is not known, but Parker's good name was clearly threatened.

The Business of Retailing

A retailer's greatest asset was his or her reputation. Defoe emphasized this but also drew attention to some of the practical aspects of successful retailing. These included choosing the right situation, not crowding a shop with too many goods, finding good staff but not allowing them too much liberty and not overspending on lavish display.[96] Shopkeepers were certainly aware of the importance of having the right premises. The best shops in towns of any size tended increasingly during the eighteenth century to cluster in principal shopping streets or around the market place. In Chester the prime locations were the rows on the south side of Eastgate Street and the east side of Bridge Street. Yet even here it was not impossible for a row level linen draper to be located above a street-level butcher or, as in

92	SRO, Quarter Sessions Files, QS/B 1812 M/586.
93	CALS, Chester Quarter Sessions Examinations, 1766, ZQSE/15/28.
94	Defoe, *Complete English Tradesman*, p. 227.
95	NA, CHES 16/129.
96	Defoe, *Complete English Tradesman*.

Batenham's etching of Bridge Street (Figure 2.1), for a druggist's shop to have a fashionable bow window next to an old-fashioned shop door.

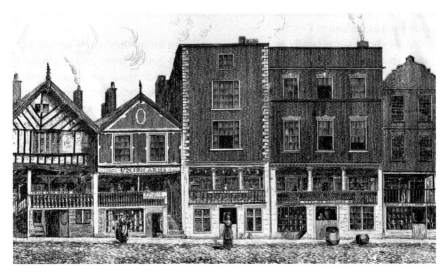

Figure 2.1   Part of the east side of Bridge Street, Chester

Source: Ancient Chester. Reproduced by permission of Manchester Libraries, Information and Archives, Manchester City Council.

The city's Assembly regularly dealt with petitions from retailers looking to improve their shop premises. One concern was improved lighting, which often meant extending a street-level shop so that it was flush with the row above, and removing any makeshift buildings that had projected into the street. For example, the grocer Thomas Griffith sought permission in 1768 to extend his Bridge Street shop, then in the possession of John Edwards, four feet four inches into the street so as to lighten it and ornament it to public view.[97] In 1790 John Bulkeley claimed that unless the front of his wine vaults was brought forward 'as others are' he would be unable to conduct his business properly and would need to use candles two hours sooner than any other wine vaults.[98] Unauthorized improvements were not encouraged. Matthew Hinton, a druggist, and Mrs Edwards, a milliner, were ordered to reduce or remove windows in the 1760s and in 1779 there was a general order that those who had made projections by means of bow windows were to remove them.[99] While all of this suggests that glazing and window displays were very much the norm by the last third of the eighteenth century, there were still shops where goods were sold though unglazed open windows and where shop fittings amounted to little more than

---

97   CALS, Assembly Minutes, ZA/B/4, fol. 259v.
98   CALS, Assembly Files, ZAF/57.
99   CALS, Assembly Minutes, ZA/B/4 fols 246v, 257, 336.

shelves, counter and drawers.[100] Falkingham Gawthorne of Derby stocked a range of metalware and japanned ware in the 1760s and counted Lord Scarsdale of Kedleston among his customers. His quite modest shop fittings comprised two counters, a nest of drawers, a glass case with a compass end, two other glass cases and shelves and other shelves, valued at £4 15s.[101]

Most shops were family businesses, possibly with an apprentice or two or a journeyman. Advertisements for apprentices and journeymen were common. Examples from the growing town of Stockport include those for a journeyman bookbinder and an apprentice wanted by John Reddish, bookseller; a journeyman tallow chandler who should also be accustomed to the grocery business and of good character wanted by James Mayers; and a journeyman grocer and an apprentice (preferably a youth from the country) wanted by Edward Turner.[102] In Chester, apprentices were still being formally enrolled in the early nineteenth century. They were more common in the producer-retailer trades than among pure retailers, but Hugh Lloyd, a druggist, took eight apprentices between 1799 and 1814 and Thomas Griffiths, a woollen draper, seven between 1805 and 1815.[103] Apprentices were no doubt used as cheap labour, but apprenticeship could be the entry point to a successful career in retailing.[104] In Stockport, Robert Rostron established a major drapery business in the centre of the town after being apprenticed to James Leech, a linen and woollen draper and marrying his daughter.[105] Benjamin Clubbe, a Chester grocer, somewhat unusually gave his apprentice William Hilditch first option on buying his stock in trade after his death.[106]

Although credit was ubiquitous in retailing, there is evidence of fixed price and cash sales from at least the early eighteenth century, particularly for patent medicines and goods like tea and coffee.[107] Retailers often made a point of mentioning prices in their advertisements. Samuel Fox, a Derby bookseller, sold paper hanging 'on as low terms as it can be bought in London'.[108] Henry Gibson and Benjamin Taylor announced their new grocery shop in Derby's fashionable

---

[100]   Jon Stobart, 'A History of Shopping: The Missing Link between Retail and Consumer Revolutions', *Journal of Historical Research in Marketing*, 2/3 (2010): 342–9.

[101]   Lichfield Record Office, Inventory of Falkingham Gawthorne of Derby, Brazier, B/C/5/1769/89.

[102]   *Manchester Mercury*, 15 February 1785, 12 April 1785, *Macclesfield Courier*, 27 April 1811.

[103]   CALS, Mayor of Chester, Apprenticeship Register, 1798–1819, ZMAB/3.

[104]   See Jane Humphries, *Childhood and Child Labour in the British Industrial Revolution* (Cambridge: Cambridge University Press, 2010), ch. 9 for a reappraisal of apprenticeship.

[105]   William Astle (ed.), *'Stockport Advertiser' Centenary History of Stockport* (Stockport, 1922), p. 112.

[106]   CALS, Will of Benjamin Clubbe, 20 June 1812 (WS Series).

[107]   Cox, *Complete Tradesman*, pp. 103–4.

[108]   *Derby Mercury*, 2 August 1765.

Irongate in 1785. Their tea, coffee, chocolate, sugar and all other groceries would sell 'at the most reasonable rates'. Their respectability was perhaps suggested by their having been 'late servants to Mr John Hardcastle'.[109] Hannah Storer, a widow who was now trading with her daughter, also in the fashionable heart of Derby advertised cut and plain glasses, jasper and Egyptian ware on the lowest terms.[110] Advertisements of this type were all too common and tend to lend weight to the Muis' assertion that by the end of the eighteenth century price ticketing, leading articles, ready money sales, mail order, free delivery and money-back guarantees were all used by some shopkeepers.[111] Yet it was also the case that even fashionable shops did most of their business on market days, that retailers found it helpful in establishing their reputation to refer to the person they had previously worked with or purchased premises from and that only a minority of retailers saw the need to promote themselves through newspaper advertising. Nor were shops particularly busy, at least in terms of numbers of customers. Thomas Dickenson, the Worcester grocer, rarely recorded sales to more than 10 customers a day and often had fewer than 5, at least in his early years.[112] Even allowing for time spent packing up and despatching orders, shopkeepers like this must have had ample leisure to entertain favoured customers in a back room.

What sort of image of themselves did retailers wish to present? Advertisements and trade cards offer some clues. Some advertisements seem to have been intended to be essentially informative, helping potential customers to become aware of what was available by listing the commodities on offer. Others, through a mixture of text and image, presented shopping as a pleasurable and fashionable activity. The language of politeness was often used, both to appeal to a higher class of customers and to imply that the purchase of the right goods could provide access to a polite lifestyle.[113] Trade cards, where the visual imagery could be at least as important as the text, were used not so much to promote particular goods as to encourage repeat business. Their language tended to be seductive rather than informative, using words and phrases like 'superior' and 'of best quality'.[114] An advertisement from Stockport, hardly the most fashionable of towns in the early nineteenth century, illustrates some of this. J. Tidmas 'respectfully' told the town's inhabitants that he had recently taken over Mr Wood's linen and woollen drapery shop and intended to reopen it with a 'new and fashionable assortment of goods'

---

[109]   Ibid., 24 November–1 December 1785.

[110]   Ibid., 1 January 1795.

[111]   Mui and Mui, *Shops and Shopkeeping*, p. 247.

[112]   SRO, Thomas Dickenson Account Book, 1740–47, D1798/HM/29/2. There may have been unrecorded petty cash customers.

[113]   Stobart, Hann and Morgan, *Spaces of Consumption*, pp. 171–84; Stobart, 'Selling (through) Politeness'.

[114]   Maxine Berg and Helen Clifford, 'Selling Consumption in the Eighteenth Century: Advertising and the Trade Card in Britain and France', *Cultural and Social History*, 4/2 (2007): 145–70.

which he had 'selected from the first Markets for cash' and which he would sell on such terms as he hoped would give him 'the same liberal Patronage and Support as enjoyed by his predecessor'.[115] The language is deferential, implies that Tidmas, though new, is to be trusted and assumes that customers desire fashion, quality and good value for money. It is difficult to judge the extent to which this sort of self-promotion was typical of retailers in general given that most did not use newspaper advertisements. Perhaps some considered it too vulgar and preferred to let their shops speak for themselves while others were content to wait in dark and old-fashioned premises for their handful of regular customers to enter.

Whether or not they perceived themselves as fashionable, retailers were in a risky business. Trade directories suggest that shops were continually appearing and disappearing. This could reflect changing criteria for inclusion in the directory, a change of location, the death of the owner, sale of the business or business failure.

Table 2.2   Survival rates of retail businesses in Chester, 1783–1797

Trade group	Number in 1783	% remaining in 1787	% remaining in 1797
Bakers, flour dealers and confectioners	26	65	31
Butchers	21	95	24
Grocers and tea dealers	32	81	37.5
Mercers and drapers	26	65	42
Milliners	11	55	9
Shoemakers	20	90	40
Furniture trades	10	80	50
Gold and silver smiths	5	100	60

Source: P. Broster, *The Chester Guide* (Chester, 1783, 1787, 1797).

Table 2.2 uses the Broster series of Chester directories to offer an indication of survival rates for different types of retail businesses in the 1780s and 1790s.[116] In most trades over half of those listed in 1783 had disappeared by 1797, and in some trades, particularly milliners, very few survived. On the other hand, retailers could become very wealthy, although it is often impossible to know how much of that wealth was derived from retailing. Mercers and drapers were usually among the wealthiest with one Stockport draper leaving over £1,400 in specific legacies

---

[115]   *Macclesfield Courier*, 3 April 1813.

[116]   In common with most late eighteenth-century directories the Broster series provides better coverage of higher-status city centre traders than it does of producer-retailers or those on the fringes of the city. Internal evidence from the directories suggests, however, that they were regularly updated and that inter-directory comparisons can be made with a reasonable degree of confidence.

in 1736 and one Chester mercer £3,600 in 1760.[117] A Chester grocer left £3,200 in legacies in 1751.[118] Personal wealth of over £1,000 was, however, rare. There is more evidence of wealthy retailers by the early nineteenth century. Three Chester mercers and drapers left personal wealth of around or over £1,000 between 1811 and 1815, including John Brown who was probably worth over £10,000; as did one Chester butcher, a Stockport grocer, a Chester grocer and a Chester glass dealer.[119] Thomas Poole, a Chester bookseller and stationer, had houses in Northgate Street, Crane Street and Pepper Street and his widow swore on oath in 1818 that his personal effects were worth up to £6,000.[120] On the other hand, Peter Broster's personal estate was put at no more than £600.[121]

Conclusions

It is almost impossible to generalize about urban retailing in the eighteenth century and early nineteenth. There were numerous retailers who positioned themselves as part of polite society. They improved their shops, advertised their fashionable wares in suitably polite language, produced elaborately illustrated trade cards and billheads and mixed with the cultural elite of their locality. Even the fairly conservative Broster and Son advertised that they were booksellers and stationers to the Duke of Gloucester (Figure 2.2).[122]

Retailers like these were ready to change with the times, although few of them experimented with radically different trading methods. For the most part change was evolutionary rather than innovatory although some, like Abner Scholes the Chester upholsterer, had radical ideas about display. Fashionable retailers were not only found in leisure towns but also in the growing industrial cities of Manchester or Sheffield and in a town like Stockport.[123]

It is, however, questionable whether these were typical of urban retailers. Are we perhaps more aware of them because of their investment in self-promotion? Most eighteenth-century retailers remain in relative obscurity, often no more than a name in a trade directory or other listing. Many still combined production with retailing. Their main concern was to make a living, preserve their reputation and good credit and perhaps take some part in community life, including membership

---

[117] CALS, Wills of John Sidebotham, 1736 and Robert Davies, 1760, WS Series.
[118] Will of William Goodwin, 1751, WS Series.
[119] Derived from the figures for wealth not exceeding a specified amount in the Cheshire probate records.
[120] CALS, Will of Thomas Poole, 1818, WS Series.
[121] CALS, Will of Peter Broster, 1816, WS Series.
[122] CALS, Dean and Chapter of Chester, Vouchers to Account, 1810–13, EDD 3/8/7.
[123] Although Manchester (but perhaps not Sheffield) was still perceived in the eighteenth century as a pleasant and cultured place to live (Cox and Dannehl (eds), *Perceptions of Retailing in Early Modern England*, p. 100).

Figure 2.2   Broster and Son, Chester, billhead, 1810

Source: Cheshire Archives and Local Studies, Dean and Chapter of Chester, Vouchers, 1810
–13, EDD 3/8/7. Reproduced by permission of Cheshire Archives and Local Studies.

of a guild or trade body. They were solid and reliable rather than showy and insubstantial, and as such were the bedrock of the urban economy and the pillars of the local community.

Longer-term trends included an increasing separation of production and retailing functions, at least in terms of what went on in any particular shop. There was also a tendency for certain types of shops, mainly those selling fashion items or more expensive household goods, to cluster on key shopping streets while shops selling more everyday items became dispersed throughout growing towns.[124] Guild membership declined in importance but involvement in local government continued. Indeed following the 1832 Reform Act and the 1835 Municipal Reform Act shopkeepers were often able to consolidate their position both in reformed boroughs and in other institutions like Poor Law Guardians and Improvement Commissions.[125] A good reputation remained of the greatest importance for those who wanted to be part of respectable society. At the same time, rapidly growing industrial towns offered increased opportunities to make a precarious living at the margins of retailing. Chapter 3 explores these opportunities.

---

[124]   See, for example, M.T. Wild and Gareth Shaw, 'Locational Behaviour of Urban Retailing during the Nineteenth Century: the Example of Kingston upon Hull', *Transactions of the Institute of British Geographers*, 61 (1974): 101–18.

[125]   Winstanley, *Shopkeeper's World*, p. 19.

Chapter 3
On the Margins: Itinerant Traders and Neighbourhood Shopkeepers

In Charlotte Brontë's novel *Shirley*, set in the time of the Luddite disturbances of 1812, the Vicar of Nunnely asks William Farren who has been laid off by the mill owner Robert Moore 'And if somebody lent you a pound or two, could you make good use of it? Could you get into a new way of doing something?' After his wife's prompting, Farren responds 'Please God ... I could buy groceries, and bits o' tapes, and thread, and what I thought would sell, and I could begin hawking at first'.[1] It was not only in fiction that those who fell on hard times thought of turning to hawking as a temporary solution to their difficulties. The 'poor poetess' Jane Jowitt described in her memoirs how towards the end of the eighteenth century she arrived in Liverpool from Ireland and, failing to find work as a servant because she was Irish, was advised to buy some light goods and travel on foot to London in easy stages. Once in London she bought muslins, silk handkerchiefs and similar articles with a view to travelling around the countryside and selling them. While doing this she met one of her Irish acquaintances, married and moved to Sheffield.[2]

Jowitt and the fictional Farren were very different from the high street retailers described in the previous chapter. They were on the margins of retailing, drifting into it probably without any prior experience or training and possibly hoping that it would only be for a short time. Not all hawkers were marginal in this sense. Some were quite wealthy and some used hawking as a stepping stone to owning a shop in a market town. They were, however, still somewhat mistrusted as threatening the livelihood of shopkeepers or as being suspected of dubious if not illegal practices. Other retailers could be regarded as operating on the margins because they were not quite respectable, because they had no fixed premises, because of the small scale of their businesses or because retailing was not their main occupation. This chapter turns away from the settled and respectable world of urban retailing, including its more innovative and fashionable practitioners, to look at some of those who were on the margins. These include hawkers and pedlars, street traders, second-hand dealers and backstreet shops in growing towns. It also considers village shopkeepers who represented another facet of the world of traditional retailing and serve as a reminder that shops were geographically

---

[1]   Charlotte Brontë, *Shirley: A Tale, by Currer Bell* (1849; Oxford World's Classics edn, Oxford: Oxford University Press, 2007), pp. 120–1.

[2]   Jane Jowitt, *Memoirs of Jane Jowitt, the Poor Poetess, Aged 74 years, Written by Herself* (Sheffield, 1844), pp. 17–19.

widespread. The traders looked at in this chapter were even more diverse than the urban shopkeepers discussed in Chapter 2 but they were very important to the daily life of their communities. What they tended to have in common was an ability to adapt to changing circumstances and seize the opportunities presented by changing demand, including that from the lower orders of society.

Hawkers and Pedlars

There can be no doubt that itinerant traders were a familiar sight in early modern England. It is, however, impossible to estimate how many of them there were at any given time. Some 2,500 were initially licensed when this was introduced in 1697 but the number of unlicensed hawkers must have far exceeded this.[3] A hostile pamphlet from around 20 years later put their number at 30,000 of whom it was said not 2,000 took out licences. The writer suggested that if hawkers were suppressed the 2,000 would probably become shopkeepers and rest either become their servants or join the army.[4] It seems likely that it was the more substantial pedlars who took out licences and indeed that they may have welcomed the licensing system as a way of distinguishing themselves from rogues and vagabonds.[5] Some of these licensed hawkers had substantial businesses, including those from in and around Macclesfield who, unlike most hawkers who travelled on foot or had just one horse, often had three, four or even five horses.[6] According to official figures there were 6,319 licensed hawkers in England in 1820 and 7,057 in 1840 but again this is like to be a substantial underestimate.[7]

The number of hawkers and pedlars may be hard to determine, but the hostility towards them continued unabated throughout much of the eighteenth century and early nineteenth. A typical pamphlet was unequivocal in its condemnation:

> The Hawker, Pedlar, and Petty-Chapman ... are a Body of strolling, idle Vagrants, wandering about from Town to Town, and from House to House, vending deceitful Wares and Merchandizes, imposing upon the Ignorant and Unwary, and by artful Insinuations trick them of their Ready-Money in Exchange for Toys and Trifles of a bad Manufacture; wherein they are supported, to the great

---

[3]   Margaret Spufford, *The Great Reclothing of Rural England: Petty Chapmen and Their Wares in the Seventeenth Century* (London: Hambledon, 1984), p. 16.

[4]   *The Case of the Fair-Trader* (London, 1720?).

[5]   Spufford, *Great Reclothing of Rural England*, p. 9.

[6]   NA, Register of Hawkers' Licences, AO 3/370.

[7]   BPP, *Return of the Number of Hawkers Licensed in England, Scotland and Ireland, in Each of the Years 1800, 1810, 1820, 1830, 1840 and 1843*, 1844, vol. XXXII (123), p. 377.

Disreputation of Trade, by a few Wholesale Men, who find their Account in
contributing to the Imposition.[8]

The writer went on to describe the practices of what he called 'travelling retailers'.
These arrived in a town and took up residence in an inn, notionally renting a room
for a year to avoid being classed as a hawker. They then advertised their cheap
goods, enticing those with ready money to come and buy. After about two months
they would leave the area having drained it of its cash. Such travellers stood
accused of paying minimal rent, avoiding taxes and disrupting trade.[9] A slightly
later pamphlet claimed that hawkers and pedlars were the chief cause of the decay
of trade, and of debt and bankruptcy among shopkeepers.[10] Other accusations were
that they harmed carriers and inns by carrying packs from house to house and that
the only goods they sold cheaply were smuggled.[11]

Shopkeepers also petitioned the House of Commons for legislation to suppress
hawkers. There was a flurry of such petitions in 1730–31 including one from the
traders and shopkeepers of Chester, 'complaining of great Decays in their Trades,
occasioned by the clandestine Trade and Dealings, carried on by Hawkers, Pedlars
and petty Chapmen, and praying, that they may be suppressed, or such other
Relief given against them, as to the House shall seem meet'.[12] Shopkeeper–hawker
hostility peaked again in the 1780s in connection with the proposals for a tax on
shops. The licence fee for hawkers was increased in 1785 and they were forbidden
to sell by auction or in market towns except in the public market. In return they
would be allowed to set up in trade in the town where they resided without having
been apprenticed. These impositions were short-lived with the additional fee
being removed in 1789 and the restriction on trading in a market town in 1795.[13]
Shopkeepers returned to the fray in 1821–22 with further petitions like this one
from 'several Tradesmen and Retail Dealers' in Macclesfield:

The Petitioners suffer very great injury and loss in their respective trades and
business, from the practices of persons trading or professing to trade, under
colours of the various Acts relating to Hawkers and Pedlars, and the more
especially by persons travelling from town to town, and selling goods by public
auction, such goods being generally of inferior quality, and only calculated to

---

8   *Case of the Fair-Trader*, p. 1.
9   Ibid., p. 2.
10   *A Brief State of the Inland or Home Trade of England* (London, 1730), p. 59.
11   *The Case of the Shopkeepers, Manufacturers and Fair Traders of England, against the Hawkers, Pedlars, and other Clandestine Traders* (London, 1730).
12   BPP, Journals of the House of Commons, vol. 21, p. 448.
13   Mui and Mui, *Shops and Shopkeeping in Eighteenth-Century England*, pp. 78–81. Mui and Mui offer a comprehensive account of the politics of shopkeeping in the 1780s.

deceive the unwary; and praying the House to take steps for the protection of the Petitioners, and other tradesmen and retail dealers.[14]

A letter in the *Stockport Advertizer* criticized the practice of hawkers 'exposing various kinds of Goods for sale, not only at our fairs and markets, but also, almost daily, at private houses, to the great injury of the fair traders and dealers' and suggested that a similar petition to that from Macclesfield would be numerously signed.[15]

So who were these hawkers and pedlars whose activity aroused so much opposition but some of whose number conformed to a romantic image of rural life and were deemed acceptable to the 'picturesque eye'?[16] What is abundantly clear is that contemporaries included many very different types of trader in the phrase. Laurence Fontaine suggests a typology of European pedlars comprising destitute pedlars, regular pedlars and merchant pedlars. The first group were on the fringes of peddling but were often the most visible and the most disturbing to the authorities; the second group had established suppliers, regular customers and were able to offer credit; and the third group rented shops but were prepared to go back on the road if necessary. In the English context she added a fourth group who worked almost exclusively for their firm.[17] Fontaine also dated the decline of pedlars in England from the middle of the eighteenth century.[18] This is questionable, even if peddling changed its character during the century. It is also helpful to adapt Fontaine's typology in the English context and to look firstly at those who might be described as temporary shopkeepers (somewhat like merchant pedlars), secondly at the traditional man or woman with a pack or a cart (both destitute and regular) and then at the specialist pedlars who increasingly worked as agents.

Much of the hostility to pedlars in the earlier part of the eighteenth century was focused on those who rented rooms in a town for a few weeks to sell goods before moving on. A typical example was Samuel Reddish, a travelling dealer in upholstery goods, who came to Macclesfield in 1738. He hired a room in the Angel Inn and distributed printed handbills advertising his goods. The arrangement was presumably a satisfactory one. Reddish gained access to a wider market, the people of Macclesfield had more household furnishings to choose from and the proprietor of the inn got some rent. The borough authorities, however, wanted Reddish to pay 12 pence for the privilege of trading in Macclesfield. When he refused they seized a carpet. Despite this, Reddish returned in 1739 and 1740. Again he refused to pay toll and again goods were seized from him. Finally Reddish lost patience

---

[14]   Journals of the House of Commons, vol. 77, p. 91.

[15]   *Stockport Advertizer*, 26 March 1822.

[16]   Cox and Dannehl, *Perceptions of Retailing in Early Modern England*, p. 46.

[17]   Laurence Fontaine, *History of Pedlars in Europe* (Cambridge: Polity, 1996), pp. 79–93.

[18]   Ibid., p. 137.

with the borough authorities and brought an action against them for seizing a carpet worth 20 shillings, a coverlet worth 15 shillings and a saddle worth 20 shillings.[19] A typical advertisement provides an indication of the range of goods that such traders might offer. John Walker was at the Wheat Sheaf in Derby during the cheese fair there and then at the Flying Horse in Nottingham during their fair. He quoted prices for bed curtains, quilts, blankets, rugs, coverlets and French and Turkey floor carpets. He claimed that 'The Goods are all Fresh and New, and you may buy Goods here as cheap as in London, the Prices are fix'd so very low, for the Sake of ready Money, that small Abatement will be made'.[20] Although itinerant, Walker had a range of goods to rival those of many fixed shops and his sales techniques had many 'modern' features.

Large fairs continued to provide opportunities for traders of this type throughout the eighteenth century. Those who only traded at fairs were outside the legislation surrounding hawkers and pedlars, although it seems likely that some took a fairly flexible approach to how long the fair lasted. Thomas Minshull advertised in 1751 that he would be at Mr Maddox's cork cutter's shop during the Chester fairs selling a 'great Choice of China Ware, of the best and newest fashions'.[21] Zephaniah Kinsey of Bristol was a regular at the Chester fairs in the 1760s, taking a shop by the Eastgate and selling goods such as handkerchiefs, ribbons, muslins and linen cloth. He was unfortunate enough to be robbed in 1765 by one Margaret Taylor who subsequently sold the goods to several old clothes dealers in the city.[22] Traders like this were at the respectable end of the itinerant spectrum even if there was a growing feeling among some customers that the city's shopkeepers sold goods just as cheaply as those who attended the fairs.[23] Less respectable were those who found themselves in trouble with the authorities in the early nineteenth century for renting rooms in inns and trading without having the appropriate licence. Examples of this were Robert Parkinson, described as a stranger, and Samuel Pattison of Middlewich in Cheshire who were trading at Burslem. Pattison was said to have paid one guinea rent for his room at an inn and to have occasionally resided there but never paid taxes.[24]

Traders like these could equally well have been selling out of a pack or a cart. They were the archetypal hawkers and pedlars, little changed from the man with a pack arrested in Chesterfield in 1661 on suspicion of felony, and who had a variety of cloths in his hawking bag as well as buttons, needles, children's rattles,

---

[19]   CALS, Earwaker Collection, Case of the Corporation of Macclesfield re Tolls, 1742, CR63/2/341.

[20]   *Derby Mercury*, 11 September 1740.

[21]   *Adam's Chester Courant*, 24 September 1751.

[22]   CALS, Chester Quarter Sessions Examinations, 1766, ZQSE/15/62, 106–7.

[23]   Ian Mitchell, 'The Changing Role of Fairs in the Long Eighteenth Century: Evidence from the North Midlands', *Economic History Review*, 60/3 (2007): 545–73 (568).

[24]   SRO, Quarter Sessions Files, Q/SB 1804 A/25 and Q/SB 1808 M/342.

combs and thimbles in his trunk.[25] Some hawkers could become very wealthy. There was a large concentration of perhaps 400 in and around Alstonefield in the Staffordshire moorlands in the eighteenth century. They mainly sold textiles and were not linked to any one manufacturer or town. John Lomas bought printed cottons from Manchester and silk from Macclesfield. His itinerary took him through Lincolnshire, Cambridgeshire and Suffolk, selling goods and preaching at nonconformist meetings.[26] In a letter to Sir George Crewe in 1820 Lomas recounted how his parents had been poor pedlars and how he had travelled with them until he was 16 years old when his father entrusted him with a pack of goods and bought him his first licence. He obtained credit from Manchester traders and built up his business until he had 10 men travelling under him. In due course he became a wholesaler with a cart and horses. Such was his status that he was one of those involved in the petitions against the restrictions on pedlars imposed in 1785 and obtained an audience with William Pitt in the company of several opulent Manchester manufacturers.[27]

Lomas was not a typical hawker. Others from the same Staffordshire colony fell on hard times and found themselves imprisoned for debt. Samuel Salt of Goldsich in Alstonefield was one such who had with him in prison in 1778 a quantity of Manchester and Leicester goods 'very much damaged by carriage' and some miscellaneous household articles.[28] Salt and those like him were often owed money by other hawkers both from the Alstonefield area and further afield suggesting that there was an element of exchanging of goods within the pedlar community. Life could be very hard. John Brocklehurst of Alstonefield was arrested in the late 1760s for debts of about £40 due to Messrs McCain and Wright, button merchants of Macclesfield. He spent 12 months in Stafford gaol before being discharged. He and his brother Anthony then continued to work as hawkers until John died at Braintree in October 1771. Anthony then took all the goods they were hawking and John's widow complained that all she had received was an old coat, an old pair of breeches, shoes and a hat.[29] A 'Jew pedlar' named Jacob Israel and imprisoned at Chester for debt in 1801 had three travelling boxes together

---

[25]   Nottinghamshire Archives, Portland Papers, Inventory of William Johnson, DD/4/P/68/9.

[26]   David Brown, 'The Autobiography of a Pedlar: John Lomas of Hollinsclough, Staffordshire (1747–1823)', *Midland History*, 21 (1996): 156–66; David Brown, '"Persons of Infamous Character" or "An Honest, Industrious and Useful Description of People"? The Textile Pedlars of Alstonfield and the Role of Peddling in Industrialization', *Textile History*, 31/1 (2000): 1–26.

[27]   DRO, Harpur Crewe Papers, D2375/M87/19.

[28]   SRO, Quarter Sessions Files, Q/SB 1778 T/207.

[29]   SRO, Records of Challinor and Shaw, Inventory of John Brocklehurst and Related Letters, D3359/12/1/100.

with tools for trunk making in his possession. He attempted to maintain himself in prison by making boxes and sweetmeats.[30]

Thomas Holcroft described something of the life of a hawker in the mid eighteenth century. His mother, who had dealt in greens and oysters in London, started peddling goods like needles, tape, garters and small haberdashery around the outskirts and neighbourhood of the metropolis. His father left off shoemaking when Thomas was aged six and travelled around the villages and fairs of Cambridgeshire and then parts of the midlands selling similar goods. He sold wooden ware and trenchers at Macclesfield and then began to deal in buckles, buttons and pewter spoons. Subsequently he fetched pottery from the neighbourhood of Stone and hawked it throughout the north of England and the midlands. In due course he returned to shoemaking with Thomas offering some assistance. There is little of the romance or picturesque in this account: it was a harsh and precarious life.[31]

Hawkers like these were also subject to scrutiny by the authorities. In the late eighteenth century and early nineteenth those trading in and around market places had to take special care to stay within the law. This included having a licence and having the words 'licensed hawker' and the licence number on their pack or cart. Some town shopkeepers were keen to report offenders. For example in 1787 James Hordern, a Wolverhampton draper, accused William James of being an unlicensed hawker of iron and steel goods who had unlawfully set up a stall in Wolverhampton. James was fined £10 despite claiming that he had manufactured some of the goods sold.[32] Two convictions at Leek in 1810 involved a hawker who sold japanned ware but had no licence and one who sold linen cloth without having 'licensed hawker' on his pack.[33] Another incident in Wolverhampton, this time in 1802, involved one John Jones, a hawker from Manchester who was selling stockings, spectacles and razors in the market place. Jones was accused of exchanging sound coins for counterfeit money and when searched was found to have 6 counterfeit half-guineas, some counterfeit seven-shilling pieces and 66 counterfeit shillings in his pockets.[34] Those who suspected hawkers of dishonesty were not always wrong. There were complaints in the small market town of Oswestry in 1817 about Irish hawkers selling linen in the market place. Five of them were brought before the mayor and, being unable to pay the fine imposed, had linen seized. The town authorities claimed that traders who were not burgesses or licensed as hawkers

[30] NA, Palatinate of Chester, Papers in Causes, Bankruptcy, CHES 10/1/2.

[31] *Memoirs of the Late Thomas Holcroft Written by Himself, and Continued to the Time of His Death from His Diary, Notes, and Other Papers* (3 vols, London, 1816), vol. 1, pp. 4–60.

[32] SRO, Q/SB 1787 E/26.

[33] SRO, Q/SB 1810 E/212–13.

[34] SRO, Q/SB 1803 A/12.

could only sell non-foodstuffs at fairs.[35] The shopkeepers of Halifax complained in 1818 that they were much injured by hawkers, pedlars and tea dealers who sold 'very inferior and damaged' goods. They asked the proprietors of the market either to refuse standings to these hawkers or to charge them such rents as would put them on a more equal footing with shopkeepers.[36] When the corporation of Newport in Shropshire considered buying the market rights in the 1830s they were advised against trying to increase the revenues from the market by increasing the number of stalls for hawkers as this would harm shopkeepers in the town.[37]

By the early nineteenth century hawkers were increasingly seizing opportunities to trade in and around the markets of growing towns. The line between them and street traders was sometimes quite blurred. The hostility they faced from shopkeepers implies that they could be a real threat by competing on price. There were, however, still those who tramped the countryside or travelled by horse and cart. George Elson who was born in 1835 in Northampton told in his autobiography how his parents hawked drapery and haberdashery carried in wickerwork baskets slung over their backs. They sold Coventry ribbons, lace and silk, cottons and linens for cash at the door, setting off each Monday to work the surrounding countryside. Unlike the tallymen of later years they received a warm welcome from their customers.[38] Elson is perhaps guilty of romanticizing some aspects of hawker life as may have been the writer of *The Life and Adventures of a Cheap Jack*. Mid nineteenth-century cheap jacks would travel around fairs and markets with a good horse, a good carriage and £100 worth of goods, including tea and coffee services, pocket knives, spoons, men's waistcoats, books, bridles and saddles. Profits were between 20 and 40 per cent and the secret of success was to look for quick returns and only deal in ready money. Many had shares in entertainments and wild beast shows. By the 1870s when the book was published the coming of the railways and the increased number of shops were said to have damaged the trade.[39]

These autobiographies indicate the importance for many hawkers of being able to switch from one product to another depending on their customers. They needed to be adaptable and keenly aware of market conditions. Others were more specialized and might in time become tied to a single supplier. There had been travelling ballad singers since the sixteenth century who sold printed copies of the ballads they sang and hawkers were involved in the distribution of chapbooks in the seventeenth and eighteenth centuries. Some of these might simply have

[35]   Oswestry Town Council, Copies of Documents and Proceedings Relative to the Town and Liberties of the Borough of Oswestry 1818–1838, A 101, fols 20v–22.

[36]   WYAS, Calderdale, Halifax New Market Papers, Petitions, MISC 111/11/23.

[37]   SRO, Sutherland-Leveson-Gower Family, Newport Market, D593/T/4/18/18.

[38]   George Elson, *The Last of the Climbing Boys: An Autobiography* (London: J. Long, 1900), pp. 9–12.

[39]   Charles Hindley (ed.), *The Life and Adventures of a Cheap Jack by One of the Fraternity* (London: Tinsley Brothers, 1876).

carried a few books among the other items in their packs while others were closer to being distribution agents for the London chapbook publishers. Some provincial booksellers such as Neville Simmons of Sheffield acquired a hawker's licence so that they could sell books from door to door while others traded from market stalls in towns near to where they were based.[40] Hawkers defending themselves against attacks from shopkeepers drew attention to their role in promoting the toy trade. A 1731 pamphlet claimed that the great increase in toy manufacture in England in the previous 40 or 50 years was largely due to itinerant traders. Had it been confined to toy shops the 'extravagant' profits of the shopkeepers would have hindered the growth in trade and kept prices high. There is at least a hint here that some hawkers were effectively working on behalf of the toy manufacturers.[41]

The most significant group of specialist hawkers were the Manchester men who sold textile goods to shopkeepers and pedlars as well as door to door.[42] The proposed suppression of hawkers in 1785 provoked strong opposition from the manufacturers and printers of silk, linen and cotton goods. Hawkers and pedlars were a vital part of the distribution chain and 'From the Mode of their Sale, which is generally from House to House in Country Villages and Districts, remote from Towns where Shopkeepers reside, great Quantities of British Manufactures are sold which otherwise would not be disposed of'.[43] Over the subsequent half century an increasing number of textile and clothing pedlars lost something of their independence and became agents of a particular firm. In Stockport in the 1830s there were said to be many travelling clothing salesmen who called on families every three weeks or so. Some dealt with four or five such salesmen. One Manchester firm had five travellers, one of whom had 360 customers in Stockport. It was alleged that travelling salesmen charged 50 or even 100 per cent more than ready money shops but of course allowed customers to enjoy their purchases before they had paid in full.[44]

Even on a generous estimate of the number of hawkers in eighteenth-century England it is clear that they were greatly outnumbered by fixed shopkeepers.[45]

---

[40]   David Stoker, '"To All Booksellers, Country Chapmen, Hawkers and Others": How the Population of East Anglia Obtained Its Printed Materials', in Robin Myers, Michael Harris and Giles Mandelbrote (eds), *Fairs, Markets and the Itinerant Book Trade* (New Castle: Oak Knoll and London: British Library, 2007), pp. 107–36; Margaret Spufford, *Small Books and Pleasant Histories: Popular Fiction and Its Readership in Seventeenth-Century England* (London: Methuen, 1981), pp. 111–26.

[41]   *A Second Letter from a Hawker and Pedlar in the Country, to a Member of Parliament at London* (London, 1731).

[42]   Fontaine, *History of Pedlars*, pp. 92–3.

[43]   BPP, *Journals of the House of Commons*, vol. 40, p. 1001.

[44]   BPP, *Report from the Select Committee on Manufactures, Commerce and Shipping*, 1833, vol. VI (H.C.690), pp. 624–6.

[45]   Hostile estimates of numbers are up to 30,000 compared to the 130,000 or more shops in the mid eighteenth century (Mui and Mui, *Shops and Shopkeeping in Eighteenth-*

They were, however, important in the overall retail scene. Itinerant traders widened the market for consumer goods, particularly textiles, clothing and hardware, by reaching those customers who were either geographically remote from shops or who, for reasons of convenience or economics, preferred to deal with them either on a regular basis or occasionally. Hawking also offered a route into trading for those who had little capital. For some it was a temporary expedient but for others it could be the starting point for a successful career. The Staffordshire hawker John Lomas became a wholesale dealer while in the early eighteenth century William Johnson of Lincoln who started off as a pedlar with a pack of linen subsequently took a small shop in the city and then became a wholesale linen draper with a fortune of over £8,000 at his death.[46] It could be a good training ground for the acquisition of skills to do with buying wisely, having good product knowledge and being able to deal with a wide range of customers. Yet there was always something a bit marginal and not wholly respectable about even a successful itinerant. In the nineteenth century it was still hard to shake off the reputation of having been a cheap jack when trying to make a living in a more settled business.[47]

Street Traders, Second-Hand Dealers and Neighbourhood Shops

Leaving little trace in the records and occupying a murky area between licensed hawkers and legitimate market sellers were the street traders. These were the sort of people John Houghton was writing about in his defence of hawkers in 1700:

> I do think that a great Trade is far better for any Country than a little one; and I never yet met with the Man that could pretend with any Colour of Reason, that such things caused a lesser Consumption. I would fain have those that are against them consider what would become of our Milk & Makarel, our other Fish, Oranges and Lemons, Etc if no body could buy a single Penny worth, unless they went to a Market or a Shop for them; besides there are vast Quantities of damaged Goods that would never be sold, if 'twere not for carrying to the Mobb in this manner.[48]

Such petty traders might have been found on the margins of any substantial market but it is likely that they were much more common in London than elsewhere. Roger Scola found little evidence of them being particularly important in Manchester, suggesting some role in the distribution of milk and perhaps fruit and vegetables

---

Century England, p. 297).

[46]   Spufford, *Great Reclothing of Rural England*, p. 46.

[47]   *Life and Adventures of a Cheap Jack*, pp. 308–11.

[48]   J. Houghton, *A Collection for Improvement of Husbandry and Trade* (London, 1690–1703), No. 399, 15 March 1699/1700.

but with small shops rather than hawkers being the main source of supply for the working classes.[49]

Street traders, whether selling from a board or cart or hawking from a basket, were often seen as a nuisance. The inhabitants of Market Street in Sheffield complained in 1829 about carts loaded with fruit obstructing the street in front of their properties.[50] There were further complaints there in 1841 about 'hawkers' (again probably street traders) standing in front of the shops at the head of the shambles. Their violent conduct and indecent language was said to deter respectable people from buying from the shopkeepers. The hawkers were ordered to move away.[51] Some such traders felt aggrieved by the actions of the authorities. One Mrs Alcock, who made her living by selling crumpets and muffins, complained that when she was hawking a basket of them in Higher Hillgate in Stockport the toll collector demand one penny from her and seized some goods when she refused to pay.[52] In mid nineteenth-century Manchester there was pressure to remove old clothes dealers from the streets into more suitable premises. They caused an obstruction and it was suggested that such gatherings easily became places for the disposal of stolen goods.[53] Some traders started out by selling from a street stall before moving to a fixed shop. The Manchester second-hand bookseller James Weatherley began his career working for Joseph Macardy at his street stall. Weatherley soon set up on his own, selling some of his own books and those of his neighbours, which he wheeled in his wife's clothes trunk to a place in front of the Exchange. He took about 12 shillings on his first day. Weatherley progressed to a shop but through a combination of drink and business errors ended his career selling books from a board in John Dalton Street.[54]

Although non-food street traders frequently dealt in second-hand goods, the second-hand trade was by no means confined to the streets. There has long been a recognition that reusing and recycling goods was commonplace in pre-industrial England and the world of the second-hand has recently received considerable attention.[55] There were no rigid distinctions between first- and second-hand

---

[49]   Scola, *Feeding the Victorian City*, pp. 250–2.

[50]   Sheffield Archives, Arundel Castle Mss, Sheffield Market, ACM/S347.

[51]   Ibid., Market Petitions, ACM/S344/15.

[52]   *Stockport Advertizer*, 2 June 1843.

[53]   *The Guardian*, 5 January 1848; City of Manchester, *Proceedings of the Council, Nov. 1853 – Nov. 1854* (Manchester, 1855), p. 283.

[54]   Chetham's Library, Manchester, *Recollections of Manchester and Manchester Characters and Anecdotes Relating to Manchester and Lancashire from the Year 1800 to 1860 by James Weatherley*, MunA.6.30; Michael Powell and Terry Wyke, 'Penny Capitalism in the Manchester Book Trade: The Case of James Weatherley', in Peter Isaac and Barry McKay (eds), *The Reach of Print: Making, Selling and Using Books* (Winchester: St Paul's Bibliographies, 1998), pp. 135–56.

[55]   On recycling see Donald Woodward, '"Swords into Ploughshares": Recycling in Pre-Industrial England', *Economic History Review*, 38/2 (1985): 175–91. Gregson and

circulations of goods. Many retailers were content take old items in part exchange for new ones and would sell second-hand goods alongside unused ones. Motivations for buying second-hand were varied. Price might be a key factor but the second-hand market was by no means limited to those who could not afford to buy new goods. Some items, like out-of-print books, might only be available second-hand. Good quality second-hand furniture might offer better value for money than poorer quality new objects. Provenance and rarity might influence a prospective purchaser. Second-hand might then be perceived as collectable or as antique leading to the emergence of specialist dealers selling to collectors (see Chapter 6). Second-hand dealers did not necessarily operate on the margins and some could be respectable and wealthy; but many, particularly those who sold old clothes, were marginal.

Clothes, furniture together with some other household goods and books were the mainstays of second-hand retailing. The trade in old clothes was extensive but has left behind relatively little evidence. Beverly Lemire drew attention to its importance some 25 years ago and to the role of pawnbrokers, clothes brokers and itinerant wholesale dealers in disposing of old clothes.[56] Old clothes dealers rarely advertised in the newspapers and were often either not recorded at all in the earlier trade directories, or were listed as tailors or brokers. Some were included such as the 14 slopsellers in Liverpool in 1774, increasing to 42 in 1800, or the 21 slopsellers in Manchester in 1800, of whom one-third were women. Tailors often stocked old clothes, frequently accepting them in part exchange for new garments. Robert Wilkinson of Nantwich in Cheshire had 163 second-hand garments when his inventory was made in 1721. Pawnbrokers were also an important source of second-hand clothing. Clothes were by far the commonest items pledged and unredeemed pledges, which amounted to 27 per cent of the total at the York pawnbroker George Fettes, would enter the second-hand market. By the 1830s pawnbrokers might have several thousand garments in stock.[57] Stolen clothing also found its way into old clothes shops. Margaret Taylor who was accused of stealing various items from Zephaniah Kinsey at Chester in 1766 was said to have sold some ribbons to a Mrs Moreton who sold old clothes in Northgate Street, a piece of striped cotton to Mrs Orme who sold old clothes in Bridge Street and a cloak to Mrs Burrows who also dealt in old clothes.[58] Stolen clothes also circulated

---

Crewe, *Second-Hand Cultures*, and Stobart and van Damme (eds), *Modernity and the Second-Hand Trade*, are key works on the second-hand.

[56]   Beverly Lemire, 'Consumerism in Preindustrial and Early Industrial England: The Trade in Secondhand Clothes', *Journal of British Studies*, 27/1 (1988): 1–24. See Also Beverly Lemire, *Fashion's Favourite: The Cotton Trade and the Consumer in Britain, 1660–1800* (Oxford: Oxford University Press, 1991), pp. 178ff.

[57]   Miles Lambert, '"Cast-off Wearing Apparell": The Consumption and Distribution of Second-Hand Clothing in Northern England during the Long Eighteenth Century', *Textile History*, 35/1 (2004): 1–26.

[58]   CALS, Quarter Sessions Examinations 1766, ZQSE/15/106.

through more informal routes such as being sold on the highway or at a public house. All of these routes made second-clothing widely available and made it possible for poorer consumers to access the world of fashion. It is likely, however, that as the price of new clothing fell in the second quarter of the nineteenth century the second-hand trade declined in importance.[59]

Most of those who bought second-hand clothes did so out of economic necessity. This was untypical of second-hand markets in general. Middling-rank consumers chose to buy old furniture and old books for other reasons. Furniture brokers were common in towns of any size by the early nineteenth century. For example, Pigot's 1834 directory listed five in Macclesfield, nine in Chester and 12 in Stockport.[60] These probably represented the lower end of the business with better quality goods being available from auctioneers and cabinet makers who accepted old furniture in part exchange for new. Buying second-hand was a way of accessing quality, fashion and possibly provenance. It was a normal way for middling-rank consumers to furnish a house in the eighteenth century and early nineteenth.[61] Second-hand booksellers also ranged from those like James Weatherley trading on the streets of Manchester or in a cellar to specialist antiquarian dealers. Weatherley rarely handled high value books with few selling for more than £1 and in the early 1830s was probably barely making a living. Most provincial booksellers had a substantial second-hand trade and regularly issued sales catalogues giving details of prices and in some cases condition. Such catalogues could list several thousand books with prices ranging from a few pence to £10 or more for antiquarian items.[62]

The growing availability of cheap new clothes and household goods in the nineteenth century tended to push the second-hand trade either towards greater marginality or towards specializing in quality goods that were desirable because of age or provenance. Other types of back street and neighbourhood shops grew in numbers and importance. Retailers describing themselves as hucksters, provisions dealers or just as shopkeepers existed in eighteenth-century towns. For example, the *Universal British Directory* listed 94 shopkeepers in Manchester and Salford in the 1790s.[63] Coverage only really improved, although still better for town centre shops

---

[59]   Alison Toplis, 'A Stolen Garment or a Reasonable Purchase? The Male Consumer and the Illicit Clothing Market in the First Half of the Nineteenth Century', in Stobart and van Damme (eds), *Modernity and the Second-Hand Trade*, pp. 57–72.

[60]   James Pigot & Co., *National Commercial Directory ... of Chester ...* (London, 1834).

[61]   Clive Edwards and Margaret Ponsonby, 'Desirable Commodity or Practical Necessity? The Sale and Consumption of Second-Hand Furniture, 1750–1900', in Hussey and Ponsonby (eds), *Buying for the Home*, pp. 117–37.

[62]   Ian Mitchell, '"Old books – New Bound?": Selling Second-Hand Books in England, *c.*1680–1850', in Stobart and van Damme (eds), *Modernity and the Second-Hand Trade*, pp. 139–57.

[63]   See Chapter 2, n.3, on the reliability or otherwise of the *Universal British*. Some large towns were not well covered by it: no shopkeepers were listed for Newcastle or Birmingham.

than for those in growing residential areas, in the directories of the 1820s and 1830s. Thus Pigot's 1834 *Commercial Directory* listed 145 shopkeepers in Stockport and district, 78 in Macclesfield but only 49 in Chester.[64] Nor were shopkeepers particularly likely to advertise in eighteenth-century newspapers. The business run by Sarah Smith in Chester was slightly different, but in some ways marginal:

> Sarah Smith, Widow of the late William Smith, Carpenter of this City ... has laid in a Quantity of all Sorts of fine Teas, Coffee, and Chocolate, which she has procured from the most eminent Warehouses in London; and which way of Business she intends to carry on at her Dwelling-House, in Newgate-Street, which she hopes will enable her to treat upon much lower Terms than if she kept a Shop.[65]

Newgate Street was a little distance away from the fashionable heart of Chester's shopping streets and this shop that was not a shop was perhaps intended to help her maintain financial independence by trading in a modest way.

Maria Maddock who kept a huckster's shop in Foregate Street in the same city was more typical. She reported that between six and seven o'clock on a Wednesday evening a tall man dressed in blue with two rows of buttons on his waistcoat entered her shop to buy some eggs. He was accompanied by another man, also in blue, who looked like a sailor and who asked for some hung beef. Maddock explained that she did not sell this and noticed a piece of bacon in his hand which she at first thought he had brought into the shop with him but soon concluded that he had stolen it from her as she missed some bacon soon after he left the shop.[66] This sort of incident was a not infrequent hazard of keeping a small shop. Hucksters like Maddock typically sold bacon, butter, cheese, eggs and flour, with perhaps some tea, sugar and other basic groceries. Many were women including 38 per cent of the 332 grocers and general shopkeepers listed in Gore's 1805 Liverpool directory.[67] Shopkeepers like this had a crucial role in supplying provisions and household stores to the rapidly expanding working classes of major towns like Manchester, Liverpool and Sheffield as well as a host of smaller ones in the textile, pottery and metal working areas of the north and midlands. They complemented markets and, to a lesser extent, street traders.

Roger Scola's pioneering work on Manchester's food supply explored the relationship between different types of retail outlet. Although markets long remained important for fresh food, the overall trend in the nineteenth century was for an increase in the proportion of this trade taking place in shops, including butchers' shops. Potatoes were available in shops at the end of the eighteenth

---

[64]   Pigot & Co., *National Commercial Directory*.

[65]   *Adam's Chester Courant*, 6 December 1774.

[66]   CALS, Quarter Sessions Examinations 1802, ZQSE/17/24.

[67]   Sheryllynne Haggerty, 'Women, Work, and the Consumer Revolution: Liverpool in the Late Eighteenth Century', in John Benson and Laura Ugolini (eds), *A Nation of Shopkeepers: Five Centuries of British Retailing* (London, 2003), pp. 106–26 (p. 116).

century.[68] There was a sixfold increase in the number of retail outlets for non-perishable food in Manchester and Salford between 1800 and 1871.[69] General shopkeepers may have had a weekly turnover of around £50 in the early nineteenth century. They were among the first retailers to move away from the city centre, were typically found in back streets and had a high proportion of customers living within a few hundred yards of the shop.[70] James Bentley of Minshull Street in Manchester was probably a typical provisions dealer trading on a fairly substantial scale in the early nineteenth century. He sold some grocery goods like tea, sugar, treacle and currants but also general provisions such as bread, flour, butter, eggs, potatoes, bacon and cheese. His takings sometimes reached £60 a week or more but he seems to have made little profit.[71] In the middle of the nineteenth century Carr and Bagshaw in Sheffield were dealing in similar items on a relatively small scale, though perhaps with a slightly greater emphasis on grocery goods, and selling small quantities to a handful of customers a day.[72]

Shops of this sort did not change very much between the mid eighteenth century and the mid nineteenth. Sarah Brown kept one such in Stockport in the 1750s. She lived with her husband Thomas who carried on his trade of waistcoat maker in part of their house while Sarah sold cheese, butter, bacon, wheat, flour, oatmeal, potatoes, eggs, mugs, soap, candles, sugar and other goods in a different part of the house. Sarah bought goods on her husband's credit and often sold on credit. She was frequently in need of money, having to pay for items before she could reap the proceeds of selling them. In 1755 and 1756 Sarah borrowed £47 from Thomas Sidall, described as a gentleman of Stockport, and £6 from his wife. Sidall subsequently paid off £6 7s of Sarah's debts on goods she had bought for the shop and also lent her further money. She managed to pay back £34 but when Sidall asked for the remainder Sarah suggested to her husband that he should pay the debt. There was a quarrel and Sarah claimed that her husband had turned her out and taken possession of the goods in the shop, selling them for £100 and keeping the money.[73] It seems reasonable to infer that Sarah was effectively an independent businesswoman within the constraints of eighteenth-century law, that she was trading on a moderate scale, but that it was easy for such a retailer to fall into debt and hard to escape this.

Insolvency was just as much a risk at the end of the century. Two Stockport examples provide evidence of the small amounts of credit given to individual customers and of the very restricted geographical area from which most customers

---

[68]   Scola, *Feeding the Victorian City*, pp. 182–92.

[69]   Ibid., p. 205.

[70]   Ibid., pp. 211, 235–41.

[71]   Greater Manchester County Record Office, Grocer's Day Book, 1798–1828, MISC/258/1.

[72]   Sheffield Archives, Arundel Castle Mss, Sheffield Court Baron, Day Book of Carr and Bagshaw, 1845–46, ACM/S/604.

[73]   NA, Exchequer Bills and Answers, E112/1089/117.

of general provisions shops came. Thomas Shawcross, a flour dealer and shopkeeper, had a counter, shelves, corn bins and a weigh beam in his shop. His schedule listed some 90 debtors, owing various sums ranging from sixpence to just under 10 pounds for goods sold and delivered. Over half of these were for amounts of less than one pound. Shawcross lived on Hillgate and almost all his customers came from his immediate vicinity. John Jackson, a shopkeeper, listed 57 debtors in his schedule. One of these, George Lowe and Company of Stockport, owed £16 16s, but of the others, only five were for amounts greater than one pound, with 17 owing less than one shilling. This schedule does not give full addresses, but 46 of his debtors were from Stockport, 5 from Bullock Smithy a couple of miles to the south and just one from Manchester.[74] It seems that it was virtually impossible to operate this sort of small shop on a cash only basis and the widespread availability of credit only added to the riskiness of the business.

Small shopkeepers also faced competition from company shops and early cooperatives. The Heaton Mersey bleachworks on the outskirts of Stockport operated a company shop in the 1810s. The company purchased large quantities of provisions from the Stockport wholesale grocer R. and T. Walmsley, including butter, treacle, candles, sugar and tea. The tea was to be made up in one- and two-ounce packs. The shop also sold meat, potatoes, cheese, clothing and medicine. Prices for basic goods were higher than in the town's market. Shopkeepers complained that workers were compelled to use such shops, or accept part of their wages in goods, and that this depressed their trade.[75] Opposition to the payment of wages in goods resurfaced in 1830 when a meeting was called in Stockport to consider petitioning for 'the suppression of a System fraught with consequences ruinous to the middle and lower classes'.[76] The newspaper was more guarded in its response to the establishment of cooperative stores in the late 1820s. It recognized that their purpose was to help the industrious poor but feared that they were 'calculated greatly to injure the huxters and small shopkeepers'.[77] Small shopkeepers were in a precarious business, but while many individuals failed their overall numbers were destined to keep on increasing. By 1850 198 such retailers were listed in Stockport located in 65 different streets in the town.[78]

---

[74]   NA, Palatinate of Chester, Papers in Causes, Bankruptcy, CHES 10/1/2, 1801.

[75]   P.M. Giles, 'The Economic and Social Development of Stockport', unpublished MA thesis, University of Manchester, 1950, pp. 314–16, 378–9.

[76]   *Stockport Advertiser*, 9 April 1830.

[77]   Ibid., 4 December 1829.

[78]   Samuel Bagshaw, *History, Gazetteer, and Directory of the County Palatine of Chester* (Sheffield, 1850).

Village Shops

It is perhaps natural to associate shops with towns and to assume that, in general, larger towns will not only have more shops than smaller towns but also a wider range of types of shops including highly specialized ones. Towns can therefore be categorized and ranked in a hierarchy based on the functions and services offered by each town. For example, Jon Stobart ranked 32 towns in early eighteenth-century north-west England and identified six discrete levels with Manchester, Liverpool and Chester being first order places and small market towns or large villages like Tarvin and Frodsham in Cheshire being sixth order. The positioning of any given town in the hierarchy might reflect a large number of lower-order functions or a small number of higher ones.[79] Although population was a significant determinant of a town's place in the urban hierarchy, other factors such as communications links, administrative functions or the presence of urban gentry seeking leisure pursuits were also important. Some places punched above their weight relative to their population.[80] Some villages, particularly those on key routes, had a substantial number of service providers, like Tarporley with six shopkeepers and two surgeons in 1783.[81] In the nineteenth century shop location seems to have been increasingly related to population distribution, particularly with regard to food shops, although local context was always important. Smaller centres continued to have shops, but their share of the total number of shops in a region may have been declining in the second half of the century.[82]

Villages might have been at the base of the urban hierarchy, but shops were sufficiently common in them by the last quarter of the seventeenth century to be accused of contributing to the ruining of cities and markets because 'in every country village where is (it may be) not above ten houses, there is shopkeeper'.[83] There was no doubt some measure of exaggeration here, but the Muis' estimates based on the plans for a shop tax in the 1750s suggest a remarkably low ratio of people to shop: just over 40 in England as a whole and only 35 in southern England.[84] Evidence from the 1780s shop tax confirms the widespread existence of village shops. In Kent, 208 places had shops in 1788 and of these 51 had just one shop while 37 had two. In Cheshire, 62 places had shops of which 26 had one shop

---

[79]   Jon Stobart, 'The Spatial Organization of a Regional Economy: Central Places in North-West England in the Early Eighteenth Century', *Journal of Historical Geography*, 22/2 (1996): 147–59.

[80]   Stobart, *First Industrial Region*, pp. 158–66.

[81]   Ibid., p. 146.

[82]   M.T. Wild and G. Shaw, 'Population Distribution and Retail Provision: The Case of the Halifax-Calder Valley Area of West Yorkshire during the Second Half of the Nineteenth Century', *Journal of Historical Geography*, 1/2 (1975): 193–210.

[83]   *The Trade of England Revived* (London, 1681), in J. Thirsk and J.P. Cooper (eds), *Seventeenth-Century Economic Documents* (Oxford: Clarendon Press, 1972), p. 397.

[84]   Mui and Mui, *Shops and Shopkeeping in Eighteenth-Century England*, pp. 38–40.

and 12 had two while in more sparsely populated Derbyshire there were fewer shops outside market towns with just 33 places having shops of which 14 had one and 5 had two.[85] Is it fair to regard them as being on the margins? Some village shops were substantial businesses and some village shopkeepers were wealthy. Yet for many, shopkeeping was only one part of what they did for a living. They might also be farmers, carriers, alehouse keepers or involved in some aspect of local industry. Some had a bad reputation for charging high prices. The description of a village shop at Mongewell in Oxfordshire in the 1790s which was run for the benefit of the poor claimed that bacon, cheese, soap, candles and salt were all sold there at lower prices than at other shops in the neighbourhood. This can hardly have been good for their business but it was argued that if existing shopkeepers were employed to run such shops they would lose little as the gains from a normal village shop were trifling, precarious and unpleasantly acquired.[86]

Even so, the number of shops was increasing in some villages during the eighteenth century. A description of Wilmslow in east Cheshire written in 1785 noted that whereas 40 years previously there had only been a few petty shopkeepers who sold treacle, sugar, salt, tobacco, coarse linen and woollens there were by then many more selling tea, coffee, spices, printed cottons, silks, hats, bonnets and caps among other items.[87] The inventory of a Derbyshire shopkeeper taken in 1800 confirms that retailers in large villages could offer a very wide range of goods. William Bradley of Winster in the lead mining district stocked muslin, calico, lace, handkerchiefs, ribbons, thread, a range of spices, currants, raisins, tobacco, sugar, flour, candles, coffee, six different types or qualities of tea, pins, toys and some household goods. His grocery goods alone were valued at over £50 out of a total of £435. Over half of this represented the proceeds of selling land in the nearby village of Birchover.[88] John Poyser at Yoxall in Staffordshire also sold a mixture of provisions, groceries and textiles, but also a snuff box, writing paper and buttons. He occasionally made up clothes for customers and sold smock frocks and shoes. He rarely seems to have had more than five customers a day, generally spending a few pence or a few shillings at most.[89] An advertisement for a village shop to be let at Rainow, five miles from Macclesfield, gives an indication of the range of skills required to succeed in such a business. The applicant needed to understand bread baking; have the means and experience to buy in 'all such useful articles … as the regular demands of a populous

---

[85]   NA, Exchequer, Land and Assessed Taxes, E182/96, 166 and 448.

[86]   *Annals of Agriculture*, vol. 29 (1797), pp. 30–7.

[87]   Samuel Finney, 'Survey of the Parish of Wilmslow', in T.W. Barlow (ed.), *The Cheshire and Lancashire Historical Collector* (2 vols, London: W. Kent & Co., 1853), vol. 1, no. 2, pp. 5–6.

[88]   Lichfield Record Office, Inventory of William Bradley, 1800, B/C/5/1800/3.

[89]   William Salt Library, Stafford, John Poyser of Yoxall, Account Books, 1777–1804, M603.

neighbourhood at a distance from markets require'; sell for ready money only; and be capable of undertaking wholesale dealings in malt and corn.[90]

The Woods at Didsbury, south of Manchester, were typical of the multitasking village shopkeeper. The family had provided parish clerks since the sixteenth century and were associated with the Ring o' Bells Inn for generations. William Wood was landlord until his death in 1790 when his son Thomas succeeded him.[91] The Woods also farmed, acted as carriers and, at least while William was alive, ran a general shop.[92] As the Muis noted, William Wood did not stock drapery or ironmongery but ran what was essentially a provisions and groceries shop.[93] He sold items like cheese, butter, some meat, tea, coffee, currants, sugar, treacle, salt, tobacco, snuff, candles, soap and starch. The shop sold bread but Wood was also willing to bake bread for customers. There were 112 different customers at the shop and the inn during the late 1780s almost all of whom came from Didsbury or immediately adjoining townships. Many customers only bought on an occasional basis but up to 15 were regulars, some buying on an almost daily basis. It was a small business with recorded credit sales of around £70 a year. There were rarely more than six customers a day and sometimes none at all. Long credit was the norm and regular customers made payments at intervals ranging between one and six months, usually leaving a few shillings owing to Wood. He also occasionally made loans of a few shillings to his customers.[94]

The shop could hardly have provided the Woods with a living, but combined with their other businesses it enable them to maintain a significant position in the village. The inn was a much more substantial business with Wood spending around £250 a year on beer, wines and spirits as well as brewing his own. Thomas's farming activities enabled him to sell hay, pigs, potatoes, apples, plums, pears and other unnamed fruit. Hay was usually sold privately but livestock, fruit and vegetables generally went to Stockport or occasionally Manchester for sale at the market or fair. Thomas also experimented with supplying newspapers to some of the villagers in the 1790s. The first newspaper, a copy of the *St James Chronicle*, was received from Mr Harrop of Manchester in November 1792 but Wood soon began to obtain the newspaper directly from London. He gave up this enterprise in 1795.[95] If, as seems likely, Thomas gave up the shop on the death of his father this may have been because he doubted its economic viability and preferred to direct his energies elsewhere. It is most unlikely, however, that Didsbury had no shop or shops after 1790.

---

[90]   *Macclesfield Courier*, 17 April 1813.

[91]   Ivor R. Million, *A History of Didsbury* (Manchester: E.J. Morton, 1969), pp. 69–70, 94.

[92]   Greater Manchester County Record Office, Ledgers of William and Thomas Wood, 1767–1838, GB127.M 62/1/1–3.

[93]   Mui and Mui, *Shops and Shopkeeping in Eighteenth-Century England*, p. 216.

[94]   William Wood Ledger, 1767–1791, GB127.M 62/1/1.

[95]   Thomas Wood Ledgers, 1791–1801 and 1792–1838, GB127.M 62/1/2–3.

If village retailing was often marginal, then rural producer-retailers in those trades that were so numerous in many towns faced even more difficulties. Shoemakers and tailors were common in villages but would almost always have needed some other occupation in order to make a living. Many in Cheshire were involved in small-scale farming.[96] Across the Pennines, John Wilson was village shoemaker in Orston between Nottingham and Grantham in the 1820s and 1830s. Most of his work involved shoe repairs although he sold one Thomas Leake a pair of calf quarter boots costing 15s 6d in March 1823. He was rarely busy, with customer numbers in single figures in most months, although an individual customer might deal with him on several occasions in the month. Credit was the norm and some bills, such as that to John Fryer the carrier, were partly offset against services rendered.[97] George Bollington from the Ashover area in Derbyshire similarly carried out shoe repairs and sold occasional boots and shoes. While it is reasonable to assume that Wilson could not have subsisted on shoemaking alone, there is clear evidence that Bollington also dealt in hops and malt, received rent and lent money.[98] Other rural traders combined a range of activities. John Foden from the Stone area of Staffordshire was a wheelwright, carpenter and cabinet maker. Unlike William Tomlin of Barnsley who was essentially a house furnisher (p. 45) Foden had to turn his hand to whatever was available. Work included hanging pew doors in a chapel, making a dining table, shopfitting, taking a chair to pieces, fitting up an easy chair and coffin making.[99] Although Wilson, Bollington and Foden were all active in the first half of the nineteenth century there is a timelessness about much of what they were doing that suggests they would not have been out place in rural life at any time from the seventeenth century to the twentieth.

Conclusions

In her autobiography Mary Smith, who was in due course to become a schoolmistress, described how when her father's shoemaking business got into difficulties in the 1830s she and her eldest brother were placed in a small shop in a village on the Oxford canal. Her brother ran the shoe business while she sold groceries and provisions and kept poultry. When her brother married his wife took over the shop and Mary went back to her father's house.[100] Running a small shop

---

[96]   Jon Stobart, 'The Economic and Social Worlds of Rural Craftsmen-Retailers in Eighteenth-Century Cheshire', *Agricultural History Review*, 52/2 (2004): 141–60.

[97]   Nottinghamshire Archives, John Wilson of Orston, Shoemaker, Account Book, 1821–34, DD 2001/1.

[98]   DRO, Miscellaneous Ashover Documents, Ledger of George Bollington, 1818–37, D5435/3.

[99]   SRO, John Foden, Ledger, 1820–66, D3161.

[100]   *The Autobiography of Mary Smith, Schoolmistress and Nonconformist* (London: Bemrose and Sons, 1892), pp. 50–65.

could be a temporary expedient or might be combined with other occupations. Indeed if the Muis' estimate of the ratio of shops to people in the mid eighteenth century is in any way accurate, then it is hard to see how a pre-industrial economy could have sustained the level of consumer demand needed to have enabled all these shopkeepers to have made a decent living. Many must have been operating on the margins of subsistence or using income from the shop to supplement other ways of earning their living. Retailing in the eighteenth century and early nineteenth was not only about the fashionable shops of London, or indeed of provincial leisure towns, but about those who were enterprising enough to seize the opportunities offered by industrial and urban growth to rent a market stall, travel with a pack or a cart or use some space in or outside a back street dwelling to sell some basic goods. These were not necessarily full-time occupations and under-employment was intrinsic to much traditional retailing.

Many of these retailers, particularly those who had no fixed premises, were treated with suspicion by the authorities. But more upmarket shopkeepers were not necessarily well respected. Pamphlets in support of the 1780s shop tax argued that retailers were 'a detrimental class of idlers', that an increase in their numbers beyond that necessary for competition tended to raise prices and that 'a considerable proportion of them live[d] in a style of opulence and even of splendour'.[101] The latter accusation can hardly have applied to a typical shopkeeper, but in reality there was no such person as a typical shopkeeper. Some, like the Chester bookseller John Rowley who advertised in 1752 that he had just imported and was selling a large quantity of fresh oranges and lemons, would seek out any opportunity to make a profit whether or not it was part of their main business.[102] Some eighteenth-century shops perhaps resembled a modern discount store with an ever-changing selection of eclectic bargains in the centre aisles. Others stuck more closely to their traditional line of business and grumbled about the activities of their more enterprising competitors. Yet others were content with a decent living and a respected place in local society. A few made fortunes and a few went bankrupt but most were neither opulent nor impoverished. Change over time was patchy and often slow. A typical town grocer's shop in 1800 would have been likely to have had a wider range of goods than one in 1700 and might have looked smarter, but business methods and attitudes to customers would probably have changed little. The same was true of most village shops. There were exceptions, particularly among some of the clothing and household goods retailers, and these exceptions were significant but were not the norm.

The context in which retailers operated was, however, changing. It was not just that the growth in population, and particularly the urban population, meant that more people than ever before were using shops and markets. Attitudes were also changing. While it may be anachronistic to talk of 'consumerism' in the

---

[101]   *The Policy of the Tax upon Retailers Considered* (London, 1786), pp. 8, 34; *A Vindication of the Shop Tax* (London, 1786), p. 42.

[102]   *Adam's Weekly Courant*, 28 November–5 December 1752.

eighteenth century, it was the case that many consumers were becoming much more aware of what it meant to participate in the world of goods. Traditional attitudes to possessions were at least being challenged if not overthrown. Shifts in belief systems and underlying attitudes manifested themselves in behaviour. In particular, words like fashion and politeness began to take on new meanings and to affect what goods people bought and why they bought them. Sensibility and the romantic imagination had an impact on material culture and on the way in which leisure was understood. The next three chapters explore these changing attitudes and what they meant for consumption and especially polite consumption.

PART II
Disturbing Influences: Luxury, Novelty and Fashion

PART II

Chapter 4
Competing Narratives: Consumption and Contentment

The Manchester draper John Moss lost all of his first four children in early childhood. When his daughter Anne died in October 1709 he wrote in his diary, 'I think it is a visitation by way of chastisement to me for my wicked life'. He prayed that he might amend his life and that his remaining two children might be spared. He reiterated this prayer on the death of a further child in February 1710/11.[1] At about the same time, and also in Manchester, Edmund Harrold, a wigmaker, used his diary to record his drinking exploits, how he bought and sold books in alehouses and how often he 'did' his wife and in what position.[2] Both Moss and Harrold knew that they were sinners, but Harrold had a degree of awareness of the flaws in his character that feels less remote from a modern understanding of the self than does the more conventional piety of Moss. Yet both can serve to remind us of how Christianity remained at the very least a background presence in the lives of enterprising men and women in the eighteenth century and was sometimes very much in the foreground. Its position as a controlling narrative was, however, under threat.

Harrold was an avid reader. There is no evidence to suggest that he ever read works by Nicholas Barbon or Bernard Mandeville, but if he had it is possible that he would have been both intrigued and a little shocked. Writing at the end of the seventeenth century Barbon was one of the earliest writers to recognize and proclaim the benefits that might accrue from the pursuit of pleasure and 'unnecessary' consumption. He drew a distinction between the wants of the body, such as food, clothing and lodging, and those of the mind which were infinite because 'his Wants increase with his Wishes, which is for every thing that is rare, can gratifie the Senses, adorn his Body, and promote the Ease, Pleasure and Pomp of Life'. Prodigality was a vice that was prejudicial to the individual but not to the economy while 'The Promoting of New Fashions, ought to be Encouraged, because it provides a Livelihood for a good Part of Mankind'.[3] Mandeville developed the argument as he attempted to demonstrate that private vices were public virtues. In opposition to the prevailing religious wisdom he declared that frugality was 'an idle dreaming Virtue that employs no Hands, and therefore [is] very useless in a

---

[1] Greater Manchester Record Office, Diary of John Moss, Misc 966, fols 14–15.

[2] Craig Horner (ed.), *The Diary of Edmund Harrold, Wigmaker of Manchester, 1712–15* (Aldershot: Ashgate, 2008), Introduction.

[3] Nicholas Barbon, *A Discourse of Trade by N.B.M.D.* (London, 1690), pp. 15, 62–7.

trading Country' and that content was the bane of industry.[4] By contrast 'Luxury Employ'd a Million of the Poor and odious Pride a Million more'.[5] A prosperous society was only possible if some Christian virtues like that of contentment were turned upside down.

Mandeville's fundamental ideas were increasingly accepted as the eighteenth century progressed. Daniel Defoe had a strong belief in individual human endeavour that would lead to greater knowledge and material well-being. He was in favour of a high wage economy and saw work coupled with ingenuity as fundamental to progress. Consumption was good provided it did not drive out investment and he had reservations about excess and luxury. Ideas like these permeated the much published and widely read *Robinson Crusoe*.[6] David Hume was more positive about luxury. The word itself was of 'uncertain signification'. If poverty was to be understood as deprivation rather than virtuous austerity, then luxury could also lose its moral implications. Instead it promoted activity and industry while sensual gratification was a source of happiness. Commerce and luxury were generally to be associated with refinement and civilization. They reduced indolence and did not lead to military enfeeblement: one of the arguments used in the luxury debates. An opulent country was likely to be a happy and industrious one. Luxury was only a vice when pursued at the expense of virtues such as liberality or charity.[7]

Adam Smith also was not inclined to make rigid distinctions between necessities and luxuries and regarded fashion as essentially harmless. While he delighted in the ingenuity required to fashion goods of all types and argued that spending even on trinkets was preferable to spending on services or liveried retainers, he maintained a moral philosopher's distaste for frivolous consumption.[8] As is well known, Smith was a complex thinker far removed from the caricature of a dedicated proponent of laissez-faire with no heed for the moral consequences. He recognized that markets needed the underpinning of both formal laws and accepted codes of behaviour if the 'invisible hand' was to work effectively. He was optimistic about progress, looking for a time when the least of the labouring classes would be tolerably well fed, clothed and housed and when all citizens

---

[4]   Bernard Mandeville, *The Fable of the Bees*, ed. Philip Harth (Harmondsworth: Penguin, 1970), pp. 134–5, 247.

[5]   Ibid., p. 68.

[6]   Peter Mathias, 'Economic Growth and Robinson Crusoe', *European Review*, 15/1 (2007): 17–31.

[7]   On Hume see in particular Christopher J. Berry, 'Hume and Superfluous Value (or the Problem with Epictetus' Slippers) in Carl Wennerlind and Margaret Schabas (eds), *David Hume's Political Economy* (Abingdon: Routledge, 2008), pp. 49–64; and Andrew S. Cunningham, 'David Hume's Account of Luxury', *Journal of the History of Economic Thought*, 27/3 (2005): 231–50.

[8]   Neil de Manchi, 'Adam Smith's Accommodation of "Altogether Endless" Desires', in Maxine Berg and Helen Clifford (eds), *Consumers and Luxury: Consumer Culture in Europe 1650–1850* (Manchester: Manchester University Press, 1999), pp. 18–36.

might enjoy a life of secure tranquillity. This security in its turn made possible the accumulation of capital and the grasping of the opportunities presented by the market. Smith placed considerable emphasis on the importance of building character and developing a sense of duty. Although he seems to have believed in a divine creator who was responsible for the conditions in which rational human beings could develop and prosper, he was sceptical about institutional religion particularly if backed by the state. Smith was exploring issues of continuing relevance to the functioning of a modern, liberal society.[9]

The traditional Christian view that was challenged by these new ways of thinking had been spelt out in some detail by the writer of *The Whole Duty of Man*, generally thought to have been the royalist and scholar Richard Allestree. *The Whole Duty* was first published in 1658 and was the most widely read devotional book in the succeeding centuries. A typical cottager at the end of the eighteenth century who had a small collection of books such as a Bible, an almanac and a chapbook or two was likely also to have owned the *Whole Duty*.[10] The starting point for Godliness was to be content with what God had provided for you and 'never to have impatient desires of any thing in the World, but to leave it to God to fit us with such an estate and condition as He sees best for us'.[11] Being content with things as they were had implications for what it was appropriate to wear: 'all immodest fashions of Apparel, which may either argue the wantonness of the wearer, or provoke that of the beholder are to be avoided'.[12] The proper use of clothing was to hide nakedness, protect the body from cold, differentiate between the sexes and make visible one's status in society. So 'let every man cloath himself in such sober attire as befits his place and calling'.[13] Clothes did not add true worth to anyone and it was therefore wrong to spend considerable time or wealth on them.

Allestree also wrote a tract on contentment which he regarded as the source of that true happiness that God willed for his human creation. Again he emphasized the need to tame rather than satisfy the appetite for material things 'which, when they have them, they are immediately sick of'.[14] He summed up his argument as follows: 'God never articled with the ambitious to give him honour, or with the covetous to fill his baggs, or with the voluptuous to feed his luxuries. Let us therefore, if we expect to be satisfied, modestly confine our desires within the limits

---

[9]   Jerry Evensky, *Adam Smith's Moral Philosophy: A Historical and Contemporary Perspective on Markets, Law, Ethics, and Culture* (Cambridge: Cambridge University Press, 2005).

[10]   Clark, *English Society*, pp. 126, 166.

[11]   *The Whole Duty of Man* (1704 edn, London), p. 42.

[12]   Ibid., p. 211.

[13]   Ibid., p. 212.

[14]   *The Art of Contentment: By the Author of 'The Whole Duty of Man'* (Oxford, 1719), p. 167.

he has set us'.[15] Allestree's arguments were not particularly original, but were a clear statement of the classic Christian view of the perils of placing too much emphasis on material things. Similar views were expressed by many devotional writers in the late seventeenth century and early eighteenth and must have been preached in innumerable sermons in parish churches throughout England. Being content with one's lot and acknowledging the perils of 'luxury' had been the default setting for early modern society.[16]

It was hardly surprising therefore that Mandeville's writings provoked a furious response. The so-called 'luxury debates' raged for the first two-thirds of the eighteenth century with the cries against luxury loudest when people felt that they were under unusual stress.[17] Running through the debates was the question of just what was meant by luxury and how, in a world where many more types of goods were becoming widely used, it was possible to distinguish luxuries from necessities. Was there perhaps a difference between 'new' luxuries that were the product of the expansion of commerce and 'old' luxuries associated with extravagant or aristocratic display? If so were the former perhaps acceptable in a way that the latter were not?[18] Or was material progress likely to result in luxury, effeminacy and decline? Women might be regarded as prone to excessive consumption or as the harbingers of more civilized values such as compassion and refinement.[19] Those who continued to worry about luxury in the eighteenth century might do so out of a pragmatic concern about how much national income should be devoted to unproductive expenditure, or on grounds of national security, fearing both effeminacy and the influx of foreign goods, but there was invariably a moral or religious undercurrent as well.

William Law was one of the first to recoil from the seductive arguments of Mandeville's *Fable of the Bees*. Although a non-juror and so excluded from a career in the church or universities, Law was one of the most influential devotional writers of the early eighteenth century. His *Serious Call to a Devout and Holy Life* was admired by John Wesley, John Byrom and Samuel Johnson among others.[20]

---

[15]   Ibid., p. 191.

[16]   This theme was not absent from sermons preached before the merchants of the Levant Company, even if many preachers also sought to demonstrate that piety and wealth could be mutually reinforcing: see Natasha Glaisyer, *The Culture of Commerce in England 1660–1720* (Woodbridge: Boydell Press for the Royal Historical Society, 2006), pp. 69–99.

[17]   John Sekora, *Luxury: The Concept in Western Thought, Eden to Smollett* (Baltimore and London: Johns Hopkins University Press, 1977), ch. 2.

[18]   Maxine Berg and Elizabeth Eger, 'The Rise and Fall of the Luxury Debates', in Maxine Berg and Elizabeth Eger (eds), *Luxury in the Eighteenth Century: Debates, Desires and Delectable Goods* (Basingstoke: Palgrave Macmillan, 2003), pp. 7–27.

[19]   E.J. Clery, *The Feminization Debate in Eighteenth-Century England: Literature, Commerce and Luxury* (Basingstoke: Palgrave Macmillan, 2004), pp. 1–10.

[20]   Janet Louth, 'Introduction', in Janet Louth (ed.), *William Law, Selected Writings* (Manchester: Carcanet, 1990).

Law warned of the danger of the indiscreet use of innocent things, writing that 'More people are kept from a true sense and taste of religion by a regular kind of sensuality and indulgence, than by gross drunkenness'.[21] His *Remarks on the Fable of the Bees* did not engage directly with Mandeville's economics but argued that he had made moral virtue contemptible and had a deficient understanding of human nature. Performing virtuous action was the true route to pleasure and fulfilment. Law thus positioned himself as a defender of a rational, and to some degree optimistic, view of human nature. Humans had an innate capacity to know the principles of morality and to act accordingly. It was Mandeville who made a blind leap of faith in assuming that humans were governed by their passions and animal nature.[22]

Other Christian writers who attacked the views associated with Mandeville were less sophisticated than Law. John Dennis denounced Mandeville as a champion of luxury and vice never heard of before. By effectively renouncing the Christian religion he had undermined the public spirit and virtue of the nation itself. Dennis believed that the influence of the Christian religion was at a low ebb in England because luxury was at a great height. He had nothing good to say about luxury which 'weakens Mens bodies, stupefies their Minds, consumes their Substance, and wastes their Time'.[23] Some writers acknowledged that in the making of luxury items many hands were employed and families maintained and that it could be argued that luxury enriched the nation. Yet rather than engaging with this argument they tended to reiterate that the true support of the country came from religion, justice and charity.[24] In the last phase of the luxury debates in the 1760s one pamphlet writer continued to maintain that luxury 'disposes us to a general neglect of the several duties which we owe to ourselves, our family, our country, and our God'. It 'deprives us of all force of acting consistently with the dignity of reasonable activities'. He also argued that luxury damaged trade by raising wages and prices.[25]

It is hardly surprising that the consciences of some individuals were pricked by the pervasive religious critique of luxury. William Pegg, a Derby porcelain painter at the end of the eighteenth century, who became a Baptist and then a Quaker twice abandoned his trade because of his religious scruples about using his skills to minister to 'mere luxury' by decorating 'articles more of show than use'.[26] Quakers

---

[21]   Law, *Serious Call to a Devout and Holy Life*, in Louth (ed.), *Selected Writings*, p. 47.

[22]   Andrew Starkie, 'William Law and *The Fable of the Bees*', *Journal for Eighteenth-Century Studies*, 32/3 (2009): 307–19.

[23]   John Dennis, *Vice and Luxury Publick Mischiefs: or, Remarks on a Book Intituled, The Fable of the Bees* (London, 1724), quote p. 74.

[24]   For example, J. Philemerus, *Of Luxury, More Particularly with Respect to Apparel* (London, 1736).

[25]   S. Fawconer, *An Essay on Modern Luxury* (London, 1765), quotes pp. 28, 33.

[26]   Berg, *Luxury and Pleasure in Eighteenth-Century Britain*, p. 326.

and Methodists were noted for their simplicity in dress: John Wesley advised that his followers should buy no velvets, silks or fine linens.²⁷ Methodists frequently struggled with their consciences, particularly when a disciplined life produced not only spiritual consolation but also material wealth. An evangelical magazine *The Christian's Amusement* informed its readers of Methodist shopkeepers and artisans in mid eighteenth-century London whose businesses they could safely patronize. Methodists were expected to examine their consciences before they bought new goods, particularly those deemed superfluities, and ask whether they were truly necessary.²⁸ The irony of this, which was not necessarily lost on contemporaries, was that strict adherence to such a policy could harm the earthly prospects of a brother or sister Methodist who was in trade.

Some writers made a link between luxury in general and retailing in particular. Erasmus Jones who thought that good husbandry and frugality were 'quite out of fashion' maintained that, 'We have too many Tradesmen, who make it their Practice to lie a-bed till Eleven o'clock every day, then just come into the Shop, and twirl their Raffles about, and [go] next to the Tavern or Coffee-house for a Whet, or Tiff of Rice-Tea'.²⁹ The public appetite for buying luxury items from such traders was not, however, likely to diminish. Perhaps instead of trying to banish them, luxuries might be taxed. Josiah Tucker, Dean of Gloucester, proposed in 1750 that everyone wishing to consume luxuries should take out a yearly licence to enable them to do so. This would cost 1½d in the pound on their estimated annual income for each item. Thus, for example, Tucker assumed that those who wore silks or had pictures in their houses had an annual income of £50 and so would pay 6s 3d a year; those who drank tea or used china had an annual income of £25 and so would pay half as much. He suggested that this might replace all other taxes.³⁰

Even towards the end of the eighteenth century this bundle of attitudes that was hostile to luxury, suspicious of excessive displays of wealth, and generally sympathetic to hard work that had a visible outcome had implications for how retailers were perceived and treated. The introduction of a tax on shops in the 1780s provided an opportunity for pent-up resentments to be aired. One pamphlet writer, ignorant or taking no heed of arguments about efficiencies resulting from the division of labour, asked 'why should one man weave the stockings and another man sell them? Why should one man make the hat, and another man sell it, when both the maker and the seller, perhaps, reside in the same parish'.³¹ Retailers, he argued, withdrew their industry from the general stock and drew their subsistence

²⁷ Styles, *Dress of the People*, pp. 202–6.
²⁸ Eryn M. White, 'The Material World, Moderation and Methodism in Eighteenth-Century Wales', *Welsh History Review*, 23/3 (2007): 44–64.
²⁹ Erasmus Jones, *Luxury, Pride and Vanity, the Bane of the British Nation*, (3rd edn, London, 1736), quotes pp. 9, 33.
³⁰ J. Tucker, *A Brief Essay on the Advantages and Disadvantages which Respectively Attend France and Great Britain with Regard to Trade* (2nd edn, London, 1750), pp. 147–9.
³¹ Gray, *Policy of the Tax upon Retailers Considered*, p. 40.

from the industry of their fellow subjects rather than from foreign countries by means of trade.[32] Another writer attacked the presumed lifestyle of retailers:

> Do not ... a considerable portion of them live in a style of opulence and even of splendour? Do they not keep their horses, their whiskies, and their phaetons? Have they not their country lodgings, and their country villas? Have they not their clubs where they regale at ease and leisure? Their private entertainments, and their public dinners, where luxury if not riot predominate? Do they not, in general, enjoy a much greater share of the conveniences and superfluities of life, than landholders of far superior property?[33]

Although clearly much exaggerated, pamphlets like this presumably reflected some degree of popular feeling that retailers prospered disproportionately to their contribution to the wealth and well-being of the country. If England was a nation of shopkeepers then this might be something to regret rather than celebrate.

This was, however, perhaps an increasingly old-fashioned and even slightly vulgar attitude in the urbane, rationale and slightly sceptical world of Hume and Smith which seemed far removed from that of the serious devotional duties prescribed by Allestree or Law, or indeed the biting satire of Mandeville. So was it true, as Roy Porter claimed, that the big issue had turned from 'Shall I be saved?' to 'How shall I be happy?'[34] and if so that a relaxed attitude towards consumption was part of the answer? Although a very broad generalization, there is evidence to support this contention. Religious belief was tending to become more a matter of private judgement and individual choice. It was perhaps no longer the norm to see the 'hand of God' as the cause of natural events. So, for example, the sick could look to medical knowledge and skill for healing rather than to divine intervention and mental illness was less liable to be regarded as a sign of possession by evil forces.[35] There was a growing sense of personal uniqueness as witnessed in literature and drama as well as in autobiographies. Fame might be sought in this life rather than in the hereafter.[36] The emphasis was shifting from the soul to the mind and the body. The workings of the mind were capable of being studied and understood without recourse to speculation about divine origins. Human beings were a work in progress and the human self was a construct rather than a given.[37] Ideas like this made the pursuit of pleasure more acceptable, not as an occasional binge or an aristocratic privilege, but as the routine entitlement of ordinary people who looked for fulfilment in the world as it actually was. Moderation, rationality

---

[32] Ibid., p. 8.

[33] *A Vindication of the Shop Tax*, p. 42.

[34] Porter, *Flesh in the Age of Reason*, p. 23.

[35] Porter, *Enlightenment*, pp. 99, 208–17.

[36] Keith Thomas, *The Ends of Life: Roads to Fulfilment in Early Modern England* (Oxford: Oxford University Press, 2009), pp. 39, 265–6.

[37] Porter, *Flesh in the Age of Reason*, pp. 360–73.

and sociability were key words and good taste could combine with sound morals in an aesthetic of virtue.[38] Fashionable pursuits including assemblies, promenades, theatre and museums bore witness to the consumption of leisure as well as of material objects. All of this helped to stimulate the growth of the market economy which in itself promoted the sense of individual identity and widened the scope for personal choice. This was the world of useful knowledge and the 'enlightened economy'.[39]

Rationality was, however, by no means the only strand in the web of late eighteenth-century culture. Other key words were sensibility, picturesque and eventually romanticism. All of these were associated more with the imagination and with feelings than with reason. They were about being able to show appropriate degrees of empathy and pity, about being moved by natural beauty and about making the proper response to the world of literature and the arts. They might require continuous exposure to pleasurable experiences, in which novelty and creativity were accorded high value. There was likely to be an element of unsatisfied longing in all of this as romantics and others attempted to achieve through the acquisition of material things those pleasures they had sampled in their imagination. As each new purchase failed to live up to expectations, so it was necessary to try again. The ceaseless consumption of novelty that is at the heart of much modern consumerism may have had part of its origins in the romantic imagination of the late eighteenth century. At the same time sensibility and an appreciation of the romantic and the picturesque might be demonstrated by the acquisition of appropriate objects. Goods revealed who you were and also shaped your self-awareness.[40]

Moreover, the acquisition of a single new item might have implications for the rest of one's possessions. In a well-known essay Denis Diderot described how the gift of a new dressing gown caused him a week or two later to feel that his desk was not up to standard and needed replacing. Then the tapestry on his study wall seemed a little threadbare. Gradually the entire contents of his study were found wanting and made way for new items. Diderot looked back with fondness to his old dressing gown and his comfortable old study regretting the changes he had made. This was, however, not an inevitable consequence of the 'Diderot effect'.[41] Given the availability of new and potentially complementary goods the acquisition of the first transformative item could set in motion an exhilarating

---

[38]   Porter, *Enlightenment*, pp. 260–70.

[39]   As described with enthusiasm by Joel Mokyr, *Enlightened Economy*.

[40]   Colin Campbell, *The Romantic Ethic and the Spirit of Modern Consumerism* (Oxford: Basil Blackwell, 1987) is the key work here. See also Colin Campbell, 'Understanding Traditional and Modern Patterns of Consumption in Eighteenth-Century England: A Character-Action Approach', in Brewer and Porter (eds), *Consumption and the World of Goods*, pp. 40–57. John Brewer, *The Pleasures of the Imagination: English Culture in the Eighteenth Century* (London: HarperCollins, 1997), is also relevant.

[41]   McCracken, *Culture and Consumption*, pp. 118–19.

and positive change in lifestyle. The need to ensure that the one new item did not look out of place provided a strong motivation for continuing engagement with the world of novelty and of fashionable consumer goods. Being discontented with one's lot was a necessary precondition for a nascent consumer society.

Underlying attitudes and belief systems in 1800 were not the same as they had been in 1700. This did not, however, mean that some combination of enlightenment, rationality and romanticism had wiped out deeply embedded religious practices. The concept of contentment had not disappeared from Christian discourse in the 1790s or even later. For example, William Paley, better known for his re-statement of the argument from design as a proof of the divine origins of the cosmos and his use of the watchmaker analogy, tried to convince working people that they should not feel discontented when they saw the exorbitant fortunes of others. Work was a blessing and frugality a pleasure whereas the 'rich who addict themselves to indulgence lose their relish'. True contentment came from simple things like family, a garden and rural diversions. Archdeacon Paley was not, however, minded to exchange places with a poor person as that would rob both of happiness.[42] Not surprisingly those poor labourers who read the complacent Archdeacon's pamphlet were less than impressed. In 1800 Adam Sibbit, Rector of Clarendon in Jamaica, inveighed against luxury which 'has been the bane of every nation, and the efficient cause of its destruction'.[43] The blessings of contentment were the theme of another writer some 30 years later and were to be contrasted with 'the ceaseless discontents, the habitual restlessness, the laborious strivings after something more, or something different, of the seekers – of those, than whom the world sees none more strenuous in the chase of luxury, or less satisfied with their prey'.[44] This modern-sounding critique of consumerism remained an orthodox Christian viewpoint, but such viewpoints did not carry the weight they had done a century and a half earlier.

Even so, Christianity remained significant in late eighteenth- and early nineteenth-century society. There were in fact many different Christianities on offer, including several that were the creation of the period. Religion was not an additional dimension in the lives of many contemporaries, but was integral to all of what they did. Religious priorities and assumptions were therefore often implicit and unspoken. The Book of Common Prayer, which was at the heart of all Anglican worship and must have been familiar to many ordinary people, contained texts that promoted social harmony alongside those that might legitimate an

[42] William Paley, *Reasons for Contentment Addressed to the Labouring Part of the British Public* (1793).

[43] Adam Sibbit, *A Dissertation, Moral and Political, on the Influence of Luxury and Refinement on Nations, with Reflections on the Manners of the Age at the Close of the 18th Century* (London, 1800), p. 9.

[44] *What is Luxury? ... by a Lay Observer* (London, 1829), p. 1.

appeal to a moral economy.[45] The all-pervasive nature of the church can be seen in detailed local studies like that by Carolyn Steedman of the relationship between the Reverend John Murgatroyd and his servant Phoebe Beatson. Murgatroyd's religion helped him to understand Phoebe as a creature like himself and prompted him to try to make her happy. Religion did not necessarily conflict with an enlightenment influenced view of the self.[46] Nor had theology yet separated entirely from economic thought. Evangelical economics, as represented for example in the writings of Thomas Chalmers, can be seen as a reaction against the sort of political economy that was perceived as wicked and dangerous by making a virtue out of calculation and the profit motive, and thus contradicting notions of grace, self-sacrifice and worthlessness.[47] Whether noisy or implicit, religion still had a part to play in shaping the expectations of ordinary people in the early nineteenth century.

Matthew Hilton has suggested that the conflicting views about material goods that were expressed in the eighteenth-century luxury debates have cast a long shadow over subsequent periods. As a result of this, consumption remains located in the moral sphere. The terminology might have changed from virtue and vice to productive and unproductive but the ambivalence about consumption has not gone away.[48] Contemporary concerns about greed and unsustainable lifestyles can be viewed as part of this continuing discourse, although it has always been easier to induce a sense of guilt among some consumers than to persuade many people to give up the comforts of the material world. As many would now recognize, affluence has brought its challenges as well as its benefits. Well-being is not the same as wealth or economic growth.[49] Nevertheless, few would now wish to base their lifestyle on the teaching of the author of *The Whole Duty of Man*. Indeed if being content with one's lot was the default setting of early modern England it was much less so by the early nineteenth century. The same message was still being preached but it increasingly sounded counter-cultural rather than mainstream as more and more people were able, if not to enjoy the luxuries and semi-luxuries that abounded in the shops, at least to gaze on them and dream.

The shocking views initially expressed by Barbon and Mandeville and then refined by the later eighteenth-century political economists have of course

---

[45]   Gregory, 'Transforming the "Age of Reason" into "An Age of Faiths"; Jeremy Gregory, '"For All Sorts and Conditions of Men": The Social Life of the Book of Common Prayer during the Long Eighteenth Century; or, Bringing the History of Religion and Social History Together', *Social History*, 34/1 (2009): 29–54.

[46]   Steedman, *Master and Servant*.

[47]   Boyd Hilton, *The Age of Atonement: The Influence of Evangelicalism on Social and Economic Thought 1785–1865* (Oxford: Clarendon Press, 1988).

[48]   Matthew Hilton, *Consumerism in Twentieth-Century Britain: The Search for a Historical Movement* (Cambridge: Cambridge University Press, 2003), pp. 14–15.

[49]   Avner Offer, *The Challenge of Affluence: Self-Control and Well-Being in the United States and Britain since 1950* (Oxford: Oxford University Press, 2006), is a thought-provoking study of how well-being might be promoted in the modern Western world.

prevailed and it is easy to assume that this was inevitable. No doubt it was, but this would not have been obvious to those who lived at the time. There was a powerful alternative narrative, grounded in traditional Christian thought and capable of being expressed in more or less sophisticated ways. As we focus in the next chapters on the world of fashion and the connections between shopping and polite leisure it is useful to keep in mind that not everyone was dazzled by sophisticated shops on high-class shopping streets or by the accumulations of new objects that were displayed in the houses of the middling ranks and above. Some remained uneasy about the implications of 'unnecessary' consumption. Their story has not always been heard as historians have celebrated the triumph of commercial culture and ought not to be entirely lost even though it cannot be the dominant narrative.

Chapter 5
A Fashionable Assortment:
Retailing and Polite Society

Round about the year 1670 Elizabeth Gell wrote from her home in Derbyshire to her brother John in London seeking advice on current fashions:

> I have a little request for you, which is that you will furnish me with 3 peir of gloves not too big the lesser size of womens gloves usually fit me if there be such a thing as a fashionable colour pray let me h[ave] yt otherwise I like brick and cream colour … would you please to let me know whether laced shoes be out of the mode or noe. I have some lace but not enough for a pair and I would not willingly be [at] any cost to put myself out of the fashion.

She went on to ask him to observe women's clothes 'for we live [in] much ignorance and you will be apt to be ashamed to be seen with us when you come again into the country'.[1] No reply from John survives so it is not possible to assess how effective a fashion guru he proved to be. There was nothing unusual in the late seventeenth or indeed eighteenth century about a young lady in the provinces wanting to be aware of the latest London fashions and having to rely on family or friends for information.

Elizabeth Gell's interest in fashion might have provoked a gentle rebuke from Richard Allestree or the other traditionally minded moralists discussed in the previous chapter. Yet as we have seen it was her outlook on life rather than theirs that increasingly became the norm in the eighteenth century. This chapter looks at some aspects of the practical repercussions of these changes in ideas and attitudes. It explores the world of new goods and how contemporaries made use of these to construct fashionable and polite lifestyles. It also discusses the varied practices of shopping, particularly those associated with polite culture. Shops were places to be seen in as well as places to make purchases. The relationship between retailer and customer could be complex and ambiguous where each might try to manipulate the other. Even though most shopping was for essential items, the sort of shopping that was concerned with fashionable and novel items was growing in importance and was a key part of eighteenth-century culture.

---

1   DRO, Gell of Hopton, D258/38/11/7.

Fashion, Taste and Polite Culture

Fashion was frequently associated with novelty and might change very frequently.[2] Its relationship to good taste was complex: trying too hard to be fashionable might provoke ridicule, but well-crafted and expensive fashionable items could be used to display one's taste. Successfully negotiating the world of new goods and fashionable places was part of a polite lifestyle. There has been an explosion of interest in these topics in the last 20 years or so, including work on new and luxury goods; on sites of display and polite leisure; and on the meanings associated with the world of fashion and good taste. Maxine Berg has argued that fashion was important in making new goods desirable and that this included household goods as well as clothes. Fashionable products appealed to the senses through the use of colour, shape and flavour; they might be ingenious and have a sense of the exotic, but also be recognizable; and they were amenable to imitation and to being associated with other more familiar goods.[3] According to Beverly Lemire fashion has shaped markets, defined material priorities and brought profit or loss to those involved in its design, production and distribution. Writing particularly of textile and clothing fashion, Lemire regrets the neglect of fashion by the academy which for many years perceived it as female and trivial and welcomes the renewed interest in it since the 1970s.[4] The first section of this chapter explores some of this recent writing on fashion, taste and politeness.

New goods were an essential component of fashionable consumption. In England demand for imported luxuries grew from the mid sixteenth century with, for example, the value of imported silks doubling between 1560 and 1622. Porcelain and glass were also important new luxuries. Domestic luxury industries were encouraged by the state.[5] Growing demand for consumer goods was not confined to the commercial economies of north-west Europe.[6] New styles of

---

[2]   'Fashion' can have many meanings and connotations. I am using it broadly to mean the sort of new styles that a typical retailer would advertise as 'fashionable'; or that an Elizabeth Gell (and increasingly women and men of all ranks) would not feel ashamed to wear in company. This is a much wider understanding than that which links it exclusively to the cultural elite – the eighteenth-century *beau monde* (see Hannah Greig, 'Leading the Fashion: The Material Culture of London's *Beau Monde*', in John Styles and Amanda Vickery (eds), *Gender, Taste, and Material Culture in Britain and North America* 1700–1830 (New Haven: Yale Centre for British Art), 2006, pp. 293–313).

[3]   Berg, *Luxury and Pleasure*, pp. 249–51.

[4]   Beverly Lemire, 'Fashion and the Practice of History: A Political Legacy', in Lemire (ed.), *The Force of Fashion in Politics and Society: Global Perspectives from Early Modern to Contemporary Times* (Farnham: Ashgate, 2010), pp. 1–18.

[5]   Linda Levy Peck, *Consuming Splendour: Society and Culture in Seventeenth-Century England* (Cambridge: Cambridge University Press, 2005).

[6]   See de Vries, *Industrious Revolution*, ch. 4, for a survey of consumer demand mainly in the Atlantic economies.

clothing and lower quality luxury goods were increasingly available in parts of the Ottoman Empire by the mid seventeenth century.[7] There was a wide range of new commodities on sale to consumers in England and elsewhere. These included beverages like tea, coffee and chocolate as well as sugar, tobacco and some exotic foods. Although tea had been known since the mid seventeenth century, it was only after 1700 that consumption really took off. East India Company imports in 1704 were about 20,000 pounds, enough for less than 1,000 families, but had rocketed to 3,735,000 pounds a year on average in the 1750s. Tea drinking became a topic for poetry and satire in the early eighteenth century and was a widespread practice by the last third of the century.[8] Ann Gomm's grocery shop in the village of Shipton-under-Wychwood stocked over six different types of tea and three types of coffee at the end of the eighteenth century while sugar consumption had reached 20 pounds a head by 1800. Recipes for non-British dishes using Asian or Caribbean ingredients were increasingly common in the second half of the century. Curry, in particular, was widely available.[9]

If food was arguably at the heart of the emerging consumer economy, then textiles were the most visible manifestation of fashion. Linen and cotton tended to replace wool as the fabric of choice. Painted and printed Asian fabrics poured into Britain in the late seventeenth century, but cotton's triumph was not immediate. New products did not always find a ready market and Asian producers initially had to adapt their designs to suit Western taste.[10] Indian textiles were, however, perceived as a sufficient threat to home produced goods for calico to be banned for use as clothing or for household interiors in 1721. The wearing of such textiles was associated with luxury, the undermining of class distinctions and even promiscuity.[11] Printed linens may have temporarily benefited from the ban. Nevertheless during the second half of the eighteenth century cotton changed the way ordinary people dressed, particularly in terms of their outer garments, and brought fashion to the people. It could be printed, painted or dyed in washable and fast colours, looked cleaner than wool and was cheaper than silk which it could imitate in appearance. It was particularly important for waistcoats, breeches, gowns, petticoats, handkerchiefs and stockings. The victory of the printed cotton

---

[7]   Eminegül Karababa, 'Investigating Early Modern Ottoman Consumer Culture in the Light of Bursa Probate Inventories', *Economic History Review*, 65/1 (2012): 194–219.

[8]   Markham Ellis (ed.), *Tea and the Tea-Table in Eighteenth-Century England* (4 vols, London: Pickering & Chatto, 2010), vol. 1, pp. viii–xviii, xxxvi.

[9]   Troy Bickham, 'Eating the Empire: Interactions of Food, Cookery and Imperialism in Eighteenth-Century Britain', *Past and Present*, 198 (2008): 71–109. On new groceries see Jon Stobart, *Sugar and Spice: Grocers and Groceries in Provincial England, 1650–1830* (Oxford: Oxford University Press, 2013).

[10]   John Styles, 'Product Innovation in Early Modern London', *Past and Present*, 168 (2000): 124–69.

[11]   Chloe Wigston Smith, '"Calico Madams": Servants, Consumption and the Calico Crisis', *Eighteenth-Century Life*, 31/2 (2007): 29–55.

gown was just about complete by 1780. Linen's durability, however, meant that it remained important for shirts, shifts and undergarments generally. Stylish clothes were not confined to the upper and middling classes. Ordinary people were aware of fashion and at some point in their lives most managed to acquire some 'best' clothes to be worn on Sundays or at customary festivals.[12]

Domestic interiors were also subject to the desire for novelty and fashion. New goods included chinaware, glass, silver plated ware, tea tables, japanned ware and a variety of novelties. Maxine Berg has explored the design, production and marketing of these commodities many of which, having originally been castigated as luxury imports, became characteristic British products in the eighteenth century. This was especially the case with the metal working industries centred on Birmingham and Sheffield. Silver and silver plate was used for fashionable tea pots, cream boats, milk jugs and sugar trays. Steel buckles made in Birmingham were a key fashion item, while the town's brass and toy trades employed large numbers of workers in factories as well as craft workshops.[13] Chinese porcelain, consisting largely of useful articles such as cups, saucers, bowls and plates specifically designed for Western taste, flooded European markets in the first half of the eighteenth century. European produced goods, whether fine continental porcelain or the cheaper British earthenware, creamware and bone china, became increasingly important in the second half of the century.[14] Oriental lacquer ware was also imitated in the japanned papier mâché patented by Henry Clay of Birmingham.[15] Goods like these when combined with a judicious mix of old and new domestic furnishings like the blue and yellow paper for the parlour, the Hogarth prints, the new bedstead and the mahogany bookcase purchased by Gertrude Savile for her Farnsfield house in the 1730s could create an interior that advertised the good taste of the occupier.[16] The popularity of wallpaper increased significantly as the century went on. It was much cheaper than damask and allowed middle income householders to experiment with colour and pattern. Rooms intended for comfort and those intended for show were hung differently, with passages often in neutral colours while drawing and dining rooms required impressive paper.[17]

Successfully negotiating the world of fashion and good taste was about much more than simply acquiring novel goods. It was also about being in the right places and participating in the right pursuits. Irrespective of whether it is useful to designate some towns as 'leisure towns' there can be no doubt that leisure and display played an important role in much eighteenth-century urban life. Peter Borsay has written of an English 'urban renaissance' starting in the

---

[12]   Styles, *Dress of the People*, especially pp. 109–30, 303–15.

[13]   Berg, *Luxury and Pleasure*, ch. 5.

[14]   Ibid., ch. 2.

[15]   Ibid., p. 82.

[16]   Amanda Vickery, *Behind Closed Doors: At Home in Georgian England* (New Haven and London: Yale University Press, 2009), pp. 211–12.

[17]   Ibid., pp. 167–76.

late seventeenth century. As well as improvement to the physical fabric of towns including a more planned approach to the streetscape, this manifested itself in the creation of new opportunities for socializing and for being seen. Assemblies were a particularly important example of this, often taking place weekly in the winter or even twice weekly in resort towns in the summer. They were held in purpose-built rooms, in inns or in new town halls. By 1770 over 60 towns had experimented with assemblies or assembly rooms. Such locations were used not only for dances but also for plays and concerts.[18] Public walks and gardens also provided opportunities for fashionable display. There was, for example, a formal promenade to the south of Preston by end of the seventeenth century; a wide range of interlinked walks and gardens in mid eighteenth-century Bath was lined with luxury shops; while in Tunbridge Wells the Pantiles provided coffee houses and shops where toys, silver, china and other such items could be viewed or bought.[19]

Sociability was about more than mere enjoyment. Meeting and mixing with one's fellow human beings was felt by many to be a civilizing influence. Appropriate and serious social and cultural spaces promoted rationality and good taste. They were an essential component of polite society, which was itself imbued with a moral seriousness.[20] Being fashionable did not necessarily mean being frivolous. Book clubs, music societies and a variety of associations concerned with scientific matters bore witness to this serious side of polite culture. Philosophical and scientific societies were often found in county towns like Northampton where electricity was a favourite topic at meetings; Leicester where the scholarly community included medical men and booksellers; or Derby where physicians and others took a keen interest in the geology of the Peak. Erasmus Darwin was instrumental in founding the Philosophical Society there in 1783.[21] Smaller towns were not exempt from this associational culture. In Nottinghamshire, for example, theatres were to be found in middle sized towns while Mansfield had a Harmonic Society in 1782, a coffee club in the 1790s and monthly assemblies, and Retford had a book club in the 1820s.[22] Theatres, concerts and assemblies were also frequently advertised in the large and rapidly growing northern industrial towns

---

[18]   Borsay, *English Urban Renaissance*, pp. 151–61.

[19]   Ibid., pp. 162–70.

[20]   Ibid., pp. 263–8. But see Bob Harris, 'The Enlightenment, Towns and Urban Society in Scotland, *c.*1760–1820', *English Historical Review*, 126/522 (2011): 1097–136, for an emphasis on the pragmatic impulses towards urban improvement and some scepticism about the links between such improvement and enlightenment ideas.

[21]   Paul Elliott, 'The Origins of the "Creative Class": Provincial Urban Society, Scientific Culture and Socio-Political Marginality in Britain in the Eighteenth and Nineteenth Centuries', *Social History*, 28/3 (2003): 361–87; Paul Elliott, 'Towards a Geography of English Scientific Culture: Provincial Identity and Literary and Philosophical Culture in the English County Town, 1750–1850', *Urban History*, 32/3 (2005): 391–412.

[22]   Catherine A. Smith, *The Renaissance of the Nottinghamshire Market Town 1680–1840* (Chesterfield: Merton Priory Press, 2007), pp. 114–6.

like Leeds, Manchester and Sheffield. Manchester also had a thriving art market by the early nineteenth century. Northerners might have been proud to stress the importance of their town as centres of trade and industry but they also saw them as places of culture and sophistication.[23] Nor were those who perceived themselves as members of polite society absent from popular amusement such as fairs even if they tried to separate themselves mentally, if not always physically, from the mob by seeking out scientific shows and some theatrical performances. Rather like the later flâneur the respectable individual observed rather than participated in the life of the crowd.[24]

As already suggested, shops were another location where individuals could participate in fashionable and polite society. Higher status retailers tended, particularly by the later eighteenth century, to cluster in a group of shopping streets at the heart of a town, often near the market place. Such streets in 'leisure towns' like Chester or Shrewsbury might also be fashionable promenades. For this to happen streets often needed to be improved. Improvements included a better separation of functions, for example relocating market stalls, removing obstructions and some rebuilding. Published town guides might take their readers on a tour of fashionable streets, pointing out shops as well as public buildings.[25] In Derby, not usually treated as a major fashionable town but with an important cultural life, Corn Market, Iron Gate, Sadler Gate and surrounding streets formed the heart of its shopping district. Shop tax returns from the late 1780s reveal that the ward that included these streets produced over two-thirds of the town's shop tax and over half of the county's.[26] Advertisements confirm that these were desirable locations, with Iron Gate seeming to be specially favoured. For example, in 1794 S. Cook, a confectioner, announced his removal to Iron Gate and C. Cowlishaw, a grocer and tea-dealer, announced that he had taken a shop opposite All Saints' church in Iron Gate.[27]

Polite shopping streets offered opportunities for window shopping and for checking up on the latest fashions, without necessarily having to enter a shop. Those who did enter, however, also found themselves in a fashionable location. Retailers spent money on chairs, tables and looking glasses in order to create a congenial setting and to send out a message of politeness and reliability. Shops were places where customers could linger, inspect goods at leisure, gossip with

---

[23] Hannah Barker, '"Smoke Cities": Northern Industrial Towns in Late Georgian England', *Urban History*, 31/2 (2004): 175–90.

[24] Ben Heller, 'The "Mene Peuple" and the Polite Spectator: The Individual in the Crowd at Eighteenth-Century London Fairs', *Past and Present*, 208 (2010): 131–57.

[25] Stobart, Hann and Morgan, *Spaces of Consumption*, chs 3 and 4. Stobart acknowledges that improvements were patchy: Brown's in Chester was described in 1830 as 'a splendid mansion, flanked by two mud-wall cow houses' (p. 97).

[26] Figures derived from shop tax schedules in NA, Exchequer, Land and Assessed Taxes, E182/166.

[27] *Derby Mercury*, 29 May 1794, 13 November 1794.

friends and perhaps join the owner for refreshment in one of the less public areas of the shop.[28] Retailers were able to offer advice on what was fashionable and in good taste as well as responding to the demands of their customers. The intimate nature of the shop interior might, however, be problematic for the relationship between the (often) male shopkeeper and the (probably but not necessarily) female customer. Was the customer to be yielding and compliant or might she subvert the expected norms of politeness by disruptive and demanding behaviour? On the other hand might the retailer manipulate the customer into thinking that she was in control of the transaction when in reality he was? Retail spaces were replete with possibility and ambiguity.[29]

Acquiring the right goods, being seen in the right places and associating with the right people were essential ingredients of a polite lifestyle. Historians have used a variety of themes to describe and analyse this. For Woodruff Smith the concept of 'respectability' embraced both material culture and the concepts of gentility, luxury and virtue. Coffee houses provided a location and cultural milieu for men to indulge in respectable activities such as rational discourse, political discussion and the exchange of information. Self-control was a virtue and an excess of sentiment was suspect. Women, on the other hand, used the rituals of the tea table to demonstrate a domestic femininity in which sympathy and sentimental attachment were important and which promoted civilized behaviour. Respectability was about behaviour rather than status.[30] John Crowley has used the trope of 'comfort' as a way of analysing some aspects of fashionable and polite behaviour. He suggests that for much of the eighteenth century goods were acquired more to display elegance and gentility than to achieve physical comfort. Chairs, for example, were not designed primarily for ease and umbrellas were adopted more for cultural and fashionable reasons than for utility. By the end of the century comfort and convenience were becoming more prominent with discomfort being satirized by contemporaries like Cruikshank and Rowlandson. Comfort had explicit priority in the design of picturesque cottages in the last decades of the century.[31]

There are useful insights here although few would wish to claim that the multifaceted culture of polite society could be reduced to one or two key themes. Taste was another important concept. It was the antithesis of both academic pedantry and vulgar luxury and implied some knowledge of the rules of design. It might be linked with 'neatness' which implied a low-key elegance far removed

---

[28]   Hann and Stobart, 'Sites of Consumption'; Berry, 'Polite Consumption'.

[29]   On this theme see Elizabeth Kowaleski-Wallace, *Consuming Subjects: Women, Shopping and Business in the Eighteenth Century* (New York: Columbia University Press, 1997), pp. 79–98. Woodward's satirical sketch (Frontispiece) offers a more conventional view of the tribulations of polite shopping.

[30]   Smith, *Consumption and the Making of Respectability*.

[31]   John E. Crowley, *The Invention of Comfort: Sensibilities and Design in Early Modern Britain and Early America* (Baltimore and London: Johns Hopkins University Press, 2001).

from unseemly showiness.[32] Taste also implied some degree of awareness of the world of the arts and the imagination. Collecting and connoisseurship might also be part of polite culture.[33] The burgeoning world of print linked many of the different aspects of fashion and politeness. A mere 6,000 titles had been published in England in the 1620s; this had risen to 21,000 in the 1710s and 56,000 in the 1790s. A fashionable and popular novel like Richardson's *Pamela* went through five editions in 12 months.[34] Books like this were readily available in provincial bookshops even if new books remained expensive for most of the century. Almost all shopkeepers and those in similar occupations were literate by the third quarter of the eighteenth century and circulating libraries offered access to novels and other books for those who could not or did not wish to buy.[35] As well as promoting a shared literary culture, print was also one of the ways in which politeness and commerce were linked. Advertisements and trade cards were used to associate shopkeepers with the local elite either by being addressed to the gentry or by the language they used. Goods were promoted for their quality, authenticity, fashionability and good taste, but not as luxury items, while trade cards might show how objects should be grouped to create a fashionable interior.[36]

So were fashion, and even politeness, essentially constructed by shopkeepers manipulating the taste and purchasing habits of their customers? Their knowledge of new products and the role some of them had in designing polite domestic interiors were certainly important. They also, however, had to listen to their customers whose needs and wants were also shaped by what they read about in books or journals and saw in the houses of their friends.[37] Objects not only advertised their owner's self-understanding of her or his participation in polite culture but also helped to create this. They could evoke appropriate behaviour as when in Jane Austen's *Mansfield Park* Fanny Price placed in her room objects of polite society that would improve her character.[38] Consumers needed to know about fashion and taste, as well as about price and quality, if they were not to risk looking foolish in the eyes of their friends and neighbours. Goods had a cultural as well as a use value.

It is, of course, important not to get carried away by all this. Many retail transactions whether in shops or markets were about the necessities of daily existence. By no means all shops were fashionable and many shopkeepers may

[32] Vickery, *Behind Closed Doors*, pp. 18–20.
[33] Brewer, *Pleasures of the Imagination* remains invaluable on high culture.
[34] Porter, *Enlightenment*, p. 73.
[35] Brewer, *Pleasures*, pp. 168–80.
[36] Stobart, 'Selling (through) Politeness'.
[37] Ilja van Damme, 'Middlemen and the Creation of a "Fashion Revolution": The Experience of Antwerp in the Late Seventeenth and Eighteenth Centuries', in Lemire (ed.), *Force of Fashion*, pp. 21–39.
[38] Ross J. Wilson, '"The Mystical Character of Commodities": The Consumer Society in 18th-Century England', *Post-Medieval Archaeology*, 42/1 (2008): 144–56.

have known little and cared less about politeness or the symbolic meanings of their goods. Yet, much to the consternation of traditional moralists, many ordinary labouring people owned a cheap tea pot and the accompanying items needed for a simple tea party. Moreover, as John Styles has reminded us, most people owned some fashionable clothing at some stage in their life and even the relatively poor might have their 'best' clothes.[39] Shopping was part of the ordinary experience of most people and at least some of that shopping was for items that were not strictly necessities. The next section of this chapter explores some aspects of this shopping experience.

Shopping for Politeness

'J. Cooper, Woollen Draper, Bridge-Street-Row ... has just returned from London, with a large and fashionable assortment of Broad Cloths, Kerseymeres, and Fancy Waistcoatings, of the best quality and newest patterns, for the Spring Fashions, which will be sold on moderate terms'.[40] This advertisement by a fashionable Chester retailer situated in one of the city's best shopping locations is typical of many that appeared each spring. Phrases like 'elegant assortment', 'most fashionable', 'new and genteel assortment', 'all the newest fashion' and 'new and fashionable for the Spring' abounded in such advertisements. A significant number of those who advertised their return from London – or very occasionally from Manchester – were women and by no means all were listed in contemporary directories.[41] This was particularly the case with those who described themselves as milliners or dress and corset makers. Retailers who made good use of the local press to draw attention to their new and fashionable stock may have escaped the notice of (male) directory compilers, but clearly expected polite society to patronize their establishments. It was not only those in the cloth and clothing trades who promoted their fashionable goods. The Chester upholsterer and cabinet maker Samuel Nickson advertised in 1806 that he 'is just returned from London, where he has selected with the greatest care, an entirely new and superb assemblage of printed Furniture, Moreens, unwatered, with Egyptian Etruscan Borders printed on in the present fashion'. He also had carpets, chairs, window cornices 'in the Egyptian and Grecian style', beds, card tables and many other goods.[42] The whole advertisement is a good example of what Jon Stobart has called 'selling (through) politeness'.

---

[39] Styles, *Dress of the People*, pp. 305–10.
[40] *Chester Chronicle*, 9 April 1802.
[41] Based on a sample of advertisements in Chester and Derby newspapers between 1770 and 1820.
[42] *Chester Chronicle*, 28 March 1806. Furniture in this context refers to soft furnishings.

However persuasive the advertising, it was only the start of the process of getting a potential customer to make a purchase. As indicated in Chapter 2, shopkeepers were increasingly trying to make their shops attractive even to the most demanding of customers. Not that it was always necessary for the customer to go to the shop. Shopkeepers continued to visit their more important customers, while at the other end of the spectrum those from the lower orders of society might be served through the shop window rather than inside the shop.[43] Some customers might send a servant to shop for them and while this might save time there was always the risk that the servant would not be as particular as the mistress about quality or price. There might even be collusion between the servant and the shopkeeper so that the servant got some commission for loyalty.[44] It was also not uncommon to use a family member or friend who lived in London or in a large town as a proxy shopper. Some goods could be ordered by mail or by sending a note to the shopkeeper, but again this could be risky particularly if the goods were easily damaged in transit. Those who shopped in person probably did so mainly in the mornings. Higher status unmarried women would usually be chaperoned on a shopping expedition but could make short visits to respectable shops unaccompanied. Once inside the shop refreshments would be offered before the browsing and possible negotiation over price began.[45] No matter how shopping was done, it is clear that it was, and was acknowledged to be, a skilled activity. It was necessary to be aware of prices and price fluctuations, to have an eye for quality and to be aware of the ways in which shopkeepers might be economical with the truth about their goods. As such it was a task for the mistress of the household and women could not only take pride in their ability as good shoppers but would be valued for this. Men also engaged in the skilled and pleasurable aspects of shopping even if there was a greater risk of them being distracted by the female shop assistants. Nor was shopping a lone pursuit: it was useful to discuss potential purchases with others and draw on their expertise.[46]

Shoppers did not confine their purchases to one or two locations. It was convenient, but not always possible, to use local shops and sometimes it was more interesting to use the shops of a larger town even if similar goods were available closer to home. Some individuals did not venture far. George Dockwra, an annuitant from a propertied family living in north Cheshire in the 1740s, bought material for shirts and handkerchiefs from a linen draper in Warrington across the Mersey in Lancashire, suit material from a Great Budworth mercer and books and fishing tackle from a Knutsford bookseller. He also used a tailor and shoemaker in

---

[43]   Cox, *Complete Tradesman*, pp. 128–34. See also Cox and Dannehl, *Perceptions of Retailing*, ch. 7.

[44]   Walsh, 'Shopping at First Hand?'

[45]   Berry, 'Polite Consumption'.

[46]   Claire Walsh, 'Shopping at First Hand?'; Claire Walsh, 'Shops, Shopping, and the Art of Decision-Making in Eighteenth-Century England', in Styles and Vickery (eds), *Gender, Taste, and Material Culture*, pp. 151–77.

Great Budworth. None of these were more than 10 miles from his home.[47] Elizabeth Shackleton, living in north Lancashire in the mid eighteenth century, kept herself abreast of London fashions and bought tableware there, but also patronized local craftsmen in Colne and Lancaster for furniture. She characterized her possessions as 'best' or 'common' with best not necessarily meaning new or fashionable.[48] Edward Sulyard from the Stowmarket area of Suffolk bought books in Ipswich, cloth in Chelmsford and wine in Diss. He could be a troublesome customer, often neglecting to pay bills on time and receiving a complaint from a Stowmarket shopkeeper in 1751 about his dog which had caused damage to her shop.[49] Buying directly from London continued to be normal for many gentry families well into the eighteenth century even when similar goods were available locally. Provincial shopkeepers had to work hard to counter the assumption that London goods were cheaper and better quality.[50] The nineteenth-century Cornish shopkeeper Henry Grylls Thomas used his business trips to London to window-shop for his family and occasionally buy goods for them. He was tempted by a papier-mâché table in 1851 but did not buy it. In the following year he bought three expensive dresses for his wife and daughters.[51]

Although it was possible to order directly from a retailer in another town, for example by sending an existing garment as a pattern, many purchasers preferred to use a reliable friend or family member to act on their behalf. Such contacts could also transmit information about fashion.[52] Shopping on behalf of someone else could be demanding. A 1739 letter from Frances Egerton in London to Mrs Downes at Worth in Cheshire expressed the hope that 'you'll approve of what we have done' before detailing purchases of ribbons and fans and providing information about the latest styles.[53] Judith Milbanke in county Durham wrote frequently to her aunt Mary Noel in London in 1780s with requests for clothing, china and other items. In October 1783 she asked Mary to buy breakfast china including two handsome Wedgwood teapots from Coopers in Jermyn Street and to look at sets of table china, advising her of prices and which was the most eligible to buy. Mary's reply was discouraging: 'I fear you will not like your China much, but Mr Cooper has no choice … I saw only one set of twelves & that was that old

---

[47]   Charles E. Foster, *Seven Households: Life in Cheshire and Lancashire 1582–1774* (Northwich: Arley Hall Press, 2002), pp. 172–9.

[48]   Amanda Vickery, 'Women and the World of Goods: A Lancashire Consumer and her Possessions, 1751–81', in Brewer and Porter (eds), *Consumption and the World of Goods*, pp. 274–301.

[49]   SRO, Letters to Edward Sulyard, D641/4/J/14/2/7.

[50]   Cox and Dannehl, *Perceptions of Retailing*, pp. 135–40.

[51]   *A Cornish Shopkeeper's Diary*, pp. 136, 142.

[52]   Miles Lambert, '"Sent from Town": Commissioning Clothing in Britain during the Long Eighteenth Century', *Costume*, 43 (2009): 66–84.

[53]   CALS, Downes Family of Shrigley, Letter from Frances Egerton, 24 April 1739, DDS 21/4.

pattern, foreign, with a great deal of blue, & gilt edges, but he did not shew me any new or pretty patterns'. There were only remnants in the shop and no Wedgwood teapots.[54] In 1785 Judith asked her brother to order a habit for her, thinking that he would be better placed than her aunt to deal with tailors. The habit proved to be 'diabolically ugly' as even her brother acknowledged when he also sent her some harpsichord music.[55] Mary sent Judith a fashionable cap in 1790, writing 'By the Carrier comes a Cap, quite new fashion, the very first mode, which I beg you acceptance of ... L[ad]y Almeira had one & looked like an Angel, Bet Jeffrys had one & look'd like a fury, but I think it will become you. You must put it very forward at the top, so that the bow comes over the hair ...'.[56] James Wright of Eyam in Derbyshire used his brother-in-law William Sisum in London for various shopping commissions in the 1790s and 1800s including playing cards and, on a regular basis, tea from Twinings even though tea would have been readily available in any nearby market town and possibly in the village itself. The Wrights bought some provisions from Sheffield and Derby but tea from London was perhaps perceived as cheaper and better quality.[57] Those visiting Bath, like Elizabeth Penrose from Cornwall in 1767, might also be asked to buy goods for family and friends.[58]

As will have been apparent from the foregoing examples, shopping was by no means just a female activity. There were, however, significant differences in the shopping activities of men and women. In general women were responsible for most aspects of the day-to-day running of the home, including dealing with retailers supplying food, household goods, textiles and some furnishings. Married men tended to take charge of transactions with their tailors and saddlers and to buy wines, luxury foodstuffs and books. They may also have exercised overall control of household expenditure while leaving much of the detail to their wives. A prospective wife may well have had the final say in the purchase of items of furniture and in the decoration of the marital home. Scientific instruments, which were important decorative items in the eighteenth century, belonged in the male sphere as did expensive items of porcelain even though women were strongly associated with china in the Georgian imagination.[59] Men continued to be active

---

[54]   *The Noels and The Milbankes: Their Letters for Twenty-Five Years 1767–1792: Presented as a Narrative by Malcolm Elwin* (London: Macdonald, 1967), pp. 219–21.

[55]   Ibid., pp. 267–8.

[56]   Ibid., pp. 367–8.

[57]   DRO, Wright of Eyam, Letters and Accounts, D5430/131/6; Household Accounts, 1808–24, D5430/8/10.

[58]   Suzanne Adams, 'Purchasers from the Parsonage: Observations on Bath Dress and Reactive Shopping by the Penrose Family, 1766–67', *Costume*, 39 (2005): 79–90.

[59]   On this topic see in particular Amanda Vickery, *Behind Closed Doors*, and Karen Harvey, 'Men Making Home: Masculinity and Domesticity in Eighteenth-Century Britain', *Gender and History*, 21/3 (2009): 520–40. David Hussey and Margaret Ponsonby, *The Single Homemaker and Material Culture in the Long Eighteenth Century* (Farnham:

shoppers in the nineteenth century. John Thomas Brookes, squire of Flitwick in Bedfordshire, bought wine, horses, carriages, books, curios, pictures and items for the development of his garden. He used visits to London to buy gifts for his wife and daughters and all things necessary for his youngest son when he went up to Oxford in 1847. Brookes's wife was responsible for mundane shopping and household management.[60]

Organizing the shopping for a large estate was a complex and skilled task. At Stoneleigh Abbey in Warwickshire the Leigh family relied heavily on London retailers, especially for luxury goods such as silverware, art, books and high quality furnishings, but they also bought grocery and haberdashery in the metropolis. Over three-quarters of the total expenditure in a sample of 628 bills was in London with 8.7 per cent in Coventry and 11 per cent in Warwick. Local tradesmen supplied hardware, perishable foods and grocery, including a range of teas; and were responsible for skilled craft work on the Abbey. They bought similar goods from different suppliers at the same time, exercising choice rather than being constrained by necessity. Their purchases made a public statement about good taste, for example in the acquisition of books and works of art, as well as more traditional forms of display.[61] In east Cheshire in the 1720s the Leghs of Lyme Hall bought mainly from local traders in Stockport, Macclesfield and Manchester although wine and oysters were purchased in London. Grocery, including coffee and tea, paper, ironmongery, shoes and linen came from Stockport and Macclesfield while Manchester retailers supplied books, drugs, wine and fruit.[62] The Grosvenors of Eaton Hall near Chester made extensive use of that city's retailers and service providers in the early nineteenth century, sometimes spending £3,000 or more there in a single year, including £327 with Mr Powell, upholsterer, in 1810 and £440 with two cabinet makers in 1811.[63]

Further down the social scale, John and Mary Gibbard of Sharnbrook in Bedfordshire patronized local retailers as well as those in Bedford and London when shopping for clothes. William Tassel, tailor and draper in Sharnbrook, was one local trader much used by the Gibbards, billing both of them separately. Mary had regular dealings with Ann Bellamy a linen draper and milliner in Bedford, while both John and Mary dealt with London tailors and milliners who could also

Ashgate, 2012), explores the interaction between singleness and gender in the context of homemaking.

[60]   David Hussey, 'Guns, Horses and Stylish Waistcoats? Male Consumer Activity and Domestic Shopping in Late-Eighteenth- and Early Nineteenth-Century England', in Hussey and Ponsonby (eds), *Buying for the Home*, pp. 47–69.

[61]   Jon Stobart, 'Gentlemen and Shopkeepers: Supplying the Country House in Eighteenth-Century England', *Economic History Review*, 64/3 (2011): 885–904.

[62]   Stockport Local Heritage Library, Peter Legh of Lyme Hall, Steward's Overseer Accounts, 1727–38, B/JJ/6.

[63]   Eaton Estate Office, Eccleston, Grosvenor of Eaton, Eaton Household, List of Tradesmen's Bills from Chester, 1808–17, EV 376.

offer fashion advice. They were skilled shoppers, making positive decisions about where best to make purchases, but also committed to supporting shopkeepers in their own village as a way of consolidating their position in local society.[64] The Pole (later Chandos-Pole) family who lived at Radbourne about five miles from Derby frequently shopped there. For example, William Parker, who described himself as a toyman, supplied them with a plate warmer, a breakfast egg tray, a silver pencil case, some fortune telling cards, two umbrellas, a dozen silver spoons and a silver plated ladle among other items in a bill amounting to £67 10s 2d.[65] This was a good example of the sort of shop made possible by growing demand from the gentry and middle classes for a wide range of fashionable items for their homes. Other fashionable Derby shopkeepers supplying the Poles in the early nineteenth century included Thomas Breary, hatter and hosier; Cox and Weatherhead, ironmongers; John Drewry, printer; Thomas Mawkes, clock and watchmaker; Francis Roome, bookseller; and Richard Smith, Italian Warehouseman.[66] Almost all their purchases seem to have been made in Derby, with occasional use of a London cabinet maker or Bath milliner. William Parker continued to supply a range of fancy goods, including a tea urn, a toy windmill, a wax doll, a drum, a fiddle, a Jew's harp and a trumpet in 1803; and more children's toys, a brooch, a historical game, a globe and fishing tackle in 1805–07.[67]

Buying and displaying books could be an effective way of demonstrating good taste and a cultured lifestyle. Many books were purchased unseen, requiring a considerable degree of trust between collector and bookseller. When collectors had very specific demands, for example regarding bindings, there was scope for misunderstanding and bad feeling. In the late seventeenth century William Boothby from Ashbourne in Derbyshire, who was an avid book collector, was in regular contact with Michael Johnson of Lichfield. Johnson supplied him with books and acted as bookbinder. Boothby was often dissatisfied both with the price of some of the books and the quality of the bindings.[68] By the early nineteenth century not only were many more books available but bookshops were much more widespread. Even so some buyers preferred to deal directly with London booksellers despite the risks involved. One William Grove of Lichfield wrote to Lackington in 1791 requesting specific books 'if they fully answer the description given of them: I must rely therefore upon you, not to send me any but what do so'. He also asked Lackington to arrange lettering on the book bindings 'as they letter very ill in Lichfield'.[69] Correspondence from the Reverend J. Riland of Yoxall in Staffordshire to the London bookseller Baynes in 1807 also implies a concern

---

[64]   Lucy A. Bailey, 'Consumption and Status: Shopping for Clothes in a Nineteenth-Century Bedfordshire Gentry Household', *Midland History*, 36/1 (2011): 89–114.

[65]   DRO, Chandos-Pole Bills, 1788–91, D5557/10/38/3.

[66]   Ibid., Vouchers 1804, D5557/10/1–21.

[67]   D5557/10/24.

[68]   DRO, Boothby Letterbooks, Microfilm, XM 856.

[69]   Stafford, William Salt Library, S. MS. 478/7/110.

that the books sent might not be quite as ordered.[70] Visiting the shop in person could also be problematic. Roger Wilbraham from High Legh in Cheshire wrote to the Manchester antiquarian bookseller William Ford after an abortive visit: 'I mean to come to Manchester on Saturday when my principle object is to look at your books & to be with you between 11 & 12 o'clock'. On his previous visit Ford had been out and his shopman could not get at any of the curious articles as they were locked up.[71] Some bookseller – collector relationships were, however, amicable and fruitful. The Yorkshire bibliophile Francis Wrangham, later to be Archdeacon of the East Riding, regularly bought books from John Fry of Bristol and consulted him about the rarity of books he was thinking about acquiring. He also sent Fry many of his duplicates – despite the complications of conveying books from Scarborough to Bristol – probably to be exchanged for other books rather than sold.[72] Specialist booksellers not merely supplied polite society but were integral to its networks.

Conclusions

Jon Stobart has suggested that shopping is the missing link between the retail and consumer revolutions of the eighteenth century. Shopping practices as well as the actual goods purchased were important in the construction of identity. Shopping spanned the worlds of economic necessity and of culture and leisure.[73] Some aspects of shopping were also subject to substantial change. By the beginning of the nineteenth century Elizabeth Gell might still have sought advice about the latest fashions from a family member in London, but she could equally well have gone to one of many shops in Derby to view them. In Chester a shop like that run by the sisters Elizabeth and Susannah Towsey was bringing the latest London fashions to the ladies of the city from at least the 1780s. It was still doing so in the 1980s, albeit as part of the Debenhams group. Its story illustrates many of the themes of this book, such as the links between polite culture and retailing and the origins of department stores and is told in the Appendix.

Shopping was changing the mental maps that contemporaries had of their world. Trade cards with exotic images, the advertising of novel products and the references to London and Paris fashion were tending to overcome barriers of distance and time. New goods, made familiar through the media of print and image, could be acquired, fitted into existing routines and used as building blocks for a lifestyle.[74] Fashion and politeness had impacted on the world of retailing while

---

[70] Ibid., S. MS. 478/18/17.

[71] Manchester, Chetham's Library, William Ford Letterbooks, Mun. A6.78–9, vol. 2b, fol. 456.

[72] Greater Manchester Archives, John Fry Letters, 2 vols, MS GF 091F8.

[73] Stobart, 'A History of Shopping'.

[74] Cox and Dannehl, *Perceptions of Retailing*, ch. 7.

changing retail practices helped sustain polite culture. Shopping was increasingly becoming both a statement about an individual's view of themselves and of how they related to the world around them and also a means of creating these; it was something to be celebrated.[75]

Not everyone would have agreed. Those who continued to emphasise the virtues of contentment found the whole world of fashion disturbing, particularly when the lower orders joined in. Some aspects of politeness, such as the emphasis on taste and on character, were more in keeping with what had been conventional views. Yet as correspondence, household accounts and newspaper advertisements make clear, the desire to be in fashion and to be seen as part of, or at least associated with, polite society was widespread by the second half of the eighteenth century if not earlier. The attitudes and behaviour of these shoppers is in many ways recognizably modern. So also are some of the more ambiguous aspects of shopping and consumption. These include the relationship between shopping and sex, visible in eighteenth-century literary perceptions that some shops like milliners might be fronts for brothels or that dressmakers were courtesans.[76] There were also those who became obsessive in the way in which they shopped for or collected desirable objects. Some of these themes are explored in the next chapter.

---

[75]   Mary Douglas, 'In Defence of Shopping', in Pasi Falk and Colin Campbell (eds), *The Shopping Experience* (London: Sage, 1997), pp. 15–30.

[76]   Chloe Wigston Smith, 'Clothes without Bodies: Objects, Humans, and the Marketplace in Eighteenth-Century It-Narratives and Trade Cards', *Eighteenth-Century Fiction*, 23/2 (2010–11): 347–80.

Chapter 6
Showing Off: Consuming and Collecting

In John Webster's early seventeenth-century play *The Duchess of Malfi* there is a scene where the imprisoned Duchess is visited by various mad people, sent by her brother to torment her. Among them was 'an English tailor craz'd i' the brain With the study of new fashions'.[1] The idea that ever-changing and perhaps ever more extreme fashions could impact on the mental stability of an individual has had a long history. Webster's tailor would have risked even more brain fever in the eighteenth century as the pace of change grew ever quicker. Was there indeed perhaps a point at which consuming material things might turn into being consumed by them? There were some, like Thomas Beddoes the late eighteenth-century physician, who certainly thought so. Not only were there the traditional dangers of excess, but the new opportunities for consuming material goods could lead to the pursuit of pernicious lifestyles which sacrificed health to fashion and novelty. Might consumption quite literally be the wasting disease of a consuming society?[2]

Consumption and Excess

While it is reasonable to claim that consuming played a significant role in shaping eighteenth-century society and culture, this is not the same as describing the eighteenth century as a 'consumer society'. For Brewer and Porter that would mean 'social orders whose expectations, whose hopes and fears, whose prospects of integration, harmony or dissolution, increasingly depended upon the smooth operation and continued expansion of the system of goods'. It was not enough that there were simply more things to be acquired.[3] Some, like Peter Stearns, have confidently asserted that a consumer society existed by the mid eighteenth century in Britain and other parts of Western Europe.[4] Others have sounded a note of caution. Sara Pannell has warned about the danger reading twentieth century consumer society back into the eighteenth and has stressed the need to consider the act of consuming and the motives that might shape this in a given context rather than

---

[1] John Webster, *The Duchess of Malfi*, IV, ii, 51–2 (1623; New Mermaid edn, London: A. & C. Black, 1993), p. 91.

[2] Roy Porter, 'Consumption: Disease of the Consumer Society', in Brewer and Porter (eds), *Consumption and the World of Goods*, pp. 58–81.

[3] John Brewer and Roy Porter, 'Introduction' in Brewer and Porter (eds), *Consumption and the World of Goods*, pp. 1–15 (p. 2).

[4] Peter N. Stearns, *Consumerism in World History*, p. 15.

simply labelling all such acts as 'consumption'.[5] Jon Stobart has recently reminded us of the importance of looking at the individual as an active player in the world of goods, making rational choices and not driven by meta-forces like consumption.[6] Don Slater has specifically linked consumer culture with modernity and hence with choice, individualism and market relations. He sees identity as being bound up with consumption, but questions the extent to which consumers are free or manipulated.[7] John Benson, writing of the difficulty of deciding what constitutes a consumer society, notes that historians who have studied such societies have described them in broadly similar terms: choice and credit are readily available, social value is defined in terms of purchasing power and possessions, and there is a desire for the new, modern, exciting and fashionable.[8]

Eighteenth-century England displayed some of the characteristics of a consumer society. There was an expanding range of new and fashionable goods both imported and home produced as discussed in Chapter 5. The middling sorts of people had sufficient purchasing power to be able to access these and, if the concept of an 'industrious revolution' has any validity, then that would also have been the case for some of those lower down the social scale (see Introduction pp. 6–7). Being able to access consumer goods is, however, not the same as wanting to do so. The changes in outlook discussed in Chapter 4 both removed some of the obstacles to desiring more material possessions, in particular that doing so was contrary to generally accepted religious views, and promoted the association of goods with a desirable and fashionable lifestyle. Buying, using and perhaps displaying the right sort of objects in the right place demonstrated one's membership of polite society, or indeed of a particular subculture within that society. The desire to be seen doing the right thing could, however, sometimes be so strong that it seemed that the material objects were almost controlling the consumer rather than the other way round. A brief exploration of some aspects of the world of obsessive consumption, notably around fashionable dress, illustrates these ideas.

Descriptions of mid eighteenth-century Bath frequently referred to the appearance and dress of those who visited. For example, Elizabeth Montagu reported how 'The Rooms were prodigiously crowded with very uncouth figures most wonderfully dressed: those who nature designed to be homely art rendered hideous, and many, who education made awkward, mantua-makers, tailors, friseurs and milliners made monstrous'.[9] Elaborate and valuable jewellery and even more elaborate hair styles and headdresses were an important part of making

[5]   Sara Pennell, 'Consumption and Consumerism in Early Modern England', *Historical Journal*, 42/2 (1999): 549–64.

[6]   Stobart, *Sugar and Spice*, p. 2.

[7]   Don Slater, *Consumer Culture and Modernity* (Cambridge: Polity, 1997), chs 1 and 2.

[8]   John Benson, *The Rise of Consumer Society in Britain 1880–1980* (London: Longman, 1994), p. 4.

[9]   Borsay, *English Urban Renaissance*, p. 238.

an impression in the fashionable places of Bath and other resorts.[10] Fashion did not have to be this extreme to be demanding. The commercialization of fashion in the second half of the eighteenth century meant that more and more people were not only increasingly aware of what they could wear, but also felt that they had to wear the latest fashions as illustrated in the growing number of ladies' magazines and almanacs. By the 1770s fashions were regarded as changing annually and each year had its fashionable colour.[11]

Men were also subject to the vagaries and extremes of fashion. The macaroni style of the 1760s and 1770s which was briefly regarded as the latest metropolitan chic included red high-heeled shoes, coloured wigs and make-up.[12] It was not only the elite who strove to be fashionable. The sons of London artisans created distinctive dress and hair styles in the later eighteenth century, such as long hair curled on their shoulders, as a way of defining their particular place in society.[13] Highly decorative male dress was, however, on its way out. Beau Brummell was to lead a fashion revolution that would emphasize cut, fit and proportion in a restricted range of colours, predominately blue, black and white. The Brummell look may have appeared pared-down or even simple but it concealed a dedication to the demands of looking good just as extreme as did more elaborate earlier styles. In essence it comprised a plain, lightly starched shirt, a perfectly tied neckcloth that held the contours of the neck and framed the face, a pale waistcoat, tight pantaloons in a soft fabric, a dark jacket and black boots. Brummell's pose of effortless elegance was the precursor of the structured, sculptural and monochrome male fashions of the nineteenth century that made men look powerful and serious. It also influenced less restrained styles, such as those associated with the later nineteenth-century aesthetic movement, which retained the structured neoclassical elements of Brummell's tailoring.[14]

Being almost enslaved by the demands of fashion was not entirely new in the long eighteenth century. The de Villiers brothers, members of the Dutch aristocracy visiting Paris in the 1650s, were compelled to stay at home one Sunday because of their lack of appropriate clothes. Their travelling clothes were too elaborate and so they summoned a tailor to alter them and make them look suitably fashionable until new clothes were ready.[15] Increasingly, however, what one wore was not a

---

[10]   Ibid., pp. 238–40.

[11]   Neil McKendrick, 'The Commercialization of Fashion', in McKendrick, Brewer and Plumb, *The Birth of a Consumer Society*, pp. 34–99.

[12]   Ian Kelly, *Beau Brummell: The Ultimate Dandy* (London: Hodder & Stoughton, 2005), pp. 2–3.

[13]   Beverly Lemire, 'Second-Hand Beaux and "Red-armed Belles": Conflict and the Creation of Fashion in England, *c.*1660–1800', *Continuity and Change*, 15/3 (2000): 391–417.

[14]   Kelly, *Beau Brummell*, especially ch. 5 and Epilogue.

[15]   Daniel Roche, *A History of Everyday Things: The Birth of Consumption in France, 1600–1800* (Cambridge: Cambridge University Press, 2000), p. 209.

matter of aristocratic whim, nor was it constrained by sumptuary laws, but was influenced, or even dictated, by the world of commercialized fashion. No one compelled you to follow this, but an internal voice more and more told you that you should do so, even if it meant being uncomfortable or looking ridiculous. Jane Austen described the wife of a Hampshire colonel arriving for a family dinner on a freezing January night in 1801 dressed 'nakedly in white muslin' as London fashion decreed.[16] Is this so far removed from twenty-first century young people roaming the streets of their local town in mid winter dressed in t-shirts, skimpy tops and short skirts? Indulging in fashionable excess and believing that by doing so you are making a personal statement about who you are feels recognizably modern. Arguably the tension between using clothes and body shape to proclaim individuality, and the need on the other hand not to stray too far from the prevailing fashions for fear of being rejected, has its origins in the fashion revolutions and fashion excesses of the long eighteenth century.

Collecting: From Curiosities to Connoisseurship

The world of collectors and collecting also sheds light on how objects could be used to create a lifestyle or play a role in polite society. Acquiring a carefully selected collection of tasteful objects might make a statement about your ability to participate in polite culture; or it might become an obsession. Theorists distinguish the making of a collection from the simple accumulation of goods of a similar type. Collecting, however, often starts with relatively unfocused accumulating. A somewhat similar shift seems to have taken place more generally in the long eighteenth century as notions of collecting became more sophisticated. In the late seventeenth century objects tended to be prized for their age, rarity or even grotesqueness. They were curiosities and included items from the natural world as well as the products of human creativity. Categorization and classification did not necessarily play much part in such accumulations. Increasingly, however, the world of collecting fragmented and issues of learning and taste became more important. Paintings, sculpture and prints were valued in a way that fossils, shells and curiosities no longer were.[17] A partial exception to this was the collection of curiosities from other, particularly far distant, cultures which could be viewed as specimens for scientific study rather than as novelties.[18]

Collecting was a serious pursuit in the eighteenth century as in subsequent periods. Walter Benjamin has summed up the essence of collecting:

[16]   McKendrick, 'Commercialization of Fashion', p. 41.
[17]   Brewer, *Pleasures of the Imagination*, pp. 253–6.
[18]   Nicholas Thomas, 'Licensed Curiosity: Cook's Pacific Voyages', in John Elsner and Roger Cardinal (eds), *The Cultures of Collecting* (London: Reaktion, 1994) pp. 116–36.

> What is decisive in collecting is that the object is detached from all its original functions in order to enter into the closest conceivable relation to things of the same kind. This relation is the diametric opposite of any utility, and falls into the peculiar category of completeness.[19]

There are two key points here: detachment from original function and completeness. The first object acquired in what is to become a collection might have been bought for its use value or might even have been a chance purchase. Only as subsequent items of the same type are acquired and valued as part of a series, rather than for their use or beauty, is it meaningful to talk about a collection.[20] As a collection grows so does the desire for completeness. The quest for the missing item or items can become obsessive, particularly if the item in question is rare. For Benjamin this is part of the collector's struggle against dispersion and confusion and the sense that even if only one piece is missing the whole collection remains a patchwork.[21] Baudrillard explores aspects of the relationship between collector and the collection. He suggests that there is an element of fanaticism in many collectors coupled with a tendency to invest in objects all that the collector finds impossible to invest in human relationships. Touching on the theme of completeness he argues that the final term in a collection is the collector.[22] Collected objects tend to be those with a high fetish value in that they are imbued with a value far in excess of what use or exchange would justify. Such objects are likely to be displayed, not hidden in specimen cabinets, and proclaim that I am what I own.[23]

Objects in a collection might have been removed from their original context, but they are not thereby distanced from the collector. Rather the practice of collecting tends to be performative, embodied and sensual.[24] In Benjamin's words, 'collectors are beings with tactile instincts'.[25] They have also needed good taste and aesthetic appreciation. This became increasingly true as the eighteenth century progressed and collectors were able to regard themselves as connoisseurs. It was important to have visited other lands, particularly around the Mediterranean, and immersed oneself in their high culture. Early members of the Society of

---

[19]   Walter Benjamin, *The Arcades Project*, trans. Howard Eiland and Kevin McLaughlin (Cambridge, MA: Belknap Press, 1999), p. 204.

[20]   Mieke Bal, 'Telling Objects: A Narrative Perspective on Collecting', in Elsner and Cardinal, *Cultures of Collecting*, pp. 97–115.

[21]   Benjamin, *Arcades Project*, p. 211.

[22]   Jean Baudrillard, 'The System of Collecting', in Elsner and Cardinal, *Cultures of Collecting*, pp. 7–24.

[23]   John Windsor, 'Identity Parades', in Elsner and Cardinal, *Cultures of Collecting*, pp. 49–67.

[24]   John Potvin and Alla Myzelev, 'Introduction: The Material of Visual Cultures', in Potvin and Myzelev (eds), *Material Cultures 1740–1920: The Meanings and Pleasures of Collecting* (Farnham: Ashgate, 2009), pp. 1–17.

[25]   Benjamin, *Arcades Project*, p. 206.

Dilettantes founded in 1734 had all done so. Collectors of this sort were capable of producing treatises, organizing expeditions and acting as arbiters of taste.[26] They had little in common with those who accumulated curiosities. Serious collecting was one way of both creating and demonstrating what Pierre Bourdieu has called 'distinction': that system of differences that distinguishes one group of people from another on the basis of inherited cultural capital and acquired knowledge or taste. Works of art, for example, would only reveal their full meaning to those who had the cultural competence to decode them.[27] The display of good taste and aesthetic sensibility among eighteenth-century collectors marked them out as an elite. This was demonstrated in the construction and furnishing of a show house like Kedleston Hall by Nathaniel Curzon in the 1760s as a temple of the arts.[28]

The collecting of porcelain illustrates some these general themes. Porcelain itself had more than a whiff of the mysterious and exotic. Although significant in Chinese culture from the tenth century, many sixteenth-century Europeans were unsure how to classify it and thought that it arose from some sort of natural process. Porcelain was also, however, the defining product of seventeenth-century shopping culture in London and Amsterdam and essential to the milieus of the coffee house and tea table.[29] At the same time porcelain was fragile and as such could become a metaphor for the supposed frailty of women and their tendency to be besotted by exotic goods and fripperies. Chinoiserie was perceived by some as being in poor artistic taste, breaching the classical virtues of harmony and proportion, and capable only of providing sensuous and emotional pleasure. In popular imagination china was associated with sexuality and with woman as hollow vessels waiting to be filled. Yet the same piece of china that symbolized indiscriminate female taste when seen among the amassed clutter of a dressing table might speak of the good taste of a male collector when displayed in a cabinet in close proximity to books, maps or carefully chosen *objets d'art*.[30] How and by whom goods were used or displayed was just as important as what they were when trying to understand the significance of material culture. Even serious male china collectors were, however, not entirely above suspicion. In 1757 when Admiral

---

[26]   Brewer, *Pleasures of the Imagination*, pp. 257–60.

[27]   Pierre Bourdieu, *Distinction: A Social Critique of the Judgement of Taste*, trans. Richard Nice (London: Routledge & Kegan Paul, 1984).

[28]   National Trust, *Kedleston Hall* (London: The National Trust, 1988), pp. 7–8.

[29]   Robert Batchelor, 'On the Movement of Porcelains', in John Brewer and Frank Trentmann (eds), *Consuming Cultures, Global Perspectives: Historical Trajectories, Transnational Exchanges* (Oxford: Berg, 2006), pp. 95–121.

[30]   Kowaleski-Wallace, *Consuming Subjects*, pp. 52–69; Vanessa Alayrac-Fielding. '"Frailty, Thy Name is China": Women, Chinoiserie and the Threat of Low Culture in Eighteenth-Century England', *Women's History Review*, 18/4 (2009): 659–68; Stacey Slobada, 'Porcelain Bodies: Gender, Acquisitiveness, and Taste in Eighteenth-Century England', in Potvin and Myzelev (eds), *Material Cultures*, pp. 19–36.

John Byng was shot for failing to recover Minorca, caricaturists represented his ineffectiveness by showing him surrounded by his collection of porcelain.[31]

Book Collecting and Book Madness

The rapid growth of print culture and book ownership was briefly described in Chapter 5 (p. 104). Books were, however, more than texts to be read and shared. They were also objects that could be collected and displayed. Alongside items like paintings, sculpture, prints and appropriately chosen and displayed porcelain, they could proclaim the connoisseurship and good taste of their owner. There was nothing new in the eighteenth century about wanting to display books, even if simply displaying them without taking due account of what was inside them had always tended to attract criticism and even ridicule. As early as the 1590s it was said that: 'We see many private men also which have gathered many [books] together, well printed, bound and gilded: to serve only for ornaments, which they never look in themselves, nor suffer others for feare of fowling them'.[32] The seventeenth-century Derbyshire book collector Sir William Boothby certainly read his books, but was also concerned about their appearance, writing in an April 1684 letter to Michael Johnson in Lichfield, 'I designe my books for posterity'.[33] Some buyers seem to have had no interest in the content of the books they purchased such as the customer of an Oxford bookseller who in 1710 'purchase[d] a yard or ell of books as they stood, because that was the exact amount of blank in his bookshelf at home.[34]

There were, of course, plenty of serious book collectors who not only read and displayed their books but also felt the need to organize and catalogue them. Classification can indeed be regarded as a prior activity to collecting: Adam classified the creatures God made and on the basis of this Noah could collect them.[35] Not all great private libraries were well organized, at least not in the early eighteenth century. For example, Sir Hans Sloane's library never had a properly classified structure. Instead the accession code functioned as a shelf-mark and so the library was not intellectually browsable. A recent study describes it as a storeroom accessed by a catalogue, an object of wonder that expanded as a

---

[31]   Thomas, *Ends of Life*, p.133.

[32]   *Of the Interchangeable Course, or Variety of Things in the Whole World ... Written in French by Loys le Roy Called Regius: And Translated into English by R A.* (London, printed by Charles Yetsweirt, 1594), p. 129.

[33]   DRO, Boothby Letterbooks, Microfilm, XM 856, 15 April 1684.

[34]   *Oxford in 1710 from the Travels of Zacharias Conrad von Uffenbach*, ed. W.H. Quarrell and W.J.C. Quarrell (Oxford: Blackwell, 1928).

[35]   John Elsner and Roger Cardinal, 'Introduction', in Elsner and Cardinal (eds), *Cultures of Collecting*, p. 1.

collector's compulsive fetish.[36] Classifying a major collection of books could be a laborious task as the Duke of Portland's agent, William Gould, noted when he returned to Welbeck in Nottinghamshire in 1785 and found a Mr Jeffrys taking a catalogue of the books there. By the following day Jeffrys had taken all the books down and partially put them into different classes. According to Gould, all was confusion and Jeffrys would have a 'tedious job' before he was finished – for which he was paid 4 shillings a day. The catalogue took about 10 days to prepare.[37] 'Honest Tom' Martin, the Suffolk book collector who had one of the most valuable private libraries in England in the mid eighteenth century which he enjoyed making available to scholars, loved arranging and classifying his collections and compiled many lists and catalogues. Martin did nothing in moderation, whether collecting or his other great passion, drink.[38]

Book collecting was not only an elite pursuit. For example, in Derbyshire in 1722 Titus Wheatcroft, the parish clerk and village schoolmaster of Ashover, wrote out a list of the nearly 400 books he possessed. Many were religious works or classical literature, but they also included some he had written himself, such as 'Wheatcroft's daily meditations'.[39] Somewhat later in the century the Sussex shopkeeper and regular frequenter of alehouses, Thomas Turner, also recorded a wide range of texts that he and his wife read to each other, including classical literature, religious works and contemporary novels.[40] John Ratcliffe, who according to Dibdin originally bought old books to use as wrapping paper in his chandler's shop but then started reading them, eventually amassed what was described as the 'largest and most choice Collection of the rare old English Black Letters, in fine Preservation and in elegant Bindings'.[41] This collection was sold over a nine-day period in March and April 1776 and included a substantial number of Caxtons. Prices were not excessive: one of the most expensive was *The*

---

[36]   William Poole, 'The Duplicates of Sir Hans Sloane in the Bodleian Library: A Detective Story, with Some Comments on Library Organisation', *Bodleian Library Record*, 23/2 (2010): 192–213.

[37]   Michael Hanson (ed.), *Ducal Estate Management in Georgian Nottinghamshire and Derbyshire: The Diary of William Gould 1783–1788*, Thoroton Society, Record Series, 44 (2006): 139–40.

[38]   David Stoker, 'The Ill-Gotten Library of "Honest Tom" Martin', in Robin Myers and Michael Harris (eds), *Property of a Gentleman: The Formation, Organisation and Dispersal of the Private Library 1620–1920* (Winchester and Delaware: St Paul's Bibliographies, 1991), pp. 91–111.

[39]   DRO, Titus Wheatcroft of Ashover, Memorandum Book, D5433/2.

[40]   Thomas Turner, *The Diary of a Georgian Shopkeeper: A Selection by R.W. Blencowe and M.A. Lower*, ed. G.H. Jennings (Oxford: Oxford University Press, 1979).

[41]   Thomas Frognall Dibdin, *The Bibliomania or Book Madness*, ed. Peter Danckwerts (1809, Richmond: Tiger of the Stripe, 2007), p. 148, n.233; *Bibliotheca Ratcliffiana, A Catalogue of the Elegant and Truly Valuable Library of John Ratcliffe, Esq ... Which Will be Sold by Auction by Mr Christie ...* (London, 1776), title page.

dyctes and notable wyse sayenges of the philosophers printed in 1477 by Caxton, described as black letter, morocco bound with gilt leaves and sold for £15 15s. A 1474 Caxton, *The game of chesse playe* fetched £16. But by comparison with the usual run of second-hand books, this was a remarkable and valuable collection.[42]

Important elite collections included that of the Curzons at Kedleston. By the mid eighteenth century libraries were becoming one of the main informal living rooms in large country houses, accessible to guests and containing games and pictures as well as hundreds or thousands of books. They displayed the culture of the owner whether or not the books were taken down from the shelves and read.[43] Robert Adam designed the Kedleston library and bookcases in the 1760s with bronzed plaster busts of Greek and Latin poets on pedestals (Figure 6.1).

Figure 6.1   The Library at Kedleston Hall, Derbyshire

Source: Image supplied by and reproduced by permission of National Trust Images.

---

[42]   *Bibliotheca Ratcliffiana*, British Library copy with manuscript prices, 270.k.30.

[43]   Mark Girouard, *Life in the English Country House: A Social and Architectural History* (New Haven and London: Yale University Press, 1978), pp. 164–70, 179–80.

The book collection itself seems initially to have reflected the first Lord Scarsdale's intellectual interests but quickly became stocked with collectors' items acquired by the second Baron, including incunables, French Renaissance books and rarities from baroque Antwerp.[44] The second Earl Spencer, who was probably the greatest collector of the late eighteenth century and early nineteenth, had a whole series of libraries at Althorp which also served as spaces for entertaining guests. His attitude to his books, however, would no doubt offend modern conservation sensibilities. For example, he had no compunction about having incunables rebound to ensure a visually cohesive look, or about moving leaves from one Caxton to another to create a complete work. Perhaps Francis Douce had a point in complaining about idle noble owners who reduced books to objects of luxury.[45]

There were others who thought that late eighteenth- and early nineteenth-century book collecting had gone beyond the bounds of what was reasonable and had become book madness. Thomas Frognall Dibdin's *Bibliomania* which was first published in 1809 satirized the excesses of book collecting. Bibliomania, which was not Dibdin's word but derived from a poem by the Manchester physician John Ferriar, was the 'passion for collecting books; not so much to be instructed by them, as to gratify the eye by looking at them'.[46] Symptoms of the 'disease' included a passion for large paper copies of books with wide margins, especially if only a very limited number had been printed; collecting uncut copies; seeking out illustrated editions even if the illustrations were poor; wanting books printed on vellum; prizing first editions even if superseded by more accurate ones; and above all a love of black letter print.[47] Dibdin provided brief accounts of book collectors, mainly from the eighteenth century but some earlier, to illustrate his theme and claimed that the disease mainly attacked the male sex in the higher and middling classes of society.[48]

Delightful as is Dibdin's satire, is there any evidence that book collectors in his era suffered from what he called bibliomania? Dibdin himself, with his liking for uncut books and first editions, could perhaps be regarded as a bibliomaniac. So perhaps was Richard Heber who was a close friend of Dibdin and who had eight houses overflowing with books when he died.[49] Some collectors recognized that their love of books could become a consuming and expensive passion. In 1812 a 1471 edition of the *Decameron* printed in Venice sold at auction to the Marquis of

---

[44]   National Trust, *Kedleston*, pp. 29–30 and National Trust Memo 7 February 2003.

[45]   Kristian Jensen, *Revolution and the Antiquarian Book: Reshaping the Past, 1730–1815* (Cambridge: Cambridge University Press, 2011), pp. 144, 165, 180.

[46]   Dibdin, *The Bibliomania*, p. 55, quoting Peignot's *Dictionnaire*.

[47]   Ibid., pp. 56–74.

[48]   Ibid., p. 14 and throughout.

[49]   Ibid., p. 158, note 278 (editor's comments).

Blandford for £2,260.[50] Samuel Egerton Brydges writing to Dibdin soon after the publication of *Bibliomania* proclaimed that: 'to me, life would be a paradise, did my fate permit me to pass my time at my ease in the luxury of London literature, unrestrained in my passion for seeing and collecting books'; and asked 'can wealth be more nobly employed than in collecting food for the mind'.[51] And the consummate collector William Beckford complained in July 1831 of the difficulty he had in finding room for his books which were lying piled up two ranks deep. Yet he could not part with any, not only because of his collector's instinct, but because he wished to refer to most of those he had in his house.[52] Perhaps it was increasingly true that 'buying books would be a good thing if one could also buy the time in which to read them'.[53]

On the other hand, scholarly book collectors who did not exhibit signs of bibliomania were also to be found in the late eighteenth century and early nineteenth. For example, in Liverpool, William Roscoe, an attorney with a passion for the history of the Italian Renaissance, was creating a private library very strong in early Italian printing and in botanical works.[54] In Manchester, John Leigh Philips was the most important collector to emerge from the town's trading and manufacturing community in the late eighteenth century. His book collection was especially strong in natural history and included many copies with manuscript notes and additional illustrations.[55] There may have been an element of conspicuous consumption and the display of good taste here, but scholarship was predominant. The age of excess was perhaps giving way to a more mature network of relationships between collectors and antiquarian book dealers. Among these was William Ford of Manchester who started out as a collector. Writing to Dibdin to thank him for the 'handsome manner' he spoke of him as a bookseller, he explained that his 'love of books not lucre' first induced him to become one. He had been a collector for many years before he became one of the 'honorable fraternity'.[56] Ford's background meant that he was well placed to supply books to and buy them from serious collectors. He bought books at the sales of both

---

[50]   Philip Connell, 'Bibliomania: Book Collecting, Cultural Politics, and the Rise of Literary Heritage in Romantic Britain', *Representations*, 71 (Summer 2000): 24–47 (25 and n.3).

[51]   British Library, Collection of Original Letters Written to Revd Thos Frognall Dibdin on the publication of his Bibliomania, Egerton Mss 2974, fol. 85, 16 January 1812.

[52]   Robert J. Gemmett (ed.), *The Consummate Collector: William Beckford's Letters to His Bookseller* (Norwich: Michael Russell, 2000), p. 78.

[53]   de Vries, *Industrious Revolution*, p. 27, n.67, quoting Arthur Schopenhauer.

[54]   Arline Wilson, *William Roscoe: Commerce and Culture* (Liverpool: Liverpool University Press, 2008), pp. 47–8.

[55]   Michael Powell, 'Towards a History of Book-Ownership in Manchester', *Transactions of the Lancashire and Cheshire Antiquarian Society*, 97 (2001): 121–36 (p. 134).

[56]   British Library, *Letters to Dibdin*, Egerton Ms. 2974, fol. 57, 16 June 1811.

John Legh Philips's and William Roscoe's libraries.[57]Among his customers were William Monck Mason, the Dublin historian and Earl Spencer as well as local Lancashire and Cheshire book collectors.[58]

According to Walter Benjamin, 'It would be interesting to study the bibliophile as the only type of collector who has not completely withdrawn his treasures from their functional context'.[59] Generally speaking this was true of English book collectors in the long eighteenth century. They were interested both in the content and the appearance of their books, even if some became obsessed by the book as a physical object and by the collectors' passion for completeness. It was also the case that participating in literary society could be set alongside the consumption of other luxury and semi-luxury goods that both created and denoted social and cultural status. Book ownership demonstrated good taste and the ability to participate in polite society, but with a particular emphasis on appearing cultured and well read. Pierre Bourdieu's concept of 'distinction' is perhaps applicable here. On the other hand this line of thinking should not be taken too far. Book collecting may have been a serious, and usually male, activity distinguishable from acquiring china or proudly displaying a cabinet of curiosities. Or is that simply a reflection of how twenty-first century academics like to read the past? There was also a sense in which book collecting was very much like acquiring curios or the latest item of fashionable consumption.

Conclusions

This chapter has deliberately turned away from the mainstream of consuming in the eighteenth century and early nineteenth to look briefly at the fashionable body and then more extensively at collectors and particularly book collectors. There are three reasons for this. First, it serves as a reminder that consuming embraced a wide range of behaviour including the obsessive book collector, the proud housewife wanting to show off her best room to her guests, and the cottager treasuring a new teapot and teacups. All were part of the society of consumers, but each has a somewhat different story to tell. Secondly, it draws attention to the way in which consuming could be a disturbing and even damaging activity in the lives of those who allowed themselves to be controlled by it. If there was a consumer revolution in the eighteenth century then it was not wholly benign but also had its shadow side. Thirdly some of the behaviour considered in this chapter has more than a hint of modernity about it. This includes those whose need to be seen to be in fashion outweighed concerns for personal comfort or indeed sensible use of resources.

---

[57]   Brenda J. Scragg, 'William Ford, Manchester Bookseller', in Peter Isaac and Barry McKay (eds), *The Human Face of the Book Trade* (Winchester: St Paul's Bibliographies, 1999), pp. 155–70 (p. 165).

[58]   Manchester, Chetham's Library, William Ford Letterbooks, Mun A6.78–9.

[59]   Benjamin, *Arcades Project*, p. 207.

It also includes those who used consuming, and more particularly collecting, to make a public statement about their understanding of their own self and what made them the person they were. Knowing who you were, and displaying this to others, was increasingly bound up with how you acquired, used and displayed your possessions.

Beau Brummell, whose influence on the fashionable body was considered on p. 115 above, died from syphilis as a pauper living in exile in France in 1840. Might this have been regarded as divine punishment for his extravagant and dissolute lifestyle; or was it simply the natural consequence of having lived life to the full? Among those who noticed his demise, some would have veered towards the former view, but far fewer than would have been the case a century and a half earlier. Victorians were religious, but God's role was increasingly to give a seal of approval to national progress, and to challenge some to social action, rather than to induce feelings of guilt about the world of material goods and a comfortable lifestyle. This was one of the changes in how people understood themselves and the world around them that this and the previous two chapters have been exploring.

Others included the pervasiveness of fashion and novelty. These were becoming part of the normal, everyday experience of large numbers of people rather than being something exceptional or limited to a few. The expansion of print culture, including the growing number of provincial newspapers regularly carrying advertisements for the latest fashions, played a significant role in disseminating novelty and polite culture. Nor was this simply a matter of the middling and lower classes emulating the fashions of their betters. Some fashions were plebeian in origin and were copied up the social scale. Fashion extended well beyond clothing to include many household goods. All of this meant that more people were not only able to participate in the world of acquiring and using novel and fashionable items, but actively wanted to do so. Going shopping was a pleasurable and sociable activity as well as a necessity.

The disturbing influences discussed in this and the preceding two chapters had implications for retailing and retailers. Were there enough shops to meet growing demand? Were shops keeping up with fashion and were they making fashionable items available to a wider market? Would retailing adapt by simply doing more of the same or were more radical and structural changes needed? The next two chapters address these issues with a particular focus on the 1820–50 period. Chapter 7 looks at the varied responses of urban retailers to changing circumstances. Some changed little while others raised their profile through investment in new buildings or new and more assertive ways of marketing. There was also more radical innovation including shops having a range of different departments under the same roof. Chapter 8 explores the impact on markets of the increased demand for food and household goods in growing towns. Innovation took the form of large and showy purpose built market halls which were statements of civic pride as well as places for the working classes, and others, to shop.

PART III
Retailing, Consumption and Modernity: Adaptation and Innovation *c.* 1820–1850

PART III

Chapter 7

The Triumph of Commerce: The Changing Face of Retailing *c.*1820–1850

Writing about his boyhood in Macclesfield, T.H. Worrall recalled some of the large shops of the second quarter of the nineteenth century, including Swanwicks':

> It was a very aristocratic and first-class tailoring establishment and was called the 'top shop' in contradistinction to the 'ready-made clothes shop' which was a little lower down. All the country gentry round about used to go to Swanwicks' for their clothes. They were also the principal undertakers for the country. In those days, when silk-sashes and hat bands and gloves were sent out to the mourners and friends, they drove a very lucrative and first-class business'.[1]

Large drapers like Swanwicks' played an important part in urban retailing in the first half of the nineteenth century and will be looked at later in this chapter. Also seeking local gentry custom, but in a rather tentative manner, was the grocer Joshua Ford from the Derbyshire market town of Wirksworth. He wrote to the Gell family in 1832:

> Please to excuse me taking the liberty of soliciting you in the Grocery business as I am given to understand my late nabour Mr Stn Hall as been in the habit of supplying your house with groceries etc and should you think proper to use my shop I will indeavour to serve you on the best terms if the proposals meets your approbation in all commands.[2]

Grocers like Ford had long been present in such market towns, and shops of this type had probably changed little since the mid eighteenth century.

It is important to remember when looking at retail change in the nineteenth century that for every Swanwicks' there must have been several shops like Ford's and even more small neighbourhood shops selling food and household essentials. The world of the small shopkeeper as described in Chapters 2 and 3 was slow to change. The focus of this chapter, however, is mainly on those types of retailing where there was significant change, in particular the development of larger shops, alternative forms of retail space like arcades and bazaars and the precursors of

---

1   T.H. Worrall, *Reminiscences of Early Life Spent in My Native Town of Macclesfield* (Macclesfield, 1897), pp. 14–15

2   DRO, Gell of Hopton, Letter from Joshua Ford, 1 June 1832, D258/5/6/4.

department stores. Some of this change involved adaptation to new conditions, notably the increased number of potential consumers in growing towns. There was, however, also real innovation, particularly with regard to the use of space and the ways in which retailing was organized and managed. This chapter looks firstly at some aspects of evolutionary change including the number of shops and their size.

The Numbers Game: Counting Shops

There is no doubt that shop numbers, particularly in growing towns, increased substantially in the first half of the nineteenth century. This was particularly the case for small general or provisions dealers.[3] David Alexander demonstrated as long ago as 1970 that the percentage increase in the number of shops in nine towns[4] between 1822 and 1848–51 was significantly greater than the increase in population. The biggest increases in both shop numbers and population were in Merthyr Tydfil and Manchester, but even so Merthyr still had the worst shop numbers to population ratio in 1848–51 while York, which had experienced the smallest increase in shop numbers, had the most favourable ratio.[5] Subsequent research has tended to confirm this general picture, although Scola's work on Manchester suggested that population per retail food outlet rose in the first 30 years of the nineteenth century and then fell slowly, only reaching 1801 levels in the 1850s.[6] It was also the case that in both Shrewsbury and Wolverhampton there were more shops per 1,000 people before industrialization than afterwards and that rapid population growth tended to have an adverse effect on shop ratios, especially in Wolverhampton in the early nineteenth century.[7] On the other hand in some west Yorkshire and east Lancashire towns the number of shops per 10,000 people rose from 61.7 in 1801 to 177.9 in 1851 while in the midlands the number of retailers increased around threefold between the 1790s and 1840s with population roughly doubling.[8] Retail provision as measured in this way similarly improved

---

[3]   Stobart, *Spend, Spend, Spend!*, pp. 102–3.

[4]   Merthyr Tydfil, Manchester, Bolton, Leeds, Nottingham, Liverpool, Leicester, Norwich and York.

[5]   Alexander, *Retailing in England*, pp. 92–5.

[6]   Roger Scola, 'Retailing in the Nineteenth-Century Town: Some Problems and Possibilities', in James H. Johnson and Colin G. Pooley (eds), *The Structure of Nineteenth Century Cities* (London: Croom Helm, 1982), pp. 153–69.

[7]   Diane Collins, 'Fixed-Shop Retailing: Shrewsbury and Wolverhampton 1660–1900', unpublished PhD thesis, University of Wolverhampton, 2002, pp. 59–64.

[8]   Gareth Shaw and M.T. Wild, 'Retail Patterns in the Victorian City', *Transactions of the Institute of British Geographers*, New Series, 4 (1979): 278–91; Andrew Hann, 'Industrialisation and the Service Economy', in Jon Stobart and Neil Raven (eds), *Towns, Regions and Industries: Urban and Industrial Change in the Midlands, c.1700–1840* (Manchester: Manchester University Press, 2005), pp. 42–61.

in Stockport and Macclesfield between 1834 and 1860, but deteriorated slightly in the rapidly growing and new town of Birkenhead.[9]

Counting shop numbers has been important, particularly in terms of demonstrating that shops were widespread in towns and many villages before the acceleration of industrialization in the late eighteenth century. While it has also been valuable to calculate the overall growth in the number of shops in the first half of the nineteenth century, and the improved ratio of shops to people in most places in the second quarter of the century, the data can raise almost as many questions as it answers. For example, directories were much more comprehensive in their coverage in, say, 1850 than in 1820. This was especially so with regard to those traders described as 'shopkeepers' or 'provisions dealers'. At least some part of the perceived increase in the number of such shops simply reflects changes in the source material. Secondly, directories reveal nothing about shop size. It is quite possible that in some town centres higher-class shops were getting bigger in this period and thus that retail provision grew without numbers changing all that much. Thirdly, many eighteenth-century shops do not seem to have been very busy, with just a handful of customers a day. There was ample scope for shops to get busier and hence for growth to take the form of taking up slack rather than being measurable in terms of increased numbers. Increased productivity was one indicator of a more modern retail sector. The apparent disparity between the substantial growth in the number of general shops and the slower growth in the number of higher-class shops probably reflected increased working-class demand; it may also in part have reflected changing directory coverage and changes in the size and busyness of town centre shops.

It is hardly surprising that retail provision in the first half of the nineteenth century varied substantially from place to place. Old established service centres, like Market Harborough or Oswestry in the midlands, tended to have a higher retail ranking than their population would suggest while the reverse was true for newer industrial towns like Hanley or Wednesbury.[10] It was, however, generally the case that a much wider range of types of shop could be found in just about any town by the 1840s than would have been the case in the 1790s. In the midlands 45 towns had 20 or more categories of shopkeepers by then compared with only 13 at the earlier date. Moreover, it was the smallest market towns, not the industrial centres, that had the least diversity.[11] Even so, the market town and lead mining centre of Wirksworth in Derbyshire with a population of under 4,000 in 1821 had three booksellers, a glass warehouse, two perfumers (one of whom was also a jeweller) and two watch and clock makers in 1828 as well as the usual shoemakers, grocers, drapers and tailors.[12] There were five booksellers at nearby Ashbourne and in 1847 Sir Henry Herbert Fitzherbert of Tissington was able to

[9]   Mitchell, 'Supplying the Masses', p. 273.
[10] Hann, 'Industrialisation and the Service Economy', p. 52.
[11] Ibid., p. 55.
[12] Pigot, *Commercial Directory*, pp. 146–8.

purchase the latest part of *Dombey and Son* from his local bookshop there.[13] It was also the case that shops were becoming more widespread in the poorer residential neighbourhoods of growing towns. In Hull, 58.5 per cent of shops were in the old town in 1823 but only 28.9 per cent in 1851. Butchers, shoemakers and grocers tended to become more dispersed while ironmongers, booksellers and jewellers were more concentrated in the old town.[14] Stockport experienced a similar pattern of dispersion: in 1850 there were boot and shoemakers in 57 different streets and milliners/dressmakers in 28 streets.[15] On the other hand, Stockport's central shopping area possibly suffered because of its proximity to Manchester, particularly after the railway arrived, and had fewer big, high-class shops than a smaller but better established place like Chester.

Bigger and Better?

A new 'Cheap Boot and Shoe Warehouse' opened in Chester in 1814. Thomas Yearsley advertised that he had taken a shop opposite the end of Cow Lane and would be selling boots and shoes of 'very superior quality' at 'very reduced prices' for ready money. Yearsley also made and repaired shoes and his warehouse was just outside the city walls away from the most fashionable shops.[16] He was in direct competition with J. Whitebrook who had run a 'Cheap London Shoe Warehouse' in Watergate Street Row at the opposite end of the city for several years. Whitebrook's March advertisement gave prices ranging from 4 shillings to 8s 3d a pair for ladies' boots and pumps and for gentlemen's light and strong shoes.[17] Shoe warehouses were not new but by the nineteenth century increasingly stressed variety and fashion as well as price. They usually held large stocks such as the 'upwards of Two Thousand Pairs of Boots and Shoes' advertised by Whitebrook in 1806.[18] Some textile and clothing shops also styled themselves as 'warehouses', implying that they held substantial stocks and traded on a fixed price, ready money basis. The splendidly named Noted, Cheap and Fashionable Bonnet, Stay, Ribbon, Lace and Baby-Linen Warehouse, Cheap Drapery and Carpet Establishment in Derby was one such.[19] Significant features of town centre shops in the first half of the nineteenth century included size, variety of goods on

[13]   DRO, Fitzherbert Family of Tissington, Ashbourne Bills, 1847–8, 239/M/F/2436/21.
[14]   Wild and Shaw, 'Locational Behaviour of Urban Retailing during the Nineteenth Century'.
[15]   Bagshaw, *History, Gazetteer, and Directory of the County Palatine of Chester.*
[16]   *Chester Courant*, 8 February 1814.
[17]   Ibid., 8 March 1814.
[18]   Riello, *Foot in the Past*, pp. 98–101; *Chester Courant*, 11 July 1806.
[19]   *Derby Mercury*, 19 May 1841.

offer, aggressive marketing techniques and, in some cases, an emphasis on ready money, fixed price sales.[20]

Grocers and associated trades displayed some of these features, although in other ways not much had changed since the mid eighteenth century.[21] Derby boasted an Italian Warehouse in the early nineteenth century that sold salad oil, wine vinegars, mustards, fish sauces, essence of lemons and limes, olives, English and continental cheese, hams, pickled salmon and anchovies. Its proprietor, Richard Smith, trusted that 'Families residing in the Country find his warehouse greatly convenient as they may have every delicacy for the table upon the shortest notice, as fresh, and without the inconvenience of sending to London'.[22] The Chandos-Pole family at Radbourne were regular customers, buying oranges, lemons, capers, olives, anchovy essence, lemon pickle, Lucca oil and ginger among other items in 1809–10. The shop had passed into the hands of Jane Smith by 1813, with whom the Chandos-Poles settled a bill for £21 13s in the July of that year.[23] The emphasis here was on the easy availability of relatively unusual goods. The Sheffield grocers, Haslehurst and Son did not 'ground their pretensions to public favour upon a pompous Advertisement, which … always makes the author appear ridiculous' according to their wordy and ingratiating announcement in the *Sheffield Independent*. Instead their 1833 advertisement for Christmas fruits, tea and coffee emphasized 'fair dealing' and listed prices.[24]

Quality was emphasized or implied by some Chester retailers operating at the more fashionable end of the food trades. Thomas Gibbon announced in 1815 that he was opening a shop in Eastgate Street Row where he would carry on the confectionery and fruit business. He recommended his bride cake 'as being of a superior quality and will keep mellow and good in any climate twelve months'. He would offer 'a superior assortment of Foreign fruit, as it is his intention to purchase the best desert fruits that markets can produce'. He also promoted his 'much-admired Hot-cross Buns'.[25] Later in the century George Dutton, who styled himself 'Family Grocer and Italian Warehouseman', and who sold a wide range of different types and qualities of tea, coffee and chocolate as well as the usual grocery items, sent potential customers a circular letter couched in just the sort of polite language that had been common in advertisements at the turn of the century. Dutton charged cash prices for accounts settled at six months but offered a 2½ per cent discount to customers who paid monthly or quarterly. He moved

---

[20]   This last may have been difficult to achieve, with some ready money stores needing to offer credit to compete (Finn, *Character of Credit*, pp. 283–5).

[21]   Stobart also suggests that the mix of goods available in grocers' shops by the late eighteenth century changed little until the early twentieth (*Sugar and Spice*, pp. 63–4).

[22]   *Derby Mercury*, 24 May 1804.

[23]   DRO, Chandos-Pole Accounts, D5557/10/37/1–2.

[24]   *Sheffield Independent*, 21 December 1833. This is a splendid example of an advertisement doing just what it claims not to do.

[25]   *Chester Courant*, 21 March 1815.

his business from Lower Bridge Street to the more fashionable Eastgate Street in 1856, rebuilt his new premises in mock Tudor style and subsequently opened branches in Wrexham and Oswestry.[26] There was something slightly old-fashioned about even the more enterprising retailers in Victorian Chester.

Large-scale and innovative retailing in this period was particularly associated with drapers and similar traders and was not confined to London where it was said that some shops employed 20 or 30 people.[27] There were substantial clothing warehouses in provincial towns selling ready-made clothes, such as Richard Sanders in Worcester who had stock worth £1,892 at his death in 1837 or Daniel Evans in Hereford who used quite aggressive marketing techniques to promote his cheap clothing.[28] Richard Boswell Belcher who was born at Banbury in 1818 told in his autobiography how he was apprenticed to a draper at Stratford-upon-Avon, released after three and a half years and then spent time at drapers in Atherstone, Birmingham and Coventry before going to London. He bought a business in Kidderminster in 1841 for £2,400 and was soon returning £8,000 a year, with over £1,000 coming from funerals. On selling the business in 1846 he had book debts of £2,400 which took some time to get in. His final foray into the drapery business was at Blockley in Gloucestershire where he prospered until he decided to go into the coal business.[29] David Binns served his apprenticeship with his uncle George Binns in Sunderland, often being left in charge of the shop and three staff as well as travelling both to buy and sell goods, including Indian silk handkerchiefs. He then managed a more general store in Staindrop, selling drapery, grocery and wines and spirits, before buying his own drapery business in Halifax. The stock there had been run down, enabling him to use his contacts to buy cheaply and sell for ready money as well as supplying country shopkeepers. Although Binns was an active and committed Quaker, there is no suggestion in his autobiography that his beliefs influenced his business practices, even if they were important in his public and civic life, or that he used a Quaker network to build up his business contacts.[30]

A similar pattern of moving around to gain experience, though in this case with a stronger London focus, is described in the *Reminiscences of an Old Draper* published in 1876. The author learnt his trade in the east end of London at a time when the 'healthy system' of sticking to one price was coming in. He recalled how smart salesmen used to bully customers; and the origins of 'selling-off' either to

---

[26] Information from business papers which were in the possession of the firm before it went out of business. Their present location is unknown.

[27] Alexander, *Retailing in England*, pp. 107–8.

[28] Alison Toplis, *The Clothing Trade in Provincial England, 1800–1850* (London: Pickering & Chatto, 2011), pp. 18–55.

[29] A.W. Exell and Norah M. Marshall (eds), *Autobiography of Richard Boswell Belcher of Banbury and Blockley, 1898; and, The Riot at Blockley in 1878* (Moreton-in-Marsh: Blockley Antiquarian Society, 1976).

[30] WYAS, Calderdale, David Binns, Draper of Halifax, Autobiography, 1799–1883 (Transcript), MISC: 379/2.

dispose of old and unsalable goods or to tempt customers into the shop through cheap offers. He widened his experience by selling high-quality shawls in Fleet Street before spending time in Chatham, Bristol and Manchester. In the course of all this he learnt about the importance of good cash management, about the need not to over-stock and the value of good window displays, as well as building a network of contacts. In due course he took over a large shop in Holborn and made a success of it.[31] The emphasis here is very much on retail techniques rather than production or craft skills and on the importance of networking.

Autobiographies can present a distorted picture, particularly when they contain a significant element of self-justification. The business records of a Macclesfield draper from the early nineteenth century are valuable therefore in providing firm evidence of a large-scale business with a wide range of suppliers and customers.[32] John Swanwick occupied a shop at the north-west corner of the market place from no later than 1791. As a draper and mercer Swanwick dealt chiefly in cloth, but also stocked ladies' hoods, cloaks, gloves, stockings, buttons, hats, handkerchiefs and umbrellas. There is no evidence that he ever directly involved himself in the provision of tailoring facilities, although his successors did so and the shop had become a tailoring establishment by the 1840s. Cloth and articles of clothing were, however, not the only items supplied by Swanwick for he seems to have dealt in a limited range of household fabrics including carpets, which he was occasionally buying from manufacturers.

Swanwick bought from manufacturers in all of the major textile-producing areas of England as well as from London wholesalers. Out of 168 suppliers listed, only 23 were in London, although their importance in terms of sales may have been much greater than mere numbers suggest. He bought woollens from Yorkshire and the west of England, cotton from Lancashire, hosiery from the east midlands, buttons from Birmingham, ribbons from Leek and coverlets and rugs from Kendal. Welsh cloths came through Shrewsbury, while the Manchester wholesale houses acted as suppliers of a wide range of cloths, including lace and tape. On occasion he would buy goods from other Macclesfield retailers. These were small purchases probably either of goods he had run out of, or goods that he did not normally stock but which a customer had requested. Thus in 1794 the Macclesfield draper John Whitaker supplied him with ribbons, gloves, cloaks, thread, cloth, hose, tapes and buttons to the value of £20 9s 9d and received goods from Swanwick to the value

---

[31]   *Reminiscences of an Old Draper* (London, 1876).

[32]   This survey is based on a brief examination of a large quantity of invoices and a few other documents relating to the Swanwick business which were discovered in the premises formerly occupied by John Swanwick. They are currently in the custody of Mrs M. Moss who generously allowed me access to these papers. Information is drawn from the invoices unless otherwise stated. Although the papers are almost wholly from the 1790–1820 period, they provide an exceptional insight into the nature of a 'quality' drapery business which appears to have changed little in the succeeding quarter century and as such are highly relevant to the discussion here.

of £10 12s 9d in part payment. Another draper, Thomas Critchley, also supplied Swanwick with occasional goods, and in 1794 acted for him at the Chester October fair either settling a bill or buying on his behalf. Apart from this instance there is no other evidence of Swanwick buying in Chester, or dealing at the fairs there. He was visited by representatives of manufacturers like Wood and Cooke of Birmingham who supplied him with buttons. An 1810 invoice was annotated, 'Our T. Cooke will be at Macclesfield about Tuesday next when we hope to be favour'd with your further Commands'.

The only surviving evidence of retail sales is contained in a fragment of a day book for November and December 1819. By this date John Swanwick himself had retired from the business which was in the hands of his son Thomas Taylor Swanwick. The day book reveals a fairly busy shop with up to 30 or even more customers in a day, drawn not only from Macclesfield but also from much of the surrounding countryside. The busiest day in the shop seems normally to have been Tuesday which was market day in Macclesfield. Customers included a number of local gentry, particularly the Davenports of Capesthorne and the Greys of Dunham. Although primarily a retailer, John Swanwick did a certain amount of wholesale business. In particular he seems to have supplied drapers in the towns to the south and west of Macclesfield with goods which he had possibly received from the Manchester wholesale houses. The retailers he supplied occasionally complained about the goods they had received or the prices they had been charged. For example, Anthony Titley of Eccleshall on returning some blankets stated, 'Am sorry to return the above, but they are charg'd much too high, and can therefore do nothing with them'.[33]

Four stock books, probably from the early years of the nineteenth century, provide evidence of the size of Swanwick's stock holdings. Each book lists the stock in the shop in detail and provides a total valuation, less the amount of goods sold during the stock-taking. These net valuations are £2,974 10s 10d, at least £3,264, £3,339 16s 10d and £4,000 0s 0d. These are strikingly high figures and confirm the impression of a very large-scale business. Assuming that he turned his stock over between two and three times a year, which was by no means impossible given the need to cater for the fashions of different times of year, Swanwick's sales could in some years have been in excess of £10,000. Even at a very moderate 20 per cent gross margin this would have provided him with handsome gross profits. John Swanwick announced his retirement in 1812[34] and at the time of his death in 1832 he was described as a gentleman of Brereton in Cheshire, the Macclesfield business he established being continued by other members of the family.[35]

The retailing of household and fancy goods also showed signs of change in the first half of the nineteenth century. There was a growing emphasis on bought-in

---

[33]   Letter of 21 December 1805.

[34]   *Macclesfield Courier*, 4 April 1812.

[35]   Biographical information chiefly drawn from notes on John Swanwick by J.P. Earwaker, CALS, Earwaker Collection, ZCR 63/1/190.

items, large stocks and competitive pricing. Robert Moseley, listed as a carver and gilder in contemporary directories, traded from the heart of Derby's fashionable shopping area. He advertised in 1825 that he had received a selection of jewellery from London, including necklaces, bracelets, brooches and lockets as well as work boxes and French lamps. He had increased his stock of silver articles and as a result was selling off Sheffield plate goods such as coffee and tea pots, cream jugs, sugar bowls and dishes at prime cost. He also wanted to employ an intelligent youth who had received a liberal education.[36] Moseley was just the sort of retailer who, from directory evidence, might have been assumed to be primarily a craftsman but who in reality was also running an up-market jeweller's and silversmith's shop. He advertised in 1826 that he was selling off his stock to focus on carving and gilding but in 1828 had restocked the jewellery business.[37] He also ran a picture gallery.[38] Alfred Parker of Stockport called himself an ironmonger and jeweller in 1850 and sold a range of Birmingham-made papier mâché goods, Sheffield goods and japanned ware. He offered a set of three papier mâché tea trays for 14 shillings. Like Moseley he was trading from a prime location in the town.[39] Some retailers who described their premises as a 'bazaar' were in practice running large household and fancy goods shops. Isaac Pochin's Pantheon Bazaar in Leicester stocked dressing cases, tea trays, scissors, cases, chess boards, hair brushes, perfumery, jewellery, cutlery, wax dolls, puzzles and games. Purchasers would, it was claimed, save 20 per cent by visiting the shop.[40] Viener's *Temple of Fancy and Grand Bazaar* in Blackpool similarly offered jewellery, clocks, china, Bohemian glass and similar items with a 10 per cent reduction on all written orders.[41] Stores like this were increasingly common and paved the way for the variety goods stores of the later nineteenth century.

The first half of the nineteenth century undoubtedly saw an increase in the number of large shops and greater differentiation in retailing with some traders emphasizing quality while others were adopting a 'pile them high, sell them cheap' approach. This was not, however, the whole story. More typical perhaps was Henry White who had ambitions to become a tea and coffee dealer in Cheltenham in the middle of the century. He initially bought goods from a tea dealer friend and worked as a travelling tea salesman, making 20 to 25 shillings profit per week but having to tramp the streets in all weathers. He subsequently took a small grocer's shop, which was mainly run by his wife while he continued his door-to-door selling, and although business increased he soon had problems with cash flow,

[36]   *Derby Mercury*, 28 September 1825.

[37]   Ibid., 12 July 1826; 16 July 1828.

[38]   Ibid., 21 July 1830.

[39]   *Stockport Advertizer*, 19 July 1850.

[40]   William White, *History, Gazetteer, and Directory of Leicestershire, and the Small County of Rutland* (Sheffield, 1846), Advertisement pages.

[41]   Lancashire Archives, Miscellaneous Documents, Handbill, DX/1961.

due in part to the dishonesty of some of his customers. He was forced to give up business and take up a situation as a butler.[42]

Nor were all linen drapers as ambitious as John Swanwick. Mary Thorley in Knutsford, Cheshire was, like many market town woollen and linen drapers in the 1820s, selling tea and coffee as well as textiles and accessories, and relying on the patronage of the nearby Leicester family at Tabley House. Her attractively engraved billhead showing a funeral procession serves as a reminder that the supply of mourning wear was a significant part of the business of many drapers (Figure 7.1).[43]

Figure 7.1   Mary Thorley, Knutsford, billhead, 1823

Source: Cheshire Archives and Local Studies, Leicester-Warren Family of Tabley, Accounts with Mrs Thorley, DLT/D154. Reproduced by permission of Cheshire Archives and Local Studies.

Unlike Moseley in Derby, the Chester firm of Butt's resisted any temptation to branch out into general household and fancy goods in the 1840s and 1850s and remained a specialist jeweller, goldsmith and silversmith. Their daybook for 1843 records between 30 and 65 transactions a month, both sales and repairs, with customers drawn from Chester and its immediate vicinity.[44] For the most part, the first half of the nineteenth century was a period of growth and change rather than radical innovation or any retail revolution. There were, however, exceptions to this which are explored in the next sections.

---

[42]   Henry White, *The Record of My Life: An Autobiography* (Cheltenham, 1889), pp. 119–30.

[43]   CALS, Leicester-Warren Family of Tabley, Accounts with Mary Thorley, DLT/D154

[44]   CALS, Butt and Company Ltd, Day Book 1843–57, ZCR 92/31.

Alternative Retail Spaces

Shopping did not have to take place in a traditional shop. As well as markets and fairs, or buying on one's own doorstep, there had long been the possibility of buying at auction and, in the early nineteenth century, arcades and bazaars offered new opportunities. Household sales, including sales by auction, were frequent occurrences in early modern England and provided opportunities for acquiring modestly priced domestic goods.[45] From at least the later eighteenth century auctions provided middle-class people with a convenient way of acquiring quality furniture at reasonable prices.[46] Advertisements for auctions of china, glass and earthenware were common in the early nineteenth-century provincial press. For example, one Mr Daniel advertised in 1833 that he was selling 'The most splendid and extensive Variety of Glass, China, and Earthenware, ever introduced to the notice of the Sheffield public' at the Music Hall in the town. The goods included willow table services, china tea sets and dinner services, chimney ornaments, claret decanters and tumblers.[47]

One of the Chester auctioneers in the 1820s and 1830s was John Brown, brother to William and Henry who were the leading silk mercers and drapers in the city.[48] John Brown provided a range of services to his customers, including valuations, arranging transport of goods and organizing advertising as well as the auctions themselves. A typical sale was that for the late John Davies of Eastgate Street in November 1827. Brown had valued the goods at £185 10s 1d, charging £2 6s 4½d for doing so, and sold them for £128 13s 2d. He charged £6 8s 8d commission, £6 8s 8d King's Duty and £1 9s 0d for advertising.[49] Earlier in 1827 he had advertised a sale by auction on the order of the assignees of the stock in trade, household goods and furniture of Richard Orme, woollen draper and tailor.[50] The sale realized £232 14s 3½d but after deducting costs and bills to one William Lowe the assignees only received £135 5s 2d.[51] A typical sale in January 1827 included:

> three sets of mahogany dining tables with D ends, mahogany two-leaved, Pembroke and card tables, modern mahogany chairs with hair seats, a mahogany sofa upholstered in satin hair, four-post and camp bedsteads with furniture, mattresses, feather beds and bedding, dressing-tables, wash-stands, a mahogany

---

[45]   Sara Pennell, '"All but the Kitchen Sink": Household Sales and the Circulation of Second-Hand Goods in Early Modern England', in Stobart and van Damme (eds), *Modernity and the Second-Hand Trade*, pp. 37–56.

[46]   Edwards and Ponsonby, 'Desirable Commodity or Practical Necessity?'

[47]   *Sheffield Independent*, 21 December 1833.

[48]   See Appendix for Browns of Chester.

[49]   CALS, Browns of Chester, Ledger 1827–32, 21 November 1827, ZCR 658/1.

[50]   *Chester Chronicle*, 16 February 1827.

[51]   Browns Ledger, February 1827.

secretary and book-case with drawers underneath, some new carpeting, and a
great variety of articles.[52]

Brown also auctioned property and farm goods. Auction houses like this were an
important part of the retail provision of many towns and deserve more attention
from historians.

Two innovative forms of retail space were shopping arcades and bazaars. Arcades
were covered passages with shops on one or both sides. They had some similarities
to the earlier Exchanges, but the Parisian arcade *Jardins du Palais Royal* is generally
regarded as the earliest example of the genre. The *Galleries de Bois* on the fourth
side of this quadrangle comprised rows of wooden shops separated by covered
passageways lit by skylights. The first English arcade, the Royal Opera in London,
was opened in 1817 with small shops lining one side of the covered corridor; a
year later the Burlington Arcade opened with shops on both sides. By 1840 there
were arcades in Bath, Bristol, Glasgow, Ryde and Glossop. The proprietors of early
arcades wanted them to have an air of exclusivity and tranquillity and exercised
control over the types of trade allowed in them as well as over the behaviour of
customers. The presence of bazaars in London may have inhibited the development
of more arcades there, and it was not until the last third of the nineteenth century that
arcades became common in the industrial cities of the north and midlands.[53] Arcades
provided specialized and fashionable shopping space away from the dirt and bustle
of town centre streets. In Benjamin's words, 'The arcade is a street of lascivious
commerce only; it is wholly adapted to arousing desires'.[54]

Bazaars, particularly in London, were something of an early nineteenth-century
sensation.[55] Like arcades they were not without their antecedents. They possibly
reminded customers of shopping galleries and of fairs. Also like arcades they
presented themselves as part of the respectable, even polite, shopping scene. The
early bazaars also, however, claimed a charitable purpose, that of encouraging
female and domestic industry by providing an outlet for their products. Some offered
an element of spectacle such as exhibitions of artistic works or even the presence of
an entertainer like a magician. The first true nineteenth-century bazaar was Trotter's
in Soho Square. It had been built as a warehouse by John Trotter in 1801–4 and
opened as a bazaar in February 1816.[56] It was a substantial building of 270 feet by

---

[52]   *Chester Chronicle*, 19 January 1827.
[53]   On arcades see Kathryn A. Morrison, *English Shops and Shopping: An Architectural History* (New Haven and London: Yale University Press, 2004), pp. 99–106 and Margaret MacKeith, *The History and Conservation of Shopping Arcades* (London: Mansell, 1986).
[54]   Benjamin, *Arcades Project*, p. 42.
[55]   Ian Mitchell, 'Innovation in Non-Food Retailing in the Early Nineteenth Century: The Curious Case of the Bazaar', *Business History*, 52/6 (2010): 875–91. See also Tammy C. Whitlock, *Crime, Gender and Consumer Culture in Nineteenth-Century England* (Aldershot: Ashgate, 2005).
[56]   Morrison, *English Shops*, p. 93.

130 feet with rooms on two floors and included 750 feet of counters. Each space for rent was numbered, and some sellers rented more than one space. Counters in the bazaar were let by the day, at a price of 3d a foot, and were therefore accessible to poorer people or those just starting out in business. In accordance with the object of encouraging domestic industry, no articles of foreign manufacture were to be sold without express permission. The bazaar also provided facilities for artists wanting to display their work (free of charge) and for authors who could advertise their books rather than selling the copyright to bookseller/publishers.

The proprietor hoped to ensure respectability by insisting on testimonials as a condition of letting a counter. There were also strict rules governing sales practices, including marking goods with their ready money price and allowing no abatement from this. Meanly or dirtily dressed people were not allowed in the bazaar. Around 2,500 people a day were said to visit the bazaar. In its early days it was claimed that of the 200 people employed in Trotter's only two were men and that the bazaar therefore helped to redress the gender balance in retailing.[57] It was argued that men had usurped the place of women behind shop counters and that there were numerous men-milliners in fashionable London shops. Trotter's was soon followed by several more bazaars in the West End and the City. By 1816 another was planned at Brighton and the Reverend Joseph Nightingale, a leading advocate of bazaars, was arguing for the desirability of having bazaars in all the principal towns of England.[58]

Bazaars had their critics who argued that they offered unfair competition and might have immoral tendencies.[59] An anonymous pamphlet developed the argument that bazaars undermined fair and respectable trading. Apparently conceding that goods sold in bazaars tended to be cheap, the author argued that 'nothing can be more erroneous than the idea, that everyone has a right to get any article as cheap as he possibly can'. But cheapness had its price. Bazaars, it was said, were occupied by a motley group of here today, gone tomorrow sellers. Articles could not be returned if defective. Many goods were of poor quality. Pickpockets entered as freely as the most respectable individual. Women who rented counters at bazaars would be better off finding employment in a shop; and if the number of bazaars increased female shop staff would lose their jobs. Bazaars were 'a company or association of Hawkers and Pedlars'.[60] Distinguishing reality from propaganda is not easy, but fire insurance records indicate that most of those who insured their goods were either in the clothing trades or in what might broadly be described as fancy goods, toys, glass and china ware, with an occasional bookseller and stationer. Those who appeared in these records were not the poor women renting a counter by the day, but more established retailers using the bazaar as a secondary outlet.

---

57   If this was true at first, fire insurance records suggest that it soon changed.
58   Joseph Nightingale, *The Bazaar, Its Origin, Nature, and Objects Explained, and Recommended as an Important Branch of Political Economy* (London, 1816).
59   *Journals of the House of Commons*, vol. 72, February 1816 – June 1817, pp. 389–90.
60   *An Appeal to the Public on the Subject of Bazaars* (1816), pp. 3–7.

Bazaars were not confined to London. The Bazaar in Deansgate in Manchester operated on almost identical principles to the early London ones in that counters were to be let to respectable people who could provide appropriate references and goods were to be marked with fixed prices. Counters on the first floor were for men and on the second floor for women.[61] Its proprietors claimed that they would have on sale a 'splendid and brilliant assortment of useful, ornamental and fashionable articles in almost every branch of manufacture'. They also assured potential customers that 'Every person, even the most inexperienced, may feel confidence in any purchase they may make in the establishment'. The bazaar was open from half past nine o'clock in the morning until eight o'clock in the evening.[62] The bazaar at Brighton was described in 1826 as a spacious building on the Grand Parade which 'affords an hour's amusement to the numerous fashionable visitors, who honour it with their presence'.[63] Paintings were part of the 'amusement'. The worlds of shopping and leisure mingled in bazaars like this, as they did in London and Bath. Advertisements for the New Bazaar in Quiet Street, Bath in 1824 referred to tableaux, military bands, the reception and sale of stock in trade and household furniture, house auctions and an exhibition of paintings.[64] A bazaar could easily become a convenient space for a wide range of activities aimed at those with time and money on their hands.

The Norfolk and Norwich Bazaar in St Andrew's Street in Norwich which opened in 1831 is one of the best documented provincial bazaars. The printed descriptions were lavish, proclaiming that the bazaar would be under the patronage of the Queen and many other ladies and would be located in a 'commodious and elegant' building. It was to be run on similar lines to those in London and Manchester. The rules were strict: tenants were to be properly dressed, not to gossip, not to eat or drink at their counters, and not to frequent any eating house in the vicinity as refreshments would be provided on the premises.[65] Plans of the bazaar indicate that there were shops near the entrance and around the sides for millinery, drapery, boots and shoes and jewellery with counters in the centre of the main space. Areas were designated for different types of goods including toys, rocking horses, cutlery, bronze goods, lace, plated goods, boxes, gloves and hosiery (Figure 7.2).

There was a gallery which could be partly used for pictures, while advertisements could be placed on the stairs.[66]

---

[61]   Alison Adburgham, *Shops and Shopping 1800–1914: Where, and in What Manner the Well-Dressed Englishwoman Bought Her Clothes* (London: George Allen & Unwin, 1981), pp. 19–21.

[62]   *Manchester Guardian*, 12 March 1831. The bazaar quickly failed and the premises passed to Messrs Watts, precursors of Kendal Milne (*Manchester Times*, 27 April 1833).

[63]   J. Whittemore, *Whittemore's Royal Brighton Guide* (Brighton, 1826), pp. 88–9.

[64]   *Keene's Bath Journal*, 19 January 1824, 12 April 1824, 20 December 1824.

[65]   Norfolk Record Office, Norfolk and Norwich Bazaar, SO 18/29.

[66]   Ibid., SO 18/26, 87.

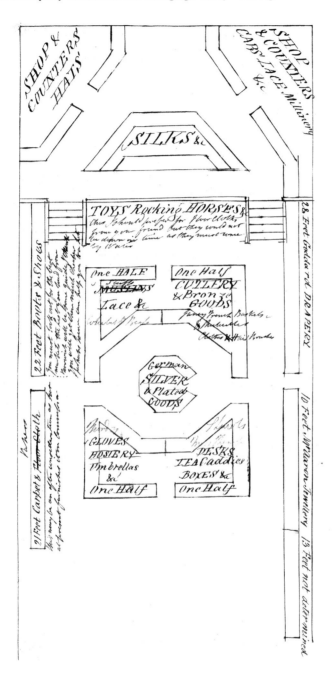

Figure 7.2   Norfolk and Norwich Bazaar, floor plan, *c.*1831

Source: Norfolk Record Office, SO 18/87. Reproduced by permission of the Record Office.

The bazaar was a speculative venture intended to be funded by the sale of 320 shares of £25 each, with £5 payable at initial subscription. The draft prospectus assumed full occupancy of the building, producing six shillings a day from shop rentals and £5 13s 4d a day from the 680 feet of counter at two pence per foot per day. Allowing for estimated expenditure, there would have been around £1,000 a year profit. It appears that not all the shares were taken up and that the £6,500 it cost to obtain the freehold and build the bazaar was greater than originally estimated. Nor were all the spaces let: daily income was only £3 2s 7d soon after opening rather than the £5 19s 4d hoped for.[67] Not all those approached to be patrons were willing with at least one declining on the grounds that it 'may prove injurious to many reputable and old established shops'.[68] Norwich retailers were hardly likely to encourage it, despite suggestions from its supporters that they might wish to become shareholders or appoint respectable females to sell on their behalf at one of its counters. By July 1832 there were problems about payments to Norwich traders and, while it was claimed that many people visited the bazaar, there were few goods on sale there. Suggestions that London shopkeepers might be encouraged to rent space in it seem to have come to nothing.[69] The hopes of the original shareholders were not realized and the bazaar soon became the property of Peter Thompson, who sold books, stationery, fancy goods and toys.

Bazaars were high-risk enterprises. Fire was a constant hazard and despite the best efforts of proprietors to provide security and ensure respectability thefts were not uncommon. There were also suggestions that some of the goods on sale may have been acquired dishonestly. Counter rents may have been higher than they would have been for similar space in a market hall.[70] Some failed quickly and hardly any survived more than a few decades. Their influence on retail developments in the nineteenth century was indirect rather than direct. Department stores cannot, with only one or two exceptions, locate their origins in a specific bazaar. On the other hand bazaars brought together in one business several important and innovative features. These included their sheer size, the variety of goods on offer, the controlled environment and the opportunity to browse without being obliged to buy. They can therefore be regarded as precursors of both department stores and large covered markets which were to be highly visible symbols of later nineteenth-century retailing.

Proto Department Stores

The department store, defined by Jefferys as 'a large retail store with 4 or more separate departments under one roof, each selling different classes of goods of

---

67 Ibid., SO 18/4, /80.
68 Ibid., SO 18/7.
69 Ibid., SO 18/84, /65.
70 Mitchell, 'Innovation in Non-Food Retailing'.

which one is women's and children's wear'[71] had iconic status as the representation of fashionable retailing in larger towns in the last third of the nineteenth century. This was the case even though department stores accounted for less than 2 per cent of total retail sales in 1900 and only around 10 per cent of sales of women's and children's wear.[72] Their novelty as a mid nineteenth-century phenomenon has been questioned. Many of the supposed novel features of department stores can be traced back to the eighteenth century including fixed prices, carefully arranged displays and showrooms, the sociable aspects of shopping and the possibility of women engaging in 'polite' shopping without being accompanied by men.[73] There were also examples in the eighteenth century of shops selling very large quantities of ready-finished goods at reasonable prices and in standardized quantities. James Lackington's book emporium, the 'Temple of the Muses' established in 1793, was said to have over a million books on display.[74] Some shops had several departments such as Harding and Howell which was established in Pall Mall in 1796. The store had five departments on the ground floor separated by glazed mahogany partitions and a refreshment room on the furnishing and fabrics floor. Stock included furs, fans, haberdashery, jewellery, perfumery and millinery.[75] This was to all intents and purposes a department store and as such represented a radical departure from what had gone before.

Although London led the way in these sort of innovations, the provinces were not all that far behind. Trying to identify the first provincial department store can be an interesting exercise, but can ultimately be a matter of definitions. It is, however, clear that drapery was often both the point of departure for the creation of a department store and tended to remain the core business.[76] Emerson Muschamp Bainbridge learnt his trade in London at the silk and shawl warehouse of Lewis and Allenby before returning to his native Newcastle-upon-Tyne and going into partnership with the draper William Dunn in 1838. Three years later he was trading on his own and by 1849 Bainbridge's had 23 departments.[77] Jolly and Son in Bath traced their origins both to the drapery trade and to the running of a bazaar. James Jolly, the son of a Norfolk linen draper, set up a shop in Winchester in the early 1800s before moving to Kent where he ran a linen draper's at Deal and then a

---

[71]   Jefferys, *Retail Trading in Britain*, p. 326.

[72]   Ibid., p. 21.

[73]   Geoffrey Crossick and Serge Jaumain, 'The World of the Department Store: Distribution, Culture and Social Change'; and Claire Walsh, 'The Newness of the Department Store: A View from the Eighteenth Century', in Crossick and Jaumain (eds), *Cathedrals of Consumption: The European Department Store, 1850–1939* (Aldershot: Ashgate, 1999), pp. 1–45, 46–71.

[74]   James Raven, *The Business of Books: Booksellers and the English Book Trade 1450–1850* (New Haven and London: Yale University Press) p. 289.

[75]   Walsh, 'Newness of the Department Store', p. 67.

[76]   Crossick and Jaumain, 'World of the Department Store', p. 10.

[77]   Adburgham, *Shops and Shopping*, p. 43.

bazaar at Margate. His son Thomas helped in the bazaar. By 1823 he had premises in Bath during the season and two years later father and son leased permanent premises there where they sold drapery and fashion items while continuing with the Margate bazaar. In the early 1830s Thomas was selling drapery, mercery, china, jewellery, toys and perfumery for ready money only from his 'Bath Emporium'.[78] Other early nineteenth-century drapery shops that eventually made the transition to department store included Mawer and Collingham in Lincoln and William Henderson in Liverpool, while the London drapery business of Clark, Debenham opened branches at Cheltenham in 1823 selling silks, muslins, shawls, gloves, lace and fancy items and at Harrogate in 1843.[79] Binns of Sunderland claimed a link to the drapery store of George Binns where David Binns of Halifax served his apprenticeship in the 1810s (p. 134). The type of skills needed to operate a large drapery business, including managing relationships with a wide range of suppliers and customers, exercising good stock control, having attractive premises and paying careful attention to cash flow, were those that were particularly useful in expanding into multiple departments. Experience of bazaar-type selling was probably also useful but less essential.

Somewhat like Jolly and Son, the Manchester department store of Kendal Milne has claimed both drapers and a bazaar as its precursors. In 1796 John Watts, who came from the village of Didsbury south of Manchester where the Woods ran the inn and village shop, opened a small draper's shop in Deansgate near the heart of Manchester's shopping district. He moved to larger premises on the opposite side of the street and in the 1820s his sons Samuel and James joined the business.[80] In 1831 the Watts family obtained the premises on the corner of Deansgate and Police Street which had previously been used as a bazaar. They refitted these for their retail and wholesale business with staff accommodation on the top floor and opened their new shop in April 1832, retaining the name 'the Bazaar'.[81] Kendal Milne did not originate in a bazaar, but the previous existence of one on the site of their shop may have helped to familiarize customers with the practice of browsing a wide range of articles in a large store.

The Watts family withdraw from the business in 1835 and it was sold to three of their employees, Thomas Kendal, James Milne and Adam Faulkner. Kendal, who was the most influential of the three, had been a draper's assistant in London. The shop reopened on 2 January 1836 with a sale of winter goods; and the bankrupt stock of T. Houghland of Stockport, including straw bonnets, was sold in August

[78] Michael Moss and Alison Turton, *A Legend of Retailing: House of Fraser* (London: Weidenfeld & Nicolson, 1989), p. 337.

[79] [Online]. Available at: http://www.housefraserarchive.ac.uk/companies [accessed: 4 May 2012].

[80] Barbara Collinson, *Kendals: One Hundred and Fifty Years 1836–1986* (Manchester, 1986); Moss and Turton, *Legend of Retailing*, p. 343.

[81] *Manchester Times*, 17 December 1831 and 7 April 1832.

of that year.[82] It was still known as 'the Bazaar' but was in practice a large draper's shop. Advertisements for subsequent years reveal a growing range of types of goods stocked and services provided. In May 1838 Kendal, Milne, and Faulkner called 'particular attention to their newly selected STOCK of MOUSSELINE DE LAINE DRESSES, the largest and most elegant assortment ever concentrated in one Establishment out of London; to be sold at prices which the most *scrupulous* will allow to be as *unprecedented* as the stock is *unsurpassed* in *magnitude* and *variety*'.[83] The following year they were advertising that they had opened an additional room for the exclusive sale of shawls both to the 'Ladies and Inhabitants of Manchester' and to country drapers.[84] By 1843 'one of the Largest and Best assorted STOCKS in the Trade (chiefly registered Designs) of BRUSSELS, KIDDERMINSTER, AXMINSTER, VENETIAN and SCOTCH CARPETS' was being sold along with printed oil cloths for hall and lobbies.[85] As with many drapers, funerals were part of the business and one acknowledgement from the 1850s stated that these had been 'conducted throughout in a manner highly creditable to that establishment'.[86] The premises were extended in the 1840s, almost doubling in size, and comprising five storeys in height rather than the previous three.[87]

Running an establishment of this size was not without its problems. Shoplifting was always a risk and employees were not always honest. It was reported in May 1838 that a young man called James Smith had entered the shop a little before it was due to be closed at nine o'clock and had stolen a large and valuable shawl from the window. The theft was seen by some of the shop assistants who pursued and detained Smith who had only been released from prison on the morning of the theft.[88] Dishonest behaviour by employees was more difficult to detect and potentially more worrying. In March 1836 one Thomas Jackson was engaged by Kendal, Milne and Faulkner, then described as silk mercers, having given a character reference. In the course of the next six weeks goods went missing from the shop and although the proprietors suspected him they could not prove anything. They found an excuse to dismiss him but he was taken on by another fashionable silk mercer, Mr Houghland. He continued to steal goods helped by a woman who posed as his wife and in due course stolen property worth £200 was found at the woman's lodgings. Jackson was then searched and found to be concealing three shawls under his waistcoat. Subsequent enquiries revealed that his accomplice was not his wife and that the reference he had produced was forged.[89] Two years later another shopman, William Walker, was tried for embezzling money. He had

---

82   Collinson, *Kendals*.
83   *Manchester Times and Lancashire and Cheshire Examiner*, 5 May 1838.
84   Ibid., 7 September 1839.
85   Ibid., 8 April 1843.
86   Ibid., 3 August 1853.
87   Ibid., 18 September 1846.
88   Ibid., 12 May 1838.
89   Ibid., 18 June 1836.

sold goods to a customer for 18s 8d, made out two invoices, one for 10s 0d and the other for 8s 8d, took them to another shopman to check as was the custom in the store. He took a sovereign from the customer but only presented one invoice to the cashier, receiving 11s 4d in change. He pocketed 10 shillings, gave the customer 1s 4d in change with another bill for the whole amount.[90] The system of checking invoices and having a cashier handle the money suggests that the partners were aware of the possibilities of fraud and had taken precautions. Walker was detected this time but other similar crimes may have gone undetected.

Expansion into a wider range of goods such as furniture did not happen until the 1860s or later and it was in the last third of the nineteenth century that Kendal Milne became Manchester's premier department store.[91] Many of the foundations for this expansion had, however, been laid by 1850. The iconic Bradford department store, Brown, Muff, also liked to emphasize its supposedly humble early nineteenth-century origins. The traditional account was that Elizabeth Brown, widow of William a saddler, opened a 'little low-browed' shop in Market Street in 1814. Elizabeth came from a Bradford trading family: one brother was an auctioneer, and another a linen draper as was her uncle John Ingham. The shop was described as having 15 feet of frontage and two bow windows with goods also displayed on hooks outside. Elizabeth was listed in Baines' 1822 directory as a clothes broker, but also as the proprietor of a circulating library. By 1828 the business was known as Brown and Son, linen drapers and was prospering.[92] The principles of cash only, giving customers their money's worth and never extending the business beyond her means were claimed as the secret of Elizabeth's success.[93] Elizabeth retired in February 1834, with her son Henry assuming full control of the shop.[94]

There is no reason to doubt the broad accuracy of the traditional account, although the emphasis on humble origins was convenient for those who wanted to tell a story of rags to riches based on hard work and honest dealing with Henry Brown as the main hero. Elizabeth Brown was clearly a formidable and astute businesswoman. She kept careful annual records of stock that reveal a rapidly expanding enterprise. The earliest of these, dating from 1818, listed a mixture of ready-made clothes such as trousers, boys suits and jackets, smocks, cloaks and gowns as well as accessories, including stockings, gloves, night caps, handkerchiefs and ribbons, table linen and lengths of cloth. The total value was £267. By the end of 1824 her stock was valued at £876 and included a similar range of goods but with an increasing emphasis on ready-made clothes, household linen, curtains

---

[90]   Ibid., 26 May 1838.

[91]   Bill Lancaster, *The Department Store: A Social History* (Leicester: Leicester University Press, 1995), p. 25.

[92]   *The Bromuff Story: A Brief Chronicle of 150 Years of Progress 1814–1964* (Bradford: Brown, Muff, 1964). Copy at WYAS, Bradford, Brown Muff Archive, 14D96/3/25.

[93]   William Scruton, *Bradford Fifty Years Ago* (Bradford: G.F. Sewell, 1897), p. 7. These 'principles' were reiterated in most subsequent accounts of Brown Muff.

[94]   *Bradford Observer*, 20 February 1834.

and carpets.[95] Reminiscing about being bought his first suit of clothes from Mrs Brown's shop, William Cudworth recalled a discussion with his parents outside the shop about whether they could afford velveteen with brass buttons or would have to settle for corduroy; and told how he was lifted on to the counter to try on the three-piece velveteen suit. The normal trying on area was a small recess screened off by a curtain.[96] Facilities may have been limited, and the target market ordinary working people and some of the middling sorts rather than polite society, but this was a substantial and increasingly profitable business.

The shop continued to prosper under Henry Brown. Stock was valued at £4,427 in November 1836 in a meticulous list arranged by location: lofts, front and back warehouse, chamber, cellar, shop and window. Ready-made clothing, particularly for men and boys, remained particularly significant.[97] At some point after he assumed control of the business Henry went into partnership with his mother's relatives Samuel Broadbent Ingham and James Broadbent Ingham, trading as Henry Brown and Company. The partnership was dissolved on 20 May 1839.[98] Henry Brown was already active in the public and commercial affairs of Bradford. His was one of the shops at which a petition for a Parliamentary Inquiry into the extent and causes of drunkenness in the kingdom could be signed in 1834; he supplied clothes to the Bradford Poor Law Union; he was active in supporting the Mechanics Institute; and he was one of 35 linen and woollen drapers and hatters who agreed in 1843 to close their shops at seven o'clock in the evening in winter and eight o'clock in summer (except on Saturdays) in order to benefit the young men in their employment.[99] At the same time, the business carried on growing. The 1841 stock take valued goods at £7,169 and by 1845 annual takings were around £20,000. It seems likely that Elizabeth Brown's insistence on ready money was still generally adhered to, although there were also some credit sales.[100] In the early 1840s Henry Brown described himself on his billheads as linen and woollen draper, hosier and tailor who sold ready-made clothes, stays, carpets and blankets. Suits were made to order in the best style and at the shortest notice.[101] Although successful and enterprising, it seems possible that by the mid 1840s Brown increasingly wanted to concentrate on his public role rather than to drive the business forward. If so, some personal tragedies in 1845 may have been decisive.

---

[95]   Brown Muff Archive, Journal of Stock Taken 1818–26, 14D96/1/1.

[96]   William Cudworth, *Yorkshire Speyks and Bradfurth Dialect Sketches* (Bradford: W.H. Brocklehurst, 1906), pp. 107–8.

[97]   Brown Muff Archive, Journal of Stock Taken 1836, 14D96/1/2.

[98]   *Bradford Observer*, 23 May 1839.

[99]   Ibid., 15 May 1834; 15 March 1838; 28 December 1843.

[100]   Brown Muff Archive, Journal of Cash Taken 1844–60, 14D96/1/3; Ledger 1838–77, 14D96/1/8.

[101]   Ibid., Customer Bills, 14D96/5/1/2.

In September of that year Brown's only child, William Henry, died at the age of seven. Three months later his mother Elizabeth died.[102] Between those two dates he entered into a partnership with Thomas Muff, brother of his wife Betsy whom he had married in 1834. The partnership agreement indicated that Brown had provided both the stock and the shop premises, for which he would receive £100 rent each year. Muff would gradually purchase up to half of the stock and each partner was to be regarded as a creditor of the firm in respect of their share of the stock, receiving 5 per cent interest on it. Muff was to 'diligently apply himself in and about the management of the said concern', receiving a salary of £100 a year as well as a half share of the profits. Brown was not required to devote time to the business beyond what he thought fit.[103] Muff gradually increased his capital in the business until in 1849 the value of the original stock was divided equally between the partners; by 1860 this £2,500 had increased to £7,122 each.[104] The transition to Brown and Muff, as the shop was styled from 1845 onwards, seems at first to have put a halt to the growth in trade with annual cash taken falling from £20,566 in 1845 to £16,116 in 1848 before increasing to £27,543 in 1851 and £35,338 in 1860.[105] The nature of the business probably changed little in these years, although there was perhaps an increasing emphasis on home furnishings and carpets alongside cloth and ready-made clothes. Brown spent £910 on alterations to the shop in 1853,[106] but Muff essentially ran the business, allowing his partner to focus on his wide range of charitable and educational interests as well as serving as Mayor of Bradford from 1856 to 1859.

If not already a fully fledged department store in the 1850s and 1860s, Brown and Muff was well on the way to becoming one. There were already several departments, the business operated on a large and growing scale, and the partners had some long-serving employees who were actively involved in the management of the firm and, when Brown withdrew in 1871, were in a position to become partners with Muff. 1871 also saw the opening of a new building of five storeys and occupying over 700 square yards. As well as providing departments for the sale of hosiery, drapery, oil cloths, clothing, shawls and mantles, curtains, upholstery, carpets, feathers and bed furnishings, there was a tailors' workshop and a large dining room for salesmen and others. According to the local newspaper it was 'a building with which not many even of the wholesale warehouses of Bradford can compete' and 'one of the largest establishments of their kind in the riding'.[107] Bradford had a department store to be proud of and, which like many others, could trace its origins to the enterprise and hard work of an earlier generation of drapers and clothes dealers seeking to bring new and affordable products to a wider market.

---

102   *Bradford Observer*, 11 September 1845; 4 December 1845.
103   Brown Muff Archive, Articles of Partnership 1845, 14D96/4/2.
104   Ibid., Ledger 1838–77, 14D96/1/8.
105   Ibid., 14D96/1/3, 5.
106   Ibid., Ledger, 14D96/1/8.
107   *Bradford Observer*, 29 April 1871.

Conclusions

The first half of the nineteenth century saw both incremental change and also some innovation in shop retailing. The overall theme of the period might be summed up as more of the same. There were undoubtedly more shops, whether fashionable ones in town centres, or general and provisions stores on the edge of the centre or in growing working-class districts. Numerical growth was probably greatest among these types of shop. There were also bigger shops, especially in the drapery and associated trades and the household goods trades. Retail methods, however, had changed little since the last decades of the eighteenth century. There was hardly any difference between the language of a typical shop advertisement from the 1780s and one from the 1830s. Ready money and fixed price selling was well established before 1800 even if practice may have sometimes departed from what was advertised. A substantial retailer like John Swanwick in Macclesfield was just as likely in the early nineteenth as in the early eighteenth century to retire from trade to concentrate on local politics or the life of a country gentleman rather than expanding into new places or new lines of business. Retailing in the early nineteenth century was sophisticated but more attuned to the needs of a highly developed commercial economy than to those of a large-scale manufacturing one.

There were, however, signs of more revolutionary changes to come. On the demand side, middle-class consumers had become used to having a range of fashionable shops readily to hand while working-class demand was becoming much more important as real wages began to increase and urban populations grew rapidly. On the supply side, commercial travellers were beginning to have a significant role in building a national market for regionally produced manufactured goods through their contacts with retailers.[108] Improved communications were also making goods more readily available. At the same time cheaper goods were available, particularly cotton textiles, some furniture and books. A changing social and economic context increasingly required structural changes in retailing. Some of these were foreshadowed in pre-1850 developments, such as the greater separation of production and retail activities; the establishment of branch shops in several towns by a handful of enterprising retailers; and the style of trading in bazaars which had some similarities to later department and variety stores. Moreover, as will be explored in the next chapter, one apparently quite traditional mode of retailing, the public market, was to be the site of significant innovation between 1820 and 1850.

---

[108] Andrew Popp, 'Building the Market: John Shaw of Wolverhampton and Commercial Travelling in Early Nineteenth-Century England', *Business History* 49/3 (2007): 321–47; Andrew Popp, 'From Town to Town: How Commercial Travel Connected Manufacturers and Markets during the Industrial Revolution', *Journal of Historical Geography*, 35/4 (2009): 642–67.

Chapter 8
Civic Pride: Market Halls

In September 1851 the Mayor of Stockport laid the foundation stone for a new market hall in the town. The local newspaper described the event in considerable detail, claiming that 'the erection of a handsome Market Hall was looked upon as so honourable to the corporate Spirit of Stockport, that even the Church Bells … became invested … with all the power of speech'.[1] The ceremony included a civic procession followed by speeches praising this new building. The Mayor declared that Stockport had now commenced the race of improvement and he hoped soon for a new town hall. The market hall itself was quite a modest building and was never very successful (Figure 8.1).

Indeed a letter to the *Cheshire Observer* in 1860 described it as 'inconvenient and ill-adapted to the purposes for which it was designed'. Traders therefore preferred 'to bear the inclemency of the weather in the open market'.[2] So why had the laying of the foundation stone been such a major event? The large, or sometimes not so large, market halls constructed in the first half of the nineteenth century were important public buildings. They often, though not always, made a real contribution to the retail provision of the town where they were built. They were almost always a statement of civic pride and urban improvement. This chapter explores the role of the market hall from both these perspectives.

Constructing the Market Hall

According to Schmiechen and Carls over 700 public market buildings have been constructed in Britain since 1750, with the market hall the predominant type after 1830. Market halls have been especially popular in Wales, the north-west of England and the midlands.[3] Many were not just large but were designed to stand out from the existing townscape rather than blend into it.[4] They were also the culmination of a process of reshaping the street and the market place according

---

[1] *Stockport Advertiser*, 19 September 1851. See also Ian Mitchell, 'Retailing Innovation and Urban Markets c.1800–1850', *Journal of Historical Research in Marketing*, 2/3 (2010): 287–99.

[2] *Cheshire Observer and General Advertiser*, 18 February 1860.

[3] James Schmiechen and Kenneth Carls, *The British Market Hall: A Social and Architectural History* (New Haven and London: Yale University Press, 1999), pp. 144–51.

[4] Ibid., p. 48.

Figure 8.1   Stockport produce market

Source: Author's own photograph.

to educated, middle-class models of respectability, social order and civic virtue.[5] They proclaimed a belief in the power of architecture to influence conduct.[6] Constructing the market hall was not just about the physical process of building, important as that was, but was also about changing the way in which buyers and sellers interacted by creating a safe spatial context that combined something of the culture of street and market trading with the controlled environment of a regulated public place. They might also be profitable, whether for a private owner or for a local authority. The prospects of earning significant income from a market hall also meant that it could be expensive for public bodies to purchase market rights from their existing owners. Stockport Borough Council, for example, paid Lord Vernon £22,500 for the market rights in 1847.[7]

Large industrial towns were among the first places to construct huge market halls. St John's Market in Liverpool has a good claim to be the earliest one. Although substantial market buildings had been erected in some towns, for example Sheffield and Halifax (see Chapter 1, pp. 30–31, 32–4), in the later eighteenth century, the sheer scale of St John's market hall marked it out as something new. It occupied an entire street block of over 8,200 square yards and was one of the largest buildings in the country when it was opened in 1822. The roof comprised five spans supported by 116 cast-iron pillars and the hall was around 180 yards long. It included 62 shops on the outer walls and 404 stalls arranged in blocks divided by avenues. As well as providing a place for the sale of a wide range of foodstuffs, St John's market hall was also important as social space. It was visited on weekday mornings by elegantly dressed ladies while evenings, particularly Saturday, were dominated by the working classes strolling and shopping.[8]

Within little more than a decade St John's market had been overtaken in size by the Grainger market in Newcastle-upon-Tyne which was opened in 1835. The market for meat, poultry, vegetables and general produce occupied just over 9,000 square yards and was probably the largest in Europe. There were 166 shops in the butchers' market and 54 in the green market.[9] Birmingham's new market hall, also opened in 1835, was only about half the size of the Grainger market but, according to White's 1849 *History of Birmingham*, was 'usually allowed to be one of the finest buildings in the kingdom'. A 'plain Grecian structure', it had six entrances, a roof with a lantern for air and light, 225 windows and room to accommodate 600 stalls. Up to 4,000 people could stroll around inside the hall.[10] Announcing its opening, the local newspaper commented that, 'It is expected that the female as well as the male heads

---

5   Ibid., p. 21.
6   Ibid., pp. 53–4.
7   Mitchell, 'Supplying the Masses', p. 267.
8   Stobart, *Spend, Spend Spend!*, pp. 97–9.
9   Thomas Oliver, *The Topographical Conductor, or Descriptive Guide to Newcastle and Gateshead* (Newcastle-on-Tyne, 1851), pp. 11–27.
10   Francis White and Co., *History and General Directory of the Borough of Birmingham* (Sheffield, 1850), p. 30.

of families, will avail themselves of the advantages thus afforded them of making, without the slightest inconvenience, their purchases in person'.[11] The market hall was to be a safe and clean environment. In Leeds markets were re-organized in the 1820s on somewhat different lines and without the building of a huge market hall. Nevertheless the town acquired a new shambles with a bazaar above it, two covered markets with a mixture of shops and stalls and an open market area. Much of this development was privately financed. This combination of dispersed markets and market halls enjoyed mixed success, with the south market and the bazaar struggling to attract traders but the shambles being very successful.[12] Even so by 1853 the town council saw an urgent need for a covered market adjoining the principal streets and sent a deputation to view the markets in Manchester, Liverpool, Birkenhead and elsewhere.[13]

Manchester had been something of an exception to this pattern of major market re-development in industrializing towns in the 1820s and 1830s. This was largely due to the intransigence of the Mosley family who owned the market rights in the town and whose first priority was to protect their legal rights and income. Instead there was a lengthy transition from a system of dispersed markets towards more centralized and purpose-built halls. An 1816 guide book listed markets in numerous locations. These included several for meat, as well as specialist markets for such items as corn, flour, fruit, cheese, butter and eggs, and shoes.[14] The Mosley's power was challenged and gradually eroded from the 1820s, but it was not until 1846 that Manchester's town council bought the market rights for the substantial sum of £200,000. Grandiose plans for two large new markets failed to come to fruition and Manchester had to settle for a major re-development of its Smithfield market in the 1850s.[15] Neighbouring Stockport similarly suffered from the unwillingness of the Vernon family to invest adequately in appropriate market facilities. A few years before the borough council finally purchased the market rights, the local newspaper attacked the levying of excessive toll in a place 'where, as yet, so little pains are taken to accommodate the frequenters of our fairs and markets'.[16]

Private ownership of market rights did not necessarily mean inferior market facilities as the case of Sheffield illustrates. The Earl of Surrey had actively supported market improvements in the 1780s (Chapter 1, pp. 32–3) and the Dukes of Norfolk continued to promote the development of new and better markets for much of the nineteenth century. The Duke's energetic Sheffield agent, Michael Ellison, produced

---

[11]   *Aris's Birmingham Gazette*, 9 February 1835.

[12]   Kevin Grady, 'Profit, Property Interests, and Public Spirit: The Provision of Markets and Commercial Amenities in Leeds, 1822–29', *Thoresby Society Publications*, 54/3 (1976): 165–95.

[13]   WYAS (Leeds), Leeds Improvement Act, Market Committee Minutes, 27 January and 16 July 1853, LLC 10/1/2, pp. 48, 63.

[14]   Joseph Aston, *A Picture of Manchester* (Manchester, 1816), pp. 216–7.

[15]   Scola, *Feeding the Victorian City*, pp. 150–70.

[16]   *Stockport Advertizer*, 2 June 1843.

a report on the state of the town's markets in 1826. These were becoming increasingly inadequate for the needs of its rapidly growing population and were not always well sited. Ellison proposed the removal of the corn, hay and cattle markets to a site away from the town centre; the erection on this new site of a corn exchange complete with offices and shops; the building of a bridge over the River Don to the new markets; and unspecified improvements to the fish, poultry and vegetable markets. He estimated the cost at £12,000 with over two-thirds of this being raised from mortgages of the rents and tolls of the new market. Ellison asked himself whether the likely return on the proposed expenditure would justify the outlay. His answer was no, except that the establishment of new markets would improve the value of the part of the Duke's Sheffield estates adjoining them.[17] The proposed work was carried out over a period of several years at a cost of £23,500, nearly double the original estimate. The corn exchange and new market cost £14,029 with the remainder made up of the building of the bridge (£4,318), solicitors' and architects' expenses, interest payments and sundries. A total of £19,100 was borrowed in amounts ranging from £250 to £2,000 on the security of the market tolls.[18]

These improvements mainly benefited the wholesale trade in agricultural products and did not provide Sheffield with the sort of retail markets that were being constructed in other growing towns. This did not pass unnoticed by those who traded in them. An 1835 letter suggested that if Ellison was to visit the fruit market he would decide that 'a more inconvenient, unseemly and ill-adapted place is not to be found in any town of equal size to this'. The Duke of Norfolk should be induced to erect similar markets to those in Liverpool and Birmingham, which the letter writer claimed somewhat disingenuously not to have been costly. He went on to add that the Duke's market rights were a bar to appropriate markets being built by public subscription.[19] Sheffield probably had fallen behind other towns in terms of market provision, perhaps as much as a consequence of its having been a pioneer of improved markets in the eighteenth century, as through any major failings by the market owners. This was soon to change. The 1847 Markets Act empowered the Duke to purchase land in the centre of Sheffield to create new markets for meal, flour, meat, fish, poultry, vegetables, cheese and all other articles.[20] The markets cost £77,150 to build, including £21,911 for purchasing land and paying compensation and £46,840 on the building account; £40,000 was borrowed to finance this and £19,859 was raised from the sale of land and premises.[21] The retail Norfolk Market was opened with lavish ceremony on Christmas Eve 1851.[22] Income from the markets and fairs in 1852 was £3,120 of which £2,041 came from the shops in the Norfolk

---

[17]   Sheffield Archives, Arundel Castle Mss, Sheffield New Market, ACM/S/346/3.

[18]   Ibid., Market Accounts, ACM/S/189/1–5.

[19]   Ibid., Letter of 20 July 1835, ACM/S/346/4.

[20]   *An Act for Removing the Market between King Street and Castle Street in the Town of Sheffield ...* 10 & 11 Victoria, cap. xlv.

[21]   Sheffield Archives, Market Accounts, ACM/S/189/6.

[22]   Blackman, 'Food Supply of an Industrial Town', p. 94.

Market. Expenditure was £598 including £150 for the superintendent's salary and £276 for gas.[23] By the mid 1870s income had increased to over £9,000 a year with expenditure averaging £3,000. Sheffield Corporation regarded them as sufficiently profitable to be prepared to offer the Duke of Norfolk £267,450 for the market rights and tolls, an amount that some regarded as excessive when compared to what other towns had spent. One opponent also suggested that the need for covered markets was decreasing as shops followed the spread of a town.[24] Despite these disagreements Sheffield was 'noted in the late nineteenth century as an exceptional instance in which the public markets were well managed in the hands of a private owner'.[25]

It was not only in a large town like Sheffield that the Dukes of Norfolk took a keen interest in marketing facilities. The small but rapidly growing Derbyshire town of Glossop also formed part of their estate. Again it was Michael Ellison who reported to the Duke on the state of trade in Glossop in 1843 and on the prospects for capital investment there that would benefit the inhabitants and be profitable to the Duke. The Manchester–Sheffield railway, due to open in 1845, would be good for the cotton industry in the town if a branch line was built from the Dinting viaduct. Ellison recommended the Duke to finance this and to obtain an Act of Parliament to establish a properly regulated market. A weekly market for the sale of provisions was already in existence and Ellison commented that for a market to succeed the need for it must have been established and that this had been done. He calculated that these improvements would cost not less than £10,000, most of which was for the branch line.[26] The market house was built but was soon found to be inadequate. Ellison reported again in 1853 that 'The present Market House – altho' when erected thought to be larger than the circumstances of the district demanded – having been found very much too small and incommodious to meet the requirements of the increased population of the Town of Glossop' needed to be extended. This was done at a cost of £4,473. Ellison, as always, was concerned about the Duke's income. He reckoned that the annual rental of the market in 1853 produced the equivalent of 8 per cent on the cost of building it and that the extension would provide 5 per cent on past and present outlay. The Duke was borrowing at 2½ per cent.[27] Market improvements like these were part of good estate management.

Elsewhere the initiative for building market halls rested with improvement commissioners operating under the authority of an Act of Parliament. The Cheshire town of Birkenhead provides a very good example of this. The town had been planted and planned on virgin soil in the 1820s and was essentially the creation of entrepreneurs, and from the 1830s onwards of improvement commissioners, many of whom were either Liverpool merchants or Birkenhead tradesmen. One of

[23]   Sheffield Archives, Market Accounts, 1852, ACM/S/189/7.

[24]   Frederick Brittain, *The Corporation and the Markets* (Sheffield, 1876). Copy at ACM/S/333.

[25]   Schmiechen and Carls, *The British Market Hall*, p. 289.

[26]   Sheffield Archives, Glossop Estate, ACM/D/31/1.

[27]   ACM/D/26/1–6.

the advantages of being a new town was that the authorities did not have to worry about existing market rights or traditional markets. Instead they could provide public markets of a high standard. The 1833 Improvement Act not only provided for a market to be established, but included detailed provisions for its conduct. At their October 1833 meeting, the commissioners appointed a sub-committee to look into building a market and almost a year later the commissioners approved plans for a market at a cost of £3,150. This was to be funded by borrowing against the expected income from rates, tolls and duties.[28] The market, which included 25 shops and numerous stalls, was opened in July 1835 to considerable celebration in the town. According to the *Liverpool Mercury*, the 'substantial, as well as delicate profusion with which the stalls were supplied, spoke well for the gastronomic capacities of the good people of Birkenhead'.[29]

In the next 10 years the population of Birkenhead grew from around 2,500 to 20,000 or more and by 1843 the commissioners were considering, and rejecting, plans to extend the market and then agreeing to the construction of a new market. Tenders in the range of £15,000 were received in September of that year.[30] This was a very much larger market, similar in design to that of St John's market in Liverpool, and comprised three arcades with space for 42 shops and 80 stalls with wrought iron shutters. There were six entrances and ample storage vaults.[31] The cost at nearly £32,000, including £8,154 for the purchase of the land, was well in excess of the earlier estimates. The money had again been borrowed, but the land owned by the commissioners for market purposes was valued at over £35,000 and it was hoped that the market, if fully occupied, would produce £2,000 a year income.[32] The *Chester Chronicle* recorded how the opening of the market hall in July 1845 had been accompanied by rejoicing in all parts of the town, how stalls and shops in the hall had been decked out, and how business had been very brisk with many of the most respectable families making purchases first thing in the morning.[33] The atmosphere in the market hall may have been somewhat less polite later in the day. Constructing a market hall on this scale was very much a statement of Birkenhead's arrival as a town to be reckoned with.

At the north-eastern tip of Cheshire improvement commissioners were also deliberating about a market, this time in the cotton textile town of Stalybridge. Their initial meeting following the Stalybridge Police and Markets Act was held at the White Hart in the town on 18 June 1828 with John Cheetham, the constable, in

---

[28] Wirral Archives, Birkenhead Improvement Commissioners, Minutes 1833–42, B/001/1, pp. 12, 25–6, 28–9.

[29] *Liverpool Mercury*, 17 July 1835.

[30] Birkenhead Improvement Commissioners, Minutes, 1842–59, B/001/2, pp. 12, 21, 23.

[31] *The Strangers' Guide through Birkenhead* (Birkenhead: Law & Pinkney, 1847), pp. 45–6.

[32] Birkenhead Improvement Commissioners, Minutes of the Birkenhead Market Committee, 1843–47, B/013/2, p. 208.

[33] *Chester Chronicle*, 18 July 1845.

the chair. They agreed in April 1829 that a market was necessary and appointed a committee to find a site and obtain plans and estimates. The land was given by Lord Stamford, money was borrowed on the security of the market tolls and in July 1830 plans were approved. A tender for £4,100 from Heywood and Johnson, stonemasons from Huddersfield, was accepted. Progress remained quite slow, with some changes made to the original plans, until in September 1831 Heywood and Johnson's proposal to erect counters, stalls and a shambles for £290 was accepted. Finally the new market was opened on 30 December 1831 and included seven shops, stalls for meat, fish and vegetables, a bazaar and an outdoor market for items such as vegetables, earthenware and glass. There was a public procession to mark the opening of the market. Once the market had been opened no stalls or standings for marketable goods were allowed elsewhere in the town.[34] There was nothing particularly grand about this market but it enabled the streets to be cleared of obstructions and the town clearly took pride in having achieved this mark of civic status. The market was extended in 1843 and replaced by a modest but elaborately decorated brick market hall in 1868.[35]

In other towns existing local authorities actively promoted market improvement and the building of market halls. On 15 July 1829 the Town Clerk of Derby invited tenders for the construction of a new market in the town adjacent to the existing market place (Figure 8.2).[36]

Figure 8.2   Derby market place

Source: Derbyshire Record Office, D369/G/Zp/532/47. Reproduced by permission of the Record Office and the Derbyshire Archaeological Society.

---

34   Tameside Archives, Stalybridge Police Commissioners Minutes, 1828–33, IC/STA/1.
35   Schmiechen and Carls, *The British Market Hall*, p. 85.
36   *Derby Mercury*, 15 July 1829.

Eleven months later he gave notice that the shops, stalls and standings in the new market were ready for inspection and that the market would be opened on 25 June 1830. An editorial in the *Mercury* commented that the 'accommodations for the convenience of both sellers and buyers are most admirable, and we have no doubt the shops, stalls and standings will be eagerly enquired after'.[37] The market included 100 shops for butchers, a butter market and a covered space for 40 fruit and vegetable stalls.[38] Although unspectacular when compared with the market halls of some other towns, this was still a valuable expansion of Derby's marketing facilities. Even before it was built a property directly opposite its entrance was being advertised as particularly desirable because of that location.[39] Derby got by with a mix of open market and these new market buildings until the 1860s when a medium-sized market hall was built at a cost of £18,000 and opened to great civic celebrations including a performance of Handel's *Messiah*.[40]

It was not always easy for a local authority to turn a proposal for a market hall, whether modest or grandiose, into reality. In the Shropshire market town of Oswestry two small market halls existed in 1849: the Cross for meat and general provisions and the Powis for butter, cheese and poultry. These were run by the town council under the provisions of an 1848 Market Act.[41] Discussions about market improvements seem, however, to have been going on for the best part of a decade. The town's Market Hall Committee considered in 1842 that it would be desirable to publish a report and accounts to repudiate charges of 'failure, haste or bad management'. They were then trying to raise £3,000 by voluntary subscription and a further £1,500 on the security of the income of the markets. The market at the Cross cost £3,661 to build, including purchasing land, and the committee estimated that the total cost of improved markets would be up to £8,000.[42] The 1848 Act provided the legal framework for the new arrangements, but did not solve all the town's problems regarding them. There were difficulties obtaining some of the land needed and the Corporation had to use its compulsory purchase powers.[43] There was also a dispute about compensation for those who had previously claimed the right to set up stalls outside their houses and let them to butchers and others on market days; these were no longer allowed when the new markets were opened. Legal advice was that no compensation was due.[44] Bye-laws

---

[37]   Ibid., 9 June 1830.

[38]   Stephen Glover, *The History and Directory of the Borough of Derby* (Derby: H. Mozley and Sons, 1843), p. 9; DRO, Cathedral Church of All Saints, Plan of New Market Place, D3372/81/3.

[39]   *Derby Mercury*, 25 November 1829.

[40]   *Illustrated London News*, 2 June 1866, p. 537; *Derby Mercury*, 30 May 1866.

[41]   Schmiechen and Carls, *The British Market Hall*, p. 284.

[42]   Oswestry Town Council, Markets, Accounts and other papers relating to new markets, 1842, F65/1.

[43]   Ibid., F65/2.

[44]   Ibid., F65/7.

for the new markets were agreed in 1853 specifying what could be sold where, the hours of opening and conditions to be observed by stall holders.[45] The town had got what it needed but not without something of a struggle.

Some towns invested considerable energy in drawing up plans for a market hall that did not come to fruition. Preston Corporation commissioned an architect to assess three possible sites for a market house in the town. The site needed to be central to the town's population; nearly level and with ease of access; moderately elevated and airy; capable of proper drainage; and as near as possible to the existing markets. The architect's 1841 report recommended the site of the existing butchers' shambles with some additional land as the easiest and, at an estimated cost of £16,930, the cheapest. The Corporation's Treasurer disagreed. He considered that site to be cramped, allowing only four entrances and precluding the Earl of Derby's proposed new street. Instead he suggested a site that would connect the corn exchange and old market, would preserve many existing buildings and, although smaller than the other options, was still double the size of the existing market place. He added the cost of purchasing land to the architect's estimate to reach a figure of £25,855 for his preferred option.[46] At the subsequent special council meeting it was proposed that a covered market, to be financed by borrowing against the security of the rents and tolls coupled with a market rate, was highly desirable and likely to be profitable as were the markets in Liverpool and Halifax. The council was, however, swayed by the arguments of those who said that a market hall would not pay and that it was not the right time to tax the town's inhabitants. An editorial in the *Preston Chronicle* expressed surprise at the decision. In its view the council had not taken proper account of those compelled to stand in the open market in all weathers or of the inconvenience caused by streets crowded with poultry higglers, butter sellers, vegetable dealers and butchers stalls.[47] Preston did not acquire a general covered market until 1875.[48]

It would be easy to find many more examples of market halls, large and small, being planned, discussed and built in towns throughout the midlands and north of England in the middle decades of the nineteenth century. They were an important, and sometimes imposing, feature of the urban landscape. Their opening was frequently marked by celebrations throughout the town. The process of constructing a market hall was, however, significantly influenced by town governance. Improvement commissioners could drive a project with enthusiasm and with the powers to do whatever it took to acquire land and funds; an energetic private owner or their representative could be similarly forceful; others could be obstructive; and a traditional or reformed corporation might find that a project became entangled in bureaucracy or fell victim to competing voices in the council

---

[45]   Ibid., F65/11.

[46]   Lancashire Archives, Preston, Miscellaneous, Report on the Proposed Covered Market, 1841, DDPR/138/50.

[47]   Ibid., Newspaper cuttings.

[48]   Schmiechen and Carls, *The British Market Hall*, p. 286.

chamber. The construction of the market hall needs to be understood in its local context. Yet whatever the symbolic status of such buildings they were ultimately places of trade, particularly supplying a growing town's population with the necessities and decencies of life. The next section looks at what was bought and sold in the market hall.

Trading in the Market Hall

According to the Muis, 'the kingpin of the weekly market was the butcher ... With the exception of butcher's meat, few items sold in the market could not be purchased more expeditiously in small quantities as needed at the chandler's shop'.[49] This may have been true for southern England in the late eighteenth century, and butchers were certainly in the majority in many markets, but as a generalization it significantly underestimates the importance of markets in the early nineteenth century and the variety of goods increasingly on offer. Birkenhead's 1845 market hall was typical of many such urban markets. When it was built it comprised 12 butchers' shops, 26 butchers' stalls, 20 vegetable stands, 8 fish shops, 6 game shops, 8 provisions shops, 8 pedlars' shops, 7 pedlars' stands, 8 flower stands, 76 farmers' tables, 7 rabbit and tripe stands and 48 vaults. Not all of these were let when the market opened. There were particular problems in letting the farmers' tables, the rabbit stalls and the vaults; and while all the butchers' shops were taken, half the stalls were initially unoccupied.[50] Adjustments were made to take account of the demand for shops and stalls. In 1846 the Market Committee ordered that the shops and open spaces occupied by pedlars be given to butchers, and the pedlars placed in vacant fish shops and other unoccupied parts of the market.[51] The committee seems to have been initially reluctant to allow a wider range of goods to be sold in the market, but in August 1848 it ordered the market superintendent to receive applications for the sale of any article that came within the meaning of the relevant Act of Parliament.[52] A furniture shop was permitted in November 1848 and a shoe shop in January 1849.[53] A glowing description of the market in the *Liverpool Mercury* in 1850 referred to toy and earthenware shops, provisions shops well stocked with cheese, hams and bacon as well as butchers, fishmongers, greengrocers and poultry shops.[54]

The bye-laws of the much smaller market hall at Oswestry also provided for the sale of a wide range of goods. The Cross Market was for the sale of

---

[49] Mui and Mui, *Shops and Shopkeeping*, p. 157.
[50] Wirral Archives, Birkenhead Improvement Commissioners, Minutes of the Market Committee, 1843–7, B/013/2, pp. 158–66.
[51] Ibid., 6 May 1846, p. 255.
[52] Minutes, 1847–51, 16 August 1848, B/013/3, p. 105.
[53] Ibid., 8 November, 1848, p. 127, 17 January 1849, p. 150.
[54] *Liverpool Mercury*, 24 December 1850.

butter, cheese, eggs, poultry, game, cakes, confectionery, meat, bacon, fruit and vegetables; and the Powis Market for corn, grain, large quantities of produce, trees, shrubs, earthenware and manufactured goods.[55] Allowing certain types of goods to be sold did not, of course, necessarily mean that they were actually sold, or indeed that everyone was happy with what was being done. Salford acquired a medium-sized new market hall in 1827 following an 1823 petition that argued the case for a market because of the town's increased population. Local shopkeepers were not happy. They claimed that markets had previously been toll free, that the inhabitants were well supplied by the existing shops and that the private owners of the new market were compelling the butchers to take stalls in it and close their shops on market days. Even so, the opening of the market was said to have been well attended.[56] After Stockport's very modest market hall opened in 1852 there were complaints from greengrocers that they had lost trade because they had been required to move their stalls to new locations. The users of the potato market also asked for it to be moved back to its original location.[57] The sort of orderly marketing arrangements that suited civic authorities did not always reflect the realities of market trading.

When Stalybridge opened its new market in 1831 it included a 'bazaar' (pp. 159–60). Counters were let there at 2s 6d a week without shelves and 3 shillings with; gas lighting was provided.[58] There are no details of the sort of goods sold there, but when alterations to the town hall and market house were proposed in 1859 there was a need to move some shops out of the bazaar.[59] Bazaar markets had been a feature of some early market halls. For example in Leeds, the new shambles built in the early 1820s had a room above the butchers' stalls about 80 yards long designated as a 'bazaar' and intended for this very purpose. The central market, completed in 1827, had a gallery around three sides of the building with a bazaar on one side.[60] Bradford also had a bazaar market. In Newcastle, where there was major market re-development in the 1830s, the Victoria Bazaar was opened in 1837 with provision for 42 shops on the ground floor.[61] A bazaar was planned for the new Exeter market built in 1835. This was to have been ranged along each side of the handsome avenue leading into the building but was not constructed.[62]

---

[55]   Oswestry Town Council, Market Bye-Laws, 7 October 1853, F65/11.

[56]   NA, Duchy of Lancaster, Salford Market, DL 41/1149.

[57]   Stockport Local Heritage Library, Stockport Borough, Manorial Tolls Committee Minute Book, 1851–60, D1814, pp. 154, 157.

[58]   Tameside Archives, IC/STA/1, 2 December 1831.

[59]   Tameside Archives, Stalybridge, Market Committee Minutes, 1858–64, 7 March 1859, CA/STA/119/17.

[60]   William White, *Directory and Topography of Leeds, Bradford, Halifax, Huddersfield, Wakefield, and the Whole of the Clothing Districts of the West Riding of Yorkshire* (Sheffield: W. White, 1847), p. 23.

[61]   Oliver, *Topographical Conductor*, pp. 65–6.

[62]   *The Architectural Magazine and Journal*, vol. 3 (London, 1836), pp. 12–16.

Somewhat unusually, trade directories for the 1830s and 1840s listed at least some of those trading in the Leeds and Bradford bazaar markets. In Bradford 23 traders were listed in 1830 and 43 in 1847; in Leeds 27 traders were listed in the central market bazaar in 1834 and 10 in the Briggate bazaar (the one over the shambles). The types of trade were quite similar to those found in Soho and the other London bazaars. In each case, traders in cloth and clothing accounted for around two-thirds or more of the total. This may of course have reflected directory bias as it is by no means clear that the directories listed all the traders in the bazaar. But there was also a scattering of fancy goods dealers and an occasional bookseller. Many of those listed were women, and some were town shopkeepers using the bazaars as an additional outlet. One such in Bradford was Thomas Waterhouse who advertised his 'cheap books' on sale at 12 Darley Street. He claimed to have 6,000 volumes of new and old books and a circulating library of over 4,000 volumes. Waterhouse was also listed as trading from 7, The Bazaar.[63]

These so-called bazaar markets seem to have met with limited success. In Leeds, the shambles was very successful, the bazaar above less so.[64] In 1837 both were purchased by a group of Leeds traders calling themselves 'The Leeds Bazaar and Shambles Joint Stock Estate' for just under £15,000. The purchase was to be funded from a £7,000 mortgage and the issue of £50 shares of which 158 were taken up.[65] The potential for a return on the investment probably came from the shambles rather than the bazaar. Although the Leeds and Bradford bazaars continued to have some tenants into the 1840s, they were clearly struggling. By 1853 it was said that the bazaar over the central market was unoccupied and that access was very inconvenient.[66] Perhaps it was simply not worthwhile for established traders on good shopping streets also to trade from these not very attractive early bazaar markets. If they wanted an additional outlet, then it was increasingly possible for them to trade in a general market.

By the mid nineteenth century some market halls were 'closer to a general shopping centre than a provisions market'.[67] At Blackburn, where a market hall was opened in 1848, much of the provisions market remained outside the hall while many of the 34 shops inside were occupied by confectioners, booksellers, furniture dealers, metalware dealers and those in the cloth and clothing trades.[68] Durham's new market, opened in 1852, accommodated clothiers, hatters, booksellers, quack medicine vendors, confectioners and hardware merchants

---

63   White, *Directory of Leeds*, advertisements, p. 17.
64   Grady, 'Profit, Property Interests, and Public Spirit', pp. 186–88.
65   WYAS (Leeds), Leeds Bazaar and Shambles Estate, Summary and Abstract of 1837 Deed, WYL 58/13, 14.
66   WYAS (Leeds), Leeds Improvement Act, Market Committee Minutes, 1848–1857, LLC10/1/2, pp. 5–6.
67   Alexander, *Retailing in England*, p. 58, referring to Blackburn market.
68   Ibid., p. 57.

as well as the usual butchers and greengrocers.[69] In mid nineteenth-century Manchester a key issue was to get second-hand dealers off the streets and into a covered market. In 1854 the Markets Committee reported that a property had been purchased for £2,450 which would be fitted out so that it could be used by dealers in old clothes and similar articles. The anticipated income from the market would be more than 5 per cent of the purchase price.[70] Three years later committee members visited Bolton market which was considered to be the nearest approach yet made to a model establishment. They recommended that £650 be spent on building a gallery in Smithfield market for dealers in artificial flowers, trinkets, ribbons and similar goods. This was expected to bring in £100 a year in rents.[71] By the 1870s farmers selling produce in Shudehill market in the city were being asked to move to make way for provisions dealers, milliners and booksellers.[72] In their Lancashire heartland, large covered markets provided a real alternative both to the corner shop and the specialist store in the second half of the nineteenth century. Two-thirds of the tenants of Bolton's market hall sold food in 1881 but half of the remaining third were clothes dealers. In Blackburn one-quarter of the market hall tenants also operated from a shop.[73]

Regulating the Market Hall

Markets halls were public space but were also subject to detailed and rigorous regulation. This was about creating a pleasant and safe environment for those who chose to shop there, including middle-class women; it was about ensuring good standards of hygiene; it was about protecting traders from unfair competition; and it was about securing a proper income for the owner of the market. The building of a market was usually followed by the making of bye-laws, often following a fairly standard format. Those for Stoke market in Staffordshire provide a typical example. They set out the opening times for the market, in this case eight o'clock in the morning until eight o'clock at night on Wednesdays, with Saturday closing being half past ten. They specified where traders were to stand in both the covered market and the open market place with the market inspector having power to order how stalls and standings were arranged. There was to be no smoking in the covered

---

[69]   Schmiechen and Carls, *The British Market Hall*, p. 175.

[70]   City of Manchester, Proceedings of the Council, November 1854 – November 1855, p. 268.

[71]   *The Guardian*, 22 January 1857.

[72]   Schmiechen and Carls, *The British Market Hall*, p. 168.

[73]   Deborah Hodson, '"The Municipal Store": Adaptation and Development in the Retail Markets of Nineteenth-Century Urban Lancashire', in Nicholas Alexander and Gary Akehurst (eds), *The Emergence of Modern Retailing, 1750–1950* (London: Frank Cass, 1999), pp. 94–114; see also Deborah Hodson, 'Civic Identity, Custom and Commerce: Victorian Market Halls in the Manchester Region', *Manchester Region History Review*, 12 (1998): 34–43.

market, no loitering, whetting of knives or posting bills and no dropping of orange peel or vegetable waste on the floor. Dogs found in the market would be seized. Blown, coloured or disguised veal, meat or fish would also be seized. Stallholders were not to leave any garbage, were to place fish refuse in the bins provided, not to wash or clean vegetables after nine o'clock in the morning and use the blocks and boards provided for chopping and cleaning. No one was to interfere with the gas light. There was a £5 penalty for breaching the bye-laws.[74] The bye-laws at Stafford were very similar, though perhaps even stricter with butchers required to wash their stalls at least twice weekly and fishmongers required to wash their slabs before eight o'clock in the morning on each market day. There was also to be no swearing or abusive language.[75]

A particular feature of market halls, particularly the larger ones, was the way in which the stalls were arranged according to type of trade. The butchers were grouped together, as were the fishmongers and vegetable sellers. Fancy goods were often placed in a gallery if there was one.[76] Similar arrangements were not unknown in smaller markets. In the Nottinghamshire market town of Worksop a private company was established in 1848 to provide a corn exchange and a market. The promoters planned to raise £5,000 from the issue of 500 shares, to purchase a site and erect the market and lease the rights to the tolls from the Duke of Newcastle. Bye-laws made in 1851 laid down where specific goods were to be sold in the covered market: butter, poultry, eggs, cheese and bacon on the west side; crockery, hardware and other goods on the east side; vegetables and fruit on the south side; and fish in the corner sheds. The company had spent just over £1,900 in providing the market while income in 1851–52 was £24 11s 3d from the butchers' shops, £82 3s 0d from the market stalls and £17 9s 0d from charges for the Assembly Rooms and sundries with annual expenditure at £46 6s 8d.[77] This was probably just about an acceptable return on the investment.

It is important not to forget that market halls needed to generate revenue. The money to build them had often been borrowed against the expected income stream. Market owners had to ensure that as much trade as possible took place within the confines of the market hall or market place and not in the surrounding streets or in a rival market. There was a dispute at Burnley in 1830 when one John Whitaker, a butcher, accused the magistrates and town improvement commissioners of illegally attempting to move stallholders from the traditional site of the market to a new site. He claimed that this new market was a monopoly scheme run by a group of shareholders and hinted at collusion between the town's gaslight company and

[74] SA, Quarter Sessions, Stoke Market Bye-Laws, 1846, Q/SB/1847 A39.
[75] SA, Borough of Stafford, Bye-Laws for Regulating the General Market and Wholesale Market, 1854, D1323/Q/1/5.
[76] Schmiechen and Carls, *The British Market Hall*, p. 168.
[77] NA, Board of Trade, Files of Joint Stock Companies, Worksop Corn Exchange and Market Company, BT 41/775/4163.

the improvement commissioners.[78] Market owners naturally wanted as many as possible of the shops and stalls in their market to be occupied. There could be a conflict between this and the ideal of segregating different trades within the market hall and it seems likely that vacant stalls were sometimes let to the wrong sort of trader. Stalls in the new market at Birkenhead had not proved that easy to let in the mid 1840s. The market authorities were initially somewhat inflexible in their letting policy, refusing one Charles Jacobson a shop for his brush selling business in February 1846 because no shop appropriated for the sale of such goods was available in the market, but relenting three months later and letting him have one of the vacant shops in the poulterers' area.[79] In the following year they allowed the Secretary of the Ladies Clothing Society to use one of the farmers' tables for the Society's annual sale of clothing in aid of the poor.[80] They did, however, refuse a request from a bookseller for two yards of a farmers' table.[81] Even so market hall interiors may not have had quite so orderly an appearance as floor plans suggest.

Deciding on lettings was only one of the many duties that fell to an active market committee reporting to a borough council or to improvement commissioners like that in Birkenhead. They had to deal with nuisances such as that caused by one Hilton at Birkenhead who was warned in 1839 and again in 1842 to desist from making tripe in his vault or be given notice to quit.[82] They had to authorize expenditure on improved facilities like the ice houses, fountain and stoves required in the new market.[83] They had to caution traders who sold the wrong goods in their shop, for example Nathaniel Knight for selling eggs in a provisions shop or John Garnett for selling poultry on his fish stand[84] They had to deal with complaints from customers. In September 1845 they received a letter from a Mr Hicklin who complained that Eleanor Coward who traded from one of the provisions shops had sold him some lard that was unfit for use. He returned it but she refused him a refund. Mrs Coward was summoned to appear before the committee and was admonished.[85] They dealt with unruly traders including John Royle and Charles Mulholland, both occupiers of egg stalls who had been fighting in the market.[86] They had to adjudicate on whether rabbits could be sold at green grocery or fish and game stalls.[87] In 1848 some butchers complained that two others had been issuing handbills to promote the sale of their meat by advertising its price. This was

[78]   Lancashire Archives, Quarter Sessions, Burnley Market, QSP/2923/35.
[79]   Wirral Archives, Minutes of the Birkenhead Market Committee, 1843–7, B/013/2, pp. 238, 257.
[80]   Ibid., 1847–51, B/013/3, p. 16.
[81]   Ibid., 27 October 1847, p. 402.
[82]   Ibid., 1835–43, B/013/1, pp. 44, 107.
[83]   Ibid., 1843–7, B/013/2, 28 September 1844, p. 66.
[84]   Ibid., 19 August 1845, p. 177; 11 March 1846, p. 243.
[85]   Ibid., 30 September 1845, p. 189.
[86]   Ibid., 18 August 1847, pp. 378–9.
[87]   Ibid., 1847–51, B/013/3, 17 and 24 November 1847, pp. 7, 9.

settled amicably but indicates the way in which traders might expect the market authorities to ensure fair competition.[88] Three years later tenants complained about the daily influx of hawkers from Liverpool selling fruit and vegetables outside the market. This was referred to the lawyers.[89] Birkenhead's market committee was particularly diligent in the exercise of its responsibilities, as was the equivalent committee at Leicester.[90] Both were concerned that the markets should be a credit to the town and should be recognized as such.

Conclusions

Some market halls were spectacular buildings, others much more ordinary. Not all of them fulfilled the highest expectations of those who built them: Birkenhead, for example, may never have been fully tenanted. All, however, were thronged at certain times of the week, particularly Saturday evenings, and at certain times of the year, particularly Christmas. All were also important to the town where they were located and were a matter of civic pride. A few years after the inhabitants of Stockport had celebrated their new market hall those of Chesterfield across the Pennines in Derbyshire did the same (Figure 8.3).

Described by Pevsner as 'The crudest show of High Victorian provincial prosperity',[91] it was opened in 1857 to great celebrations including a dinner attended by around 100 gentlemen and tradesmen. Sir Joseph Paxton proposed a toast to the market hall, in his view a 'most beautiful and appropriate building', and to the prosperity of the town.[92] A market hall was an almost essential part of the townscape of any self-respecting northern or midland town.

In 1846 the Newcastle and Carlisle Railway advertised that third-class carriages would be attached to Saturday trains at Haydon Bridge and Blaydon to take passengers to Newcastle market and to Tuesday trains at Newcastle and Haltwistle for the Hexham market.[93] The combination of rail travel, itself one of the great innovations of the nineteenth century, and purpose-built market halls, combining a traditional approach to buying and selling with innovative building design and use of space, had a major impact on the ability of ordinary people to access food, clothing and household goods and to exercise choice in how and where they shopped. There was a sense in which the great market halls did for working-class shoppers something of what fashionable shops and later department

---

[88]   Ibid., 20 September 1848, p. 115.

[89]   Ibid., 19 March 1851, pp. 322–3.

[90]   Alexander, *Retailing in England*, pp. 45–7.

[91]   Nikolaus Pevsner, *The Buildings of England: Derbyshire* (Harmondsworth: Penguin, 1986), p. 145.

[92]   *Sheffield and Rotherham Independent, Supplement*, 16 May 1857.

[93]   NA, Pre-Nationalization Railway Companies, Special Collections, Tomlinson Collection, Poster, RAIL 1157/3/13.

Figure 8.3   Chesterfield market hall

Source: Author's own photograph.

stores had done for middle-class ones. They turned shopping from being an activity that had to be undertaken in order to acquire the necessities of life into one that was pleasurable in its own right. Market halls were places to promenade, to be seen and to socialize with friends. As such they played a key role in modern shopping practices.

Chapter 9
Conclusion: Everybody's Story

In George Eliot's novel *The Mill on the Floss*, there is a description of a charity bazaar in the town of St Ogg's at which the heroine Maggie Tulliver has a stall for the sale of 'large plain articles', including gentlemen's dressing gowns, not wanting to sell 'elaborate products, of which she had but a dim understanding'. The bazaar was attended by 'All well-dressed St Ogg's and its neighbourhood' and as well as the stalls for the sale of goods there was an orchestra and a room for refreshments.[1] Charity bazaars grew in popularity from the 1820s onwards. In December 1827 a four-day fancy fair in Brighton raised £1,315 for the Sussex County Hospital while in June 1833 a four-day bazaar in the Hanover Square Rooms in London raised £5,106 for the Society of Friends of Foreigners in Distress. A typical bazaar raised perhaps £1,000 and by the middle of the century there were around 1,000 advertisements a year in the provincial press for bazaars. They were predominately organized and run by women.[2] The Anti-Corn Law League Bazaar of 1845 was the most spectacular of these. It opened on 8 May for viewing only and included stalls from 46 provincial towns and 12 London districts. Admission was 10s 6d. Selling began a week later and in the course of 17 days the bazaar was visited by 170,000 people and made £25,000. All the latest consumer goods were on display in what was described as a museum of British manufacture. It was largely organized by the wives and daughters of the local and national leaders of the Anti-Corn Law League. As well as raising money, charity bazaars conveyed a message that shopping and consumption could be virtuous pursuits not just self-indulgence.[3] This message found growing acceptance in Victorian England.

---

[1] George Eliot, *The Mill on the Floss* (1860, Collins edn; London, 1952), Book 6, ch. 9, p. 423.

[2] F.K. Prochaska, 'Charity Bazaars in Nineteenth-Century England', *Journal of British Studies*, 16/2 (1977): 62–84.

[3] Peter J. Gurney, '"The Sublime of the Bazaar": A Moment in the Making of a Consumer Culture in Mid-Nineteenth Century England', *Journal of Social History*, 40/2 (2006): 385–405. The Anti-Corn League campaigned against the Corn Laws which imposed duties on imports of foreign wheat. It argued that they favoured landowners at the expense of industrialists and working people and kept the price of basic foodstuffs unnecessarily high.

Mid Nineteenth-Century Consumption and Retailing

Six years after the Anti-Corn Law League Bazaar even greater crowds flocked to London for the Great Exhibition at the Crystal Palace in Hyde Park. An estimated 500,000 people assembled in the Park on 1 May 1851 to watch the aeronaut Charles Spencer ascend in a balloon prior to the opening of the Exhibition. At least 25,000 people visited on opening day and by the time it closed in October it was thought that around one in five Britons had been there at least once. The initial high admission charge of one pound was reduced after the first 10 days and then further reduced after 24 May to one shilling on Mondays to Thursdays. Once inside there were strict rules: no smoking, no alcohol and no dogs. On display were many of the wonders of British manufacturing, a huge range of consumer goods, exotic items from all over the world and a medieval court largely designed by Pugin and featuring many ecclesiastical items as well as his great chandelier from Alton Towers. Henry Cole had been the driving force behind the Exhibition which he effectively regarded as a key part of his crusade to improve the taste of the British public by emphasizing the importance of good and honest design. Like Pugin, he was strongly critical of objects that pretended to be what they were not, whether pine made to look like mahogany or a tin bath painted to look like marble. The Exhibition was a huge celebration of British manufacturing prowess and the benefits of free trade, but there were also lessons to be learnt from it.[4]

The 100,000 exhibits in the Crystal Palace could hardly fail to leave the visitor both awed and bewildered by the sheer number and variety of material objects that were now available for purchase. What you should purchase not only depended on price, but also had moral implications. Pugin, Cole and others despised what they regarded as deceitful goods because they believed that they made other forms of deceit acceptable.[5] By contrast, honest goods could help promote a virtuous and honest lifestyle. Cole believed that there were absolute and fixed canons of taste which could be learnt and which, if practised, would elevate character.[6] Later in the century the Reverend W.J. Loftie published *A Plea for Art in the House* which argued that the cultivation of taste was a moral and religious duty. Appropriate consumption could make people good.[7] It could also help to promote good health and good eating habits among the working classes. This was one of the reasons why local authorities saw it as their duty to promote good quality, properly regulated public markets where wholesome fresh food was available at

---

[4]   A.N. Wilson, *The Victorians* (London: Hutchinson, 2002), pp. 137–43; Rosemary Hill, *God's Architect: Pugin and the Building of Romantic Britain* (London: Allen Lane, 2008), pp. 454, 472; Deborah Cohen, *Household Gods: The British and Their Possessions* (New Haven and London: Yale University Press, 2006), pp. 14–18.

[5]   Cohen, *Household Gods*, p. 18.

[6]   Ibid., pp. 16–19.

[7]   Ibid., pp. 27–8.

reasonable prices.[8] Whether it was Birmingham manufacturers bringing affordable but tasteful jewellery to the rising middle classes; a firm like Liberty making goods with artistic integrity available to a wider public; or the bourgeois values of respectability and certitude being made concrete in the goods displayed and sold in department stores, the Victorian world of goods was imbued with positive values.[9] Christianity and consumption could go hand in hand. It was a long way from the gloomy outlook of an evangelical like Thomas Chalmers in the first half of the century:

> An affection for riches, beyond what Christianity prescribes ... is sure, at length, to visit every country, where it operates with the recoil of all those calamities, which, in the shape of beggared capitalists, and unemployed operatives, and dreary intervals of bankruptcy and alarm, are observed to follow a season of overdone speculation.[10]

The Victorians had not abolished such 'calamities' but they were more at ease than their predecessors with material possessions in excess of what strict Christians might have deemed essential.

It is of course important not to be too dazzled by the splendours of the Great Exhibition or the elegance of London's department stores and overlook the reality of shopping and consuming in villages and working-class districts of industrial towns throughout the nineteenth century. Times could still be very hard. For example, trade depression in the late 1830s and early 1840s had a significant effect on Stockport's small retailers. In 1842 Samuel Walker, a flour, corn and provisions dealer who supplied many small shopkeepers, said that these were now very irregular in their payments and that one who had failed a fortnight previously owed £128. Families who used to buy flour now only bought oatmeal. Mr Meakin, a furniture broker, said that poor people were now trying to sell him their knives, forks, old iron, Bibles and religious books as they had already disposed of their tables and chairs. Shop rents in Chestergate were said to have fallen by about one-third.[11] In Birkenhead, trade depression hit in the late 1840s when it was said that houses were left unfinished, businesses failed and the former boom town became

---

8   Schmiechen and Carls, *The British Market Hall*, pp. 134–5.

9   Francesca Carnevali, 'Luxury for the Masses: Jewellery and Jewellers in London and Birmingham in the 19th Century', *Enterprises et Histoires*, 46 (2007): 56–70; Sonia Ashmore, 'Liberty and Lifestyle: Shopping for Art and Luxury in Nineteenth-Century London', in Hussey and Ponsonby (eds), *Buying for the Home*, pp. 73–90; Grant McCracken, *Culture and Consumption*, pp. 26–7.

10   Thomas Chalmers, *Discourses on the Application of Christianity to the Commercial and Ordinary Affairs of Life* (Edinburgh: Sutherland and Knox, 1848), pp. vi–vii.

11   BPP, *A Copy of the Evidence Taken, and Report Made, by the Assistant Poor Law Commissioners Sent to Inquire into the State of the Population in Stockport*, 1842, vol. XXXV (158), pp. 26–9.

the 'city of the dead'.[12] Little changed in the world of the village shop. They continued to stock groceries, some plain articles of drapery and basic household goods. Intending shopkeepers were advised against stocking fancy articles that soon became out of date and were recommended to sell for small and sure profits.[13]

Nevertheless the longer-term trends of rising real incomes at most levels of society, the continuing growth of middle-class consumption, the importation of cheap food and the beginnings of mass production in shoes and clothing had important implications for the structure of retailing from the middle of the nineteenth century onwards.[14] These structural changes tended to reinforce the changes in consumer attitudes and behaviour discussed above and these in turn helped promote change. The origins of department stores, almost always in the drapery and associated trades, have been discussed in Chapter 7 and the transformation of urban markets through the construction of market halls in Chapter 8. There were some cooperative stores in the second quarter of the nineteenth century but it was in the post 1850 period that the movement really took off. They focused on the sale of basic goods at moderate prices and had their heartland in the north and Scotland. The English Cooperative Wholesale Society was founded in 1863 and a factory supplying shops with biscuits, sweets and similar items was opened in 1873.[15] There was nothing unusual about an early nineteenth-century retailer opening a branch shop in a neighbouring town, but firms operating 10 or more branches were again essentially a feature of the second half of the century. W.H. Smith, J. Menzies and the Singer Manufacturing Company were among the earliest companies to build up chains of shops, while in the grocery trades Walton, Hassell and Port of London had 30 branches by 1870 and in Liverpool James Pegram pioneered this sort of trading. Early growth of multiples was largely in the footwear, grocery, meat and household goods trades with clothing and chemists goods following later in the century.[16] Important as these structural changes were, independent retailers still accounted for up to 90 per cent of total sales.[17]

The beginnings of mass production, the growing importance of wholesaling and the development of branding also had implications for retailers. Manufacturing and processing skills became less important as in some cases did detailed knowledge of the product they were selling. Instead they needed to focus on marketing, display and good stock and cash management. A reputation for fair dealing remained crucial. Their political influence was also growing following the 1832 Reform Act which led to shopkeepers becoming the largest recognizable

---

[12] Agnes McCulloch, *The Headland with the Birches: A History of Birkenhead* (Birkenhead: Countywise, 1991), p. 42.
[13] H. UU, *Hints for Country Shopkeepers* (Moulton, 1847).
[14] Jefferys, *Retail Trading*, pp. 7–8.
[15] Ibid., pp. 16–18.
[16] Ibid., pp. 21–5; on the grocery trades, p. 136.
[17] Ibid., p. 29.

group of voters in many towns.[18] In Manchester, 18 of the 60 councillors elected in 1838 were retailers and all the Chartists on Leeds Council were small traders or shopkeepers.[19] They tended to favour cheap government and low taxation and were reluctant to support measures to improve public health. Their support for free trade was tempered by a desire to protect their own interests against pawnbrokers, street traders and fairs. Thus they opposed state restriction on their ability to make profits rather than state restrictions as such.[20] It is not entirely fanciful to see a degree of continuity here from the influence exercised by eighteenth-century retailers through craft guilds and their role on unreformed corporations.

Some of these broader changes in the structure of retailing in the nineteenth century had implications for consumer choice. There was nothing new in middling and upper rank consumers buying similar goods from more than one retailer, presumably making decisions based on price, quality or the precise nature of the goods on offer (see Chapter 5, pp. 109–10). Improved communications and the increased number of retail outlets meant that many more people could make such choices by the middle of the nineteenth century. Shopkeepers and others were aware of this and retailers knew that they had to be proactive in attracting customers. There were particular issues with regard to village shops which were generally regarded as being more expensive than those in market towns. It was said in the 1840s that village shops were between 10 and 25 per cent dearer than town ones yet sold inferior goods and that families in south-east England chose to travel six to eight miles rather than buy in their village. One employer from near Maidstone reported that when he began paying his workers at nine o'clock in the morning on Saturdays instead of seven o'clock in the evening they all deserted the village shops for the better and cheaper ones of Maidstone.[21]

In northern England the choice might be between a smaller or larger industrial town. It was claimed in 1840 that some Stockport inhabitants went weekly, or even daily, to Manchester to shop because they believed that items ranging from bread and potatoes to haberdashery were cheaper and better there. A local journal protested that, except in a very few cases, Manchester's retailers could not possibly be cheaper than Stockport's given that their rents and taxes were much higher, and maintained that some items of drapery were one-fifth cheaper in the smaller town. It called on the town's inhabitants to support their local traders, 'who take the lead in every project for your benefit – who are the safeguard of public security and peace – the framer and supporter of your public schools, and places of worship'.[22] When Birkenhead's new market opened in 1845 a letter in the

---

18   Winstanley, *Shopkeeper's World*, p. 19.

19   Ibid., p. 27.

20   Ibid., pp. 25–30.

21   BPP, *Reports of Special Assistant Poor Law Commissioners on the Employment of Women and Children in Agriculture*, 1843, vol. XII, [510], p. 1 (pp. 140–2 of Report).

22   *Stockport Monthly Magazine and Commercial Advertiser*, No. 8, December 1840, pp. 169–71.

Liverpool Mercury advised traders there not to charge too high prices and be left with unsold stock because their customers had been supplied from Liverpool. He noted that strawberries were priced at one shilling a quart in Birkenhead but only eight pence in Liverpool. He continued, 'Do not charge us for wet days when we cannot conveniently cross the water; nor even when you know your then customer might have done so; convince him, or her, or them, it is lost time and trouble, by proving you can serve them as well as Liverpool'.[23] Birkenhead shopkeepers were well aware of the attractions of Liverpool and frequently advertised that their prices were the same as or lower than there. A century earlier some enterprising provincial shopkeeper might have advertised that their prices were lower than those in London. Relatively few people, however, had a real choice between shopping locally or in London. By the mid nineteenth century taking a ferry across the Mersey to save money was within reach of very many people. Working-class shoppers were skilled at using different types of outlet for different purchases and at knowing the best time to shop to get the best price.[24]

Consumers and Consuming

This does not of course mean that it would be anything other than anachronistic to speak of consumer power or a consumer movement in the first half of the nineteenth century. As Frank Trentmann has argued 'consumers' were virtually absent from eighteenth-century discourse even though a great deal of consuming was going on. In nineteenth-century England consumers who regarded themselves as such emerged from specific contexts, most notably conflicts over the availability and price of water in London.[25] Water Consumers Defence Leagues sprang up all over London in the 1880s as water rates increased while the price of food and gas fell. These consumer organizations were effectively the voice of male ratepayers and landlords rather than of shoppers.[26] The popular politics of free trade helped to establish the consumer as a person with a social conscience, actively involved in politics and society and far removed from the flâneur exploring, but never fulfilling, infinite desires.[27]

---

[23]   *Liverpool Mercury*, 18 July 1845.

[24]   Hodson, 'Civic Identity, Custom and Commerce', p. 41.

[25]   Frank Trentmann, 'The Modern Genealogy of the Consumer', in Brewer and Trentmann (eds), *Consuming Cultures, Global Perspectives*, pp. 19–69.

[26]   Frank Trentmann and Vanessa Taylor, 'From Users to Consumers: Water Politics in Nineteenth-Century London', in Frank Trentmann (ed.), *The Making of the Consumer: Knowledge, Power and Identity in the Modern World* (Oxford: Berg, 2006), pp. 53–79.

[27]   Frank Trentmann, 'The Evolution of the Consumer', in Sheldon Garon and Patricia L. Maclachan (eds), *The Ambivalent Consumer: Questioning Consumption in East Asia and the West* (Ithaca and London: Cornell University Press, 2006), pp. 21–44.

Using (or not using) material goods to express a social conscience was not entirely new in the nineteenth century as is demonstrated by the late eighteenth-century sugar boycott as a way of protesting the slave trade. Christian socialism, coupled with the renewed theological emphasis on the humanity of Christ and the need for his followers actively to pursue a social justice agenda, did, however, make its mark on the world of retailing in the last third of the nineteenth century. The Anglican clergyman and Oxford don Wilfrid Richmond was keen that those who participated in the market economy should be fully aware of the consequences of their actions. He argued that the prices consumers paid for goods should afford fair wages to those whose labour produced them. Consumers had an obligation to find out whether this was the case. He had this to say about shopping:

> Supposing that I leave the wilds of Glenalmond, and come up for a day's shopping in Edinburgh, or pay a visit to London. With a pardonable desire to make the most of my resources, I make for the cheapest shops. But if I do so, what has conscience to say? Suppose I am buying furniture. I do not know what happens in Edinburgh, but I know of a part of London where men live who are employed by one of the great dealers in furniture, where, under pressure, men are employed to work twenty-four hours on end; and I suppose every one knows that overwork and underpay are regular incidents in the production of cheap wares.[28]

In his lectures on *Economic Morals* he made the same point even more directly: 'There is no good the public complaining of sweating and low wages as long as they like low prices'. He suggested that some consumers should agree together only to deal with those shops whose prices would pay fair wages to the workers in the industry in question.[29] The Christian Social Union of which Richmond was a founder member along with Henry Scott Holland attempted to put some of these principles into practice. There was at least the germ of an idea that consumers might be a force to be reckoned with.

The subsequent history of consumer movements lies well outside the scope of this book, but it is appropriate to reflect briefly on consumerism as a fundamental component of modernity. Matthew Hilton has argued that the so-called consumer society of the eighteenth century was essentially about *access* to goods: more things were available to more people for more of the time. Modern consumerism, however, has been perceived as being about *individual choice* and this has been reflected in the activities of the consumer movement. Issues of access and basic needs have risked being neglected.[30] Modern liberal society assumes that autonomous individuals are able to exercise free and rational choices through the hidden mechanisms of market exchange. Add to this a wider range of available

---

[28]   Wilfrid Richmond, *Christian Economics* (London, 1888), p. 217.
[29]   Wilfrid Richmond, *Economic Morals: Four Lectures* (London, 1890), p. 57.
[30]   Matthew Hilton, 'The Death of a Consumer Society', *Transactions of the Royal Historical Society*, 18 (2008): 211–36.

goods, more and easier ways of purchasing them and an acceptance that affluence is a proper goal of life and the elements of a consumer society are in place. The realization that the anticipation of purchase or ownership of an item is often more satisfying than the ownership itself means that the drive to consume becomes self-perpetuating no matter what standard of living is reached. In due course the possession, display and use of material goods becomes the principal means through which individuals both create and express who they are, their place in society and their aspirations: a lifestyle captured in Barbara Kruger's iconic 'I Shop therefore I am' poster. At the same time, and as other narratives like religion or politics lose some their power, aspects of life that have traditionally fallen outside the remit of market exchange or consumerist desires become subject to these. For example, religion with its sense of the given, becomes 'spirituality' with the implication that the freely choosing individual can create their own mix of spiritual beliefs and practice from the marketplace of the world's religions and new religious movements. In late modernity (or post-modernity for those who see a significant cultural break in the last decades) consumerism has become the controlling narrative into which all else has been subsumed.

It is possible to celebrate this as facilitating human creativity and freeing individuals from the dead hand of the past. There is a playfulness about the best of consumerism that can uplift the human spirit. There is also considerable skill involved in negotiating all the manipulative pressures of consumerism and emerging as an autonomous but connected individual. Those who succeed create a fulfilling lifestyle for themselves. Other commentators focus on the darker side of consumerism. They might argue that consumerism is destructive of culture and indeed that the phrase consumer culture is an oxymoron. This is because consumerism tends to produce anarchy and alienation and relativizes all values. Humans need some generally agreed values in order to build stable societies: contemporary consumerism destabilizes everything. It also makes individuals more self-obsessed than they might otherwise be. Other critics might focus on the illusory nature of the freedoms that consumer society claims to offer, arguing that most individuals are in fact manipulated by those who control the media and multinational corporate bodies. They might also bring questions of access back into the picture and emphasize the importance of not losing sight of basic needs.[31] Those on both sides of the argument would, however, tend to agree that the many of origins of modern consumerism are to be found in the changes in beliefs, attitudes and practices described in this book. These include the rationality associated with enlightenment thought; the acceptance of the power of markets associated with Adam Smith and his followers; the massive growth in the availability of and access

---

[31]   Slater, *Consumer Culture and Modernity*, provides a useful discussion of the arguments, albeit from a perspective of suspicion about consumerism. Zygmunt Bauman, *Consuming Life* (Cambridge: Polity Press, 2007) offers a thought-provoking account.

to commodities; and the increased use of commodities to express distinction and position in society.[32]

Conclusions

This does not mean that the progression to modernity was linear or unbroken. Instead it was fractured and fragmented, with numerous false starts, some reverses and many opportunities for exploring byways en route. Indeed the story being told here is less like a Victorian novel with a clear beginning, middle and end than a modernist work with multiple layers of narrative, time shifts and indeterminacy inviting the reader to make their own contribution. Among those whose story has been told or suggested were the street traders, the status conscious members of craft guilds or trade societies, the pushy forward-looking shopkeepers, the fashion conscious man or woman, the collector, the moralizing commentator, the public servant, the hungry industrial worker, the corner shop owner and the stallholder in market, fair or bazaar. The cumulative impact of these stories has been, however, to chart the sort of changes that brought retailing in England to the cusp of the recognizably modern retail world of the second half of the nineteenth century.

Some general conclusions can be drawn from this survey. First, although there is always something arbitrary about any choice of starting and end dates for a study like this one, chronology matters and some dates are more arbitrary than others. The period chosen for this book (1700 to 1850) saw major changes in the economy, society and political and intellectual life of England. It was not to be expected that either retailing or consumer behaviour would be unaffected by these changes. In general, shops were bigger, bolder and more sophisticated at the end of the period than at the beginning and there were many more of them. Markets, particularly in industrial towns, were very different in how they were controlled and, very often, how they looked and where they were located. Shoppers were more confident, had many more goods to choose from and a wider range of retail outlets in which to browse and purchase. Shopping and leisure were intertwined in a way that was not generally the case in 1700. It matters whether a particular example of shopkeeper or consumer behaviour was set in, say, 1720 or 1820. What was exceptional and interesting at one date might be normal practice at another. The choice of 1850 as the end date was not arbitrary. Historians of the long eighteenth century have often concluded their studies in 1820 or possibly 1830. Studies of 'modern' retailing have tended to start in 1850. The intervening years were important with some radical changes to retailing even if the general picture was one of more of the same, particularly with regard to small general shops. Innovation in these decades hinted at the major changes that would take place after 1850 such as the growth

---

[32] For a stimulating and provocative account of modernity see Jerrold Seigel, *Modernity and Bourgeois Life: Society, Politics, and Culture in England, France, and Germany since 1750* (Cambridge: Cambridge University Press, 2012).

of multiple shops and department stores. Going beyond 1850 would have meant exploring the very different world of late Victorian retailing; stopping at 1820 would have precluded the discussion of bazaars, early department type stores and market halls.

Secondly, the dual focus on retailing and on consumption has avoided the sort of artificial separation that can produce shopkeepers who have no need to take account of shoppers or consumers who never engage in the actual business of making purchases. It has also made possible some engagement with the changing world of attitudes and beliefs that to some extent informed customer behaviour. Eighteenth- and early nineteenth-century shoppers are elusive, particularly those below the ranks of the gentry or articulate middle classes. Even when it is hard to document their behaviour it is necessary to keep on recalling that without the activity of shoppers making innumerable individual choices there would be no history to be written here.

Thirdly, the slight shift of gaze from the fashionable and modern to the traditional and ordinary has made explicit what ought to be obvious: that most retail transactions were about basic needs rather than about showing off. Again these are the transactions that are most difficult to document. There is plenty of evidence, for example, about the building of new markets, about their regulation and about the legal disputes that dogged many eighteenth-century urban markets, but much less about the interaction between buyer and seller except when scarcity threatened to disrupt the normal operation of the market. There can be little doubt, however, that markets not only remained important throughout the period covered here but that in many northern and midland towns experienced a renaissance in the early nineteenth century. By the third quarter of the century they were providing working-class shoppers with a much wider range of goods than they had done a century earlier, including significant non-food items. There is a wealth of material about Victorian markets in local authority archives that needs to be exploited to provide a better understanding of working-class consumption in the second half of the century.

Fourthly, the variety of retail types and of consumer behaviour throughout the period suggests that scholars should be very wary of trying to reduce these to any simple explanatory model of retail change. Similarly it would dangerous to try to sum up the eighteenth century and early nineteenth in a single phrase. The long eighteenth century was religious and secular; hierarchical and democratic; polite and vulgar. It all depended on particular context and particular perspective. One implication of this is that models derived from the social sciences, and especially those derived from cultural theory, need to be used with extreme caution. People have always behaved in unexpected ways and reality is almost always more complex than theory allows. Where possible it is important to listen to the voices of those involved in buying and selling and to let a myriad of different and sometimes competing stories emerge. The result may be something of a *bricolage* rather than a tidy pattern but if so it is probably more true to the reality that the historian is trying to capture.

Finally, however, this does not absolve the author from suggesting a broad framework for the development of English provincial retailing between 1700 and 1850. The fundamental argument of this book is that eighteenth-century retailing combined both traditional and modern features. Markets remained important as did itinerant traders, but were capable of adaptation to changes in the wider economy and society. Some shops changed little while others embraced new methods of attracting and dealing with customers such as advertising, window displays and ready money, fixed price sales. None operated in an unchanging world. In particular, changing attitudes to material possessions, the greater availability of new consumer goods, and the way in which objects were acquired, combined and used to create and display a lifestyle impacted significantly on retailing. So did the rapid growth of urban populations from the late eighteenth century onwards. All of this meant that the structure of retailing would eventually have to undergo significant change. The first signs of this were apparent in the decades following the Napoleonic Wars with the emergence of larger shops, the greater separation of retailing and production functions and the growing importance of retail skills. There was also more radical innovation, particularly in the use of retail space, in the organization of the largest shops which were displaying some features of department stores, and in the building of large covered market halls. Alongside this, more traditional types of shop increased in numbers. By 1850 English retailing was on the point of undergoing the sort of major change that could be described as a retail revolution. Shopping was part of everybody's story and this book offers an account of how that came to be and what it meant.

Appendix
Browns of Chester

When the social research organization Mass Observation talked to people in Chester in 1945 about their perceptions of the department store Browns one long-standing customer looked back to the days when the store had been an exclusive meeting place and complained, 'nowadays you meet the people from the back streets there'. One woman from the back streets said, 'I never go to Browns, I leave that to the toffs. People that's got the money to spend'. Others, however, commented on the helpfulness of the assistants and the reasonableness of the prices in the shop.[1] At the time that Mass Observation was interviewing people Browns had been in existence in the heart of Chester for over a century and a half. It liked to present itself both as part of Chester's heritage and as the finest shop outside London: the Harrods of the North. The fashion designer Lady Duff Gordon visited in 1924 and was ecstatic: 'I have never seen a shop as good as this anywhere in England! It is wonderful! I have been all over London, and there is not one single shop with such beautiful things as you have here. And so cheap. If you are not well dressed it is no one's fault but your own'.[2] Its reputation for exclusivity could, however, be damaging to its future and its management recognized the need attract a wider range of customers. One of the senior assistants said to a Mass Observation researcher, 'Browns is such an unusual place – all nooks and corners, and I think that is part of its charm. Where will you find a big modern shop with an atmosphere and quaintness like Browns?'[3] Yet the pavement level entrance seemed uninviting; once potential customers got inside they found that departments were not well signposted; and, while not expensive, neither was there anything really cheap there.[4] Perhaps it was necessary to go back to the beginnings.

The origins of a shop like Browns can be hard to untangle and are often enshrouded in some degree of myth. A safe starting point is the millinery and haberdashery shop run by Elizabeth and Susannah Towsey at the corner of Eastgate Street and Bridge Street Rows and which was in existence by 1781 at the latest. They advertised their return from London in the spring of that year with 'a new and fashionable assortment' of millinery and haberdashery goods. The

[1] H.D. Willcock (ed.), *Browns and Chester: Portrait of a Shop 1780–1946* (London: Lindsay Drummond for Mass-Observation, 1947), pp. 216–17.

[2] University of Sussex, Special Collections, Mass Observation Archive, Browns of Chester, SxMOA2/24/2C, Extract from *Chester Chronicle*, 12 April 1924.

[3] Ibid., 3A, General Description of Browns, 12 December 1943.

[4] Ibid.

advertisement used conventionally polite language: the Towseys returned 'their most grateful thanks to their Friends for the favours conferred' since they started in business. They also wanted an apprentice or two.[5] Elizabeth and Susannah were the daughters of Thomas Towsey, a feltmaker, and sisters to John a hatter and hosier who kept a shop in Northgate Street. John was declared bankrupt in 1790 and died soon afterwards, with his widow, another Elizabeth, carrying on the business. Susannah's elder sister Elizabeth died in 1786 and in 1788 Susannah married John Brown, a druggist and member of a Chester producer-retailer family with a background in shoemaking.[6] Following these events the millinery business continued under the name of S. Brown. It is not clear how far Susannah's husband John involved himself in the business. He was listed as a linen draper in Holden's 1809–11 directory and styled himself as a mercer and haberdasher in his will dated 19 May 1810. This referred to the business managed by his wife and son and directed that his son William be admitted as a partner in the business alongside Susannah. Brown was a rich man at his death in October 1810 with a personal estate not exceeding, but presumably close to, £12,500.[7]

The Towsey sisters' original shop was located in the best position in Chester, right at the heart of the city and at Row level. When the business moved in 1791 Susannah Brown made sure that customers knew whose business was whose, announcing, 'That her friends and the public may not be misled by the place she lately left appearing to be occupied in the same line [she] wishes to inform them, she is removed to a commodious shop in Eastgate Street-row (late Mr Brassey's) …'.[8] Although there have been subsequent moves and expansions, Browns has always retained a prime location in Chester's shopping district. In its early days it was also notable for being run by women. This was not unusual in the millinery and haberdashery business, but Susannah seems to have been a formidable character who retained her independence as a businesswoman after her marriage into the Brown family. While still in partnership with her sister, she had given detailed instructions to an assistant who went on a buying trip to London in 1782. The assistant was to pay bills, look at items like gloves and ribbons and on occasion complain about previous orders. She must have had a busy time calling at 12 different addresses in the Cheapside and Moorgate area.[9] By 1784 the sisters

---

[5]   Willcock, *Browns and Chester*, p. 14.

[6]   NA, Exchequer, Depositions taken by Commission, E134/33Geo3/Mich14 and Hil8. Elizabeth's death seems a more likely explanation for the changes to the business than the suggestion in Willcock (p. 17) that after her sister's marriage she went to help run her father's business.

[7]   CALS, Will of John Brown of Chester, 1811, WS Series.

[8]   *Chester Chronicle*, 14 October 1791, transcript in Mass Observation Archive, MOA2/24/2E.

[9]   Willcock, *Browns and Chester*, pp. 24–5.

were calling themselves milliners, haberdashers and glovers and in the early 1800s Susannah Brown added mercer and hosier to the description.[10]

There are no surviving business records for this period, although an occasional bill can be found among household accounts. For example, in 1801 Susannah sold 8 yards of muslin for a gown to G. Boscowen of Trevalyn Hall (Figure A.1).[11]

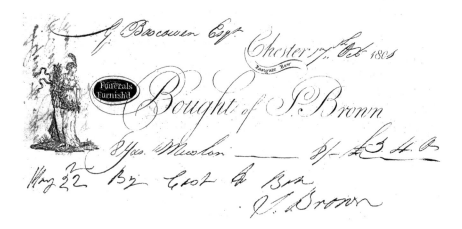

Figure A.1   S. Brown, Chester, bill, 1801

Source: Flintshire Record Office, Trevalyn Hall Manuscripts, Vouchers, D/TR/49. Reproduced by permission of the Record Office.

A typical advertisement was that for April 1802:

> S. Brown, Milliner, Haberdasher, and Glover, Eastgate-Street-Row Respectfully informs her friends, that she.has received a most extensive variety of FASHIONABLE ARTICLES, for the spring trade; and on Tuesday next she purposes having ready for their inspection, a variety of elegant Millinery, selected by her Fore-woman (now in Town) from houses of the first fashion and consequence, all of which she trusts will be found worthy their attention, and secure to her a continuance of their favours, the most grateful sense of which will ever be retained by their obliged humble servant, S. Brown.[12]

A similar advertisement the following year added, 'As in the very extensive number of Mrs Brown's friends, accidental omissions in sending out cards have happened, and offence been taken, she purposes in future, to address them through

---

10   *Adam's Weekly Courant*, 26 April 1784; *Chester Courant*, 15 October 1805.
11   Flintshire Record Office, Trevalyn Hall Mss, Vouchers, 1773–1839, D/TR/49.
12   *Chester Chronicle*, 13 April 1802.

the medium of the newspaper only'.[13] The suggestion of a very large business, whether or not entirely true, must have been a good advertising ploy. The language of all of these advertisements expresses both a recognition that a female milliner and haberdasher was not on equal terms with the local gentry; but could nevertheless play a part in ensuring that they maintained the standards appropriate to fashionable and polite society.

Susannah died in 1812 and her son William took sole charge of the business. Her sister-in-law Elizabeth had continued to trade as a hatter and hosier, regularly advertising supplies of new hats from London and that she supplied rennet skins to farmers for cheese making.[14] William called himself a mercer, draper and haberdasher in his 1814 advertisement for the autumn fashions and was selling a wide range of cloths as well as furs, shawls and other accessories.[15] His brother Henry joined the business in 1819 but there is no evidence that his sister Eliza was involved with the shop. Decades of female management gave way to a very male-dominated business. The other sibling, John, was an auctioneer trading in Northgate Street but it is unclear whether there was any connection between the two businesses.[16] Expansion of the business through property purchases was the keynote of the 1810s and 1820s. In 1814 William bought the shop, vault and cellars next door to his existing premises for £1,680 from a bankrupt draper Thomas Steele. Thirteen years later the Brown brothers purchased two more shops in Eastgate Street for £2,100 together with the cellars occupied by butchers. In 1828 they built an entirely new shop in the neoclassical style next door to Bolland's, one of Chester's leading confectioners.[17]

The business itself got bigger but did not greatly change its character. Supplying mourning wear and making arrangements for funerals were often part of a draper's business and Browns were no exceptions. In 1824 they arranged the funeral of one Matthew Travis, charging £71 19s 11d for mourning wear together with £43 4s 8d for other disbursements, including £20 for the coffin made by a Mr Gardner and 13s 6d for funeral biscuits from the confectioner Thomas Gibbons. The account was due at six months with a discount of 2½ per cent offered for ready money.[18] Like other retailers they suffered from a minority of customers who had no intention of settling their bills. A Miss Haymes was billed £9 17s 7d for goods in 1823 and by 1827 had incurred nine shillings interest. The 1827 reminder was annotated, 'Messrs William and Henry Brown cannot help expressing their extreme surprise at Miss Haymes' conduct respecting the above account. Her being a perfect stranger to them and the goods having been sent entirely on account of her connection

[13]   *Chester Chronicle*, 7 November 1806, transcript in MOA2/24/2E.

[14]   MOA2/24/2E.

[15]   *Chester Courant*, 14 November 1814.

[16]   John Brown is listed in Pigot's 1828 Directory. A ledger covering 1827–32 in the Browns archive contains entries for goods appraised and auctioned (CALS, ZCR 658/1).

[17]   Willcock, *Browns and Chester*, pp. 36, 40; MOA2/24/A1.

[18]   CALS, Browns of Chester, Vouchers, 1824, ZCR 658/4/2, 10, 11.

with so respectable …'. The note was not finished and the bill apparently never sent.[19] Keeping a careful eye on outstanding bills was a vital part of managing a growing retail business; in the 1840s around 60 per cent of their 'good debts' had been settled at 6 months and around 80 per cent at 12 months but with up to 5 per cent still outstanding after two years.[20] There were some changes in where goods were purchased after 1840. As well as buying in London, Henry travelled to Paris for the spring fashions in 1841 and subsequent years. Both brothers were involved in the public life of Chester being members of the Council and serving as Mayor, while William played a major role in bringing the railway to Chester.[21] Browns the store and Browns the family were becoming Chester institutions.

The transition from large mercer's and draper's shop to department store took place in the 1850s and 1860s. Both William and Henry died without children and the business passed to their nephews William and Charles, the sons of their auctioneer brother John, in 1853. The shop premises were valued at £6,500 the following year and further property was bought in 1856 for £3,400 prior to a rebuilding in the Gothic style. The new owners seem to have had big ideas, perhaps making use of some of the skills and contacts built up in their father's business in order to branch out. Browns began to supply ships, hotels and some individual overseas customers, occasionally acting as a sort of agent. For example, they received an order in 1853 for counterpanes, blankets, sheets, pillow cases, towels and mattresses for the ship *Amelia*. Two years later a Mr Ryder in Melbourne, Australia ordered wines, spirits, and groceries: Browns' role here was to organize the purchase of these goods and their despatch. In 1856 Mrs Frederick Whittall ordered skirts, a mantle, a straw hat, gloves and other items to be sent to her in Smyrna; in the following year shirts were sent overland to George Urmson in Hong Kong; and in 1859 Mrs Gubbins requested that silk for a lady's evening dress be packed very carefully in tin and wood and sent to her in India.[22]

The range of goods sold at home was also expanding to include table linen, blankets and curtains. Furniture was added in the 1860s with some being made in the firm's own workshops and some imported from Paris. William and Charles increasingly selected their fashions in Paris rather than London. Like their uncles they were heavily committed to the civic life of Chester and in 1868 brought in an outsider, John Goodie Holmes, as a partner. Holmes invested £1,500 and was to receive one-sixteenth of the profits. In 1869 the firm was appointed silk mercers to the Princess of Wales. By 1874 Holmes had a quarter share of the business and in 1875 the shop's name was changed to Brown, Holmes and Co. Annual takings by then were between £30,000 and £40,000 with annual profits of around £3,000.

---

[19] MOA2/24/2F.

[20] CALS, Browns of Chester, Monthly Sales Figures 1868–91 (at front of volume), ZCR 658/3.

[21] Willcock, *Browns and Chester*, pp. 44–50.

[22] CALS, Browns of Chester, Estimates and Orders, 1853–1910, ZCR 658/2.

The 1870s also saw regular annual sales.[23] Sales figures for 1868–69 reveal that the busiest months were May, October and November, no doubt still reflecting the importance of spring and autumn/winter fashions. August and the winter months from December to January were quietest. Business excluding furniture was categorized under some 20 headings, of which silks, mantles and woven dresses were the most lucrative. Shirts, jewellery, furs and umbrellas contributed least to takings.[24] By the last quarter of the nineteenth century Chester had a department store to rival any outside London.

There was, however, always something different about Browns, and that difference could be unsettling. Describing some of the shops in Chester in 1831, Joseph Hemingway made particular mention of the establishment of Messrs William and Henry Brown, silk mercers and milliners which had lately been built and was, in his eyes, equal to the shops in Regent Street.[25] He described it as:

> Stuccoed in imitation of stone, standing on huge massive pillars, projecting into the street, the roof towering above its more humble neighbours; this demi-palace being adjoined in the street on one side by a small *chandler's* and on the other, a *butcher's shop*. The association of ideas created by a view of these disparities, suggests the picture of a brace of country clowns, in tattered habilements, linked under each arm of a *dashing exquisite* of the nineteenth century – or, if the hyperbole be too strong, of a splendid family mansion flanked by a couple of mud wall cow-houses.[26]

Browns was the exception rather than the rule even in a polite and fashionable place like Chester. Some 25 years later Thomas Hughes in his *Stranger's Handbook to Chester* also provided brief descriptions of some of the shops in Eastgate Street. He mentioned in particular Platt and Son, chemists, Messrs McLellan, drapers and Bolland's the confectioners, but not Browns.[27] Were there some politics involved here, given that the Brown brothers were staunch liberals; or did the architecture of the shop displease a writer who preferred the half-timbered style that the Victorians made the hallmark of Chester? Whatever the reason, it is a strange omission in view of the leading role the Brown brothers played in Chester's economic and political life in the 1850s.

There were also those who thought the Browns were too influential in late Victorian Chester and when Mass Observation conducted their research on Browns in the 1930s and 1940s they were surprised at the strength of the tradition

---

[23]   Willcock, *Browns and Chester*, pp. 83–115; MOA 24/2/1G, 2A.

[24]   CALS, Browns of Chester, Monthly Sales Figures, 1868–91, ZCR 658/3.

[25]   Joseph Hemingway, *History of the City of Chester, from Its Foundation to the Present Time* (2 vols, Chester, 1831), vol. 1, p. 388.

[26]   Ibid., p. 410.

[27]   Thomas Hughes, *The Stranger's Handbook to Chester and Its Environs* (Chester: T. Catherall, 1856), pp. 46–9.

associated with the shop and the fact that this did not always operate in the shop's favour. The shop was perceived as powerful in the city and 'a few people closed up like a clam and refused to talk about it'.[28] The researchers also noted that it was difficult to find out much about its history other than by asking members of the firm: the only mention in guide books to the city tended to be of the old crypt.[29] A shop like Browns was more than just a place to buy fashionable items, or even to be seen engaging in shopping as a leisure pursuit. It helped to create and maintain Chester's reputation as a prime shopping location in north-west England. It was part of the way in which Chester presented itself as a city with a proud heritage yet also in the forefront of fashion. Although now part of the Debenhams group it is still 'Browns of Chester', not Debenhams.

---

[28] Willcock, *Browns and Chester*, p. 1.
[29] MOA 2/24/3A.

Bibliography

Manuscript Sources

Barnsley Archives and Local Studies, Barnsley

Barnsley Cordwainers' Society, General Ledger, 1747–1867, A/2065/G/2/1.
William Tomlin, Ledger, 1841–52, 575/B/1.

British Library, London

Ordinary of the Company of Bakers in the city of York, Add. Ms. 34,605.
Original letters, etc., addressed to the Rev. Thomas Frognall Dibdin on the publication of His Bibliomania, 1809–1813, Egerton Ms. 2974.

Cheshire Archives and Local Studies, Chester

Borough of Macclesfield, Assembly Minute Books, 1734–68, 1769–1822, LBM/1/3–4.
Browns of Chester, ZCR 658.
Butt and Company Ltd, Jewellers, Day Book, 1843–57, ZCR 92/31.
Cheshire Quarter Sessions, Sessions Books, QJB.
Cheshire Quarter Sessions, Sessions Files, QJF.
Chester City Council, Lawsuits, Rex v. Daffy and Brereton, 1758, ZCL/118.
Chester Quarter Sessions, Examinations and Depositions, ZQSE.
City of Chester Assembly Books, ZAB.
City of Chester Assembly Files, ZAF.
City of Chester, Mercers, Ironmongers, Grocers and Apothecaries Company, ZG 16.
City of Chester, Painters, Glaziers, Embroiderers and Stationers Company, ZG 17.
City of Chester, Treasurers' Account Books, ZTAB.
Dean and Chapter of Chester, Vouchers to Account, 1810–13, EDD 3/8/7.
Downes Family of Shrigley, Letters, DDS 21/4.
J.P. Earwaker Collection and Manuscripts, ZCR 63.
Leicester-Warren Family of Tabley, Accounts with Mrs Thorley, 1817–26, DLT/D154.
Mayor of Chester, Apprenticeship Registers, ZMAB.
Mayor of Chester, Assize of Bread, 1767–68, ZMBB.
Probate Records, Diocese of Chester, WC and WS Series.
Shakerley Family of Hulme and Somerford, Congleton Tolls, DSS 3991/369.

Sheriffs of Chester, Files, ZSF.
Vernon and Warren Family, Manor of Stockport, DVE 9.

Chetham's Library, Manchester

James Weatherley, Autobiography and Daybook, Mun.A.6.30–30*.
William Ford, Letterbooks, MunA.678–9.

Derby Local Studies Library, Derby

Derby Company of Mercers, Apothecaries, Grocers, Ironmongers, Upholsterers
    and Milliners, Minute Book and Other Records, 1674–1740, Parcel 200/26–30.

Derbyshire Record Office, Matlock

Cathedral Church of All Saints, Derby, Papers relating to the New Market Place,
    D3372/81.
Chandos-Pole Family of Radbourne, Accounts, D5557/10.
Fitzherbert Family of Tissington, Ashbourne Bills, 239/M/F/2436.
Friargate Unitarian Church, Minute Book, 1697–1819, D1312/A1.
Gell of Hopton Hall, D258.
Harpur Crewe Papers, John Lomas, D2375/M87/19.
Heathcote Collection, Chesterfield Court Leet, 1963–1841, D267, Box 20.
Miscellaneous Ashover Documents, Ledger of George Bollington, 1818–37,
    D5435/3.
Wheatcroft of Ashover, D5433.
William Boothby of Ashbourne, Letterbooks, 1676–89, Microfilm, XM 856.
Wright Family of Eyam Hall, D5430.

Flintshire Record Office, Hawarden

Nerquis Hall Manuscripts, D/NH.
Trevalyn Hall Manuscrips, D/TR.

Greater Manchester County Record Office, Manchester

Assheton Family of Middleton, E7.
James Bentley, Day Book, 1798–1828, MISC/258/1.
John Fry of Bristol Bookseller, Correspondence, 1809–22, Gf 091 F8.
John Moss, Diary, 1704–37, MISC/966.
Legh Family of Lyme Hall, E17.
William and Thomas Wood of Didsbury, Ledgers, 1767–1838, M62.

House of Lords Record Office, London

Committee on the Dearness of Provisions, 1765.

Lancashire Archives, Preston

Miscellaneous Documents, DX/1961.
Preston, Miscellaneous, Report on the Proposed Covered Market, 1841, DDPR/138/50.
Probate Records, Diocese of Chester, WC.
Purchased Documents, Advertisement of the Albion Bazaar, DP/282/6.
Quarter Sessions, Petitions, QSP.
Shuttleworth, Dallas and Crombleholme, Solicitors, Manor of Blackburn, DDCM/2/165.

Lichfield Record Office, Lichfield

City of Lichfield Butchers' Company, Minute Book, 1631–1865, D77/4/3.
City of Lichfield, Smiths' Company, Counsel's Opinion, D77/4/6/4.
Diocese of Lichfield, Consistory Court, Cause Papers, Inventories, B/C/5.

National Archives, London

Auditors of the Imprest, Register of Hawkers' Licences, 1697–98, AO 3/370.
Board of Trade, Files of Joint Stock Companies, BT 41.
Chancery, Master Farrer's Exhibits, Say and Pierce Letter Book, C 108/30.
Chancery, Petty Bag Office, Writ Files, C202.
Duchy of Lancaster, Salford Market, DL 9/50/1; DL 41/1149.
Exchequer, Bills and Answers, Cheshire, E 112/1089/117.
Exchequer, Depositions by Commission, E 134/33Geo3, Mich14 and Hil8.
Exchequer, Land and Assessed Taxes, Shop Tax, E 182/96, 166, 448.
Home Office, Domestic Correspondence, George III, HO 42.
Palatinate of Chester, Exchequer Pleadings (Paper), CHES 16.
Palatinate of Chester, Papers in Causes, Bankruptcy, CHES 10.
Pre-Nationalization Railway Companies, Special Collections, RAIL 1157/3/13.
Privy Council, Miscellaneous Unbound Papers, PC 1.
State Papers Domestic, Anne, SP 34/37/101.

Norfolk Record Office, Norwich

Norfolk and Norwich Bazaar, SO 18.

Nottinghamshire Archives, Nottingham

John Wilson of Orston, Shoemaker, Account Book, 1821–35, DD/2001/1.
Mansfield Municipal Borough, Improvement Commissioners Minutes, 1823–33, DC/M/2/1.
Portland Family of Welbeck, DD/P.

Oswestry Town Council, Oswestry

Records relating to Markets and Fairs, A52 – A60, A101, F65.

Sheffield Archives, Sheffield

Arundel Castle Manuscripts, ACM.
Bagshawe Collection, Market and Fairs at Hope and Castleton, Bag C/779/66.

Staffordshire Record Office, Stafford

Borough of Stafford, Market Bye-Laws, 1854, D1323/Q/1/5.
Challinor and Shaw, Solicitors, Hawker's Inventory, 1771–2, D3359/12/1/100.
Cowlishaw and Mountford, Solicitors, Uttoxeter Market, D1504/6/14/1.
Hand, Morgan and Owen, Solicitors, Thomas Dickenson of Worcester Grocer, Account Books and Purchasing Book, D1798/HM/29/2, 5.
John Foden, Ledger, 1820–66, D3161.
Quarter Sessions Files, Q/SB.
Sulyard Family, Edward Sulyard Correspondence, D641/4/J/14/2.
Sutherland-Leveson-Gower Family, Newport Market, D593/T/4/18.

Stockport Local Heritage Library, Stockport

Borough of Stockport, Manorial Tolls Committee, Minute Book, 1851–60, D1814.
Peter Legh of Lyme Hall, Steward's Overseer Accounts, 1727–38, B/JJ/6.
Thomas Claye, Photocopy of Diary, 1803–10.
Warren Papers, HX 181, 182, 229.

Tameside Local Studies and Archives Centre, Ashton-under-Lyne

Stalybridge Market Committee Minutes, 1858–64, CA/STA/119/17.
Stalybridge Police Commissioners Minutes, 1828–33, IC/STA/1.

University of Sussex Library, Brighton

Special Collections, Mass Observation Archive, Browns of Chester, SxMOA2/24.

West Yorkshire Archives Service, Bradford

Brown Muff Archive, 14D96.

West Yorkshire Archives Service, Calderdale (Halifax)

David Binns, Draper of Halifax, Autobiography, 1799–1883 (Transcript), MISC: 379/2.
Halifax New Market Papers, MISC: 111/11

West Yorkshire Archives Service, Leeds

Leeds Bazaar and Shambles Estate, WYL58/13, 14.
Leeds Improvement Act, Markets Committee Minutes, 1848–57, LLC10/1/2.

William Salt Library, Stafford

John Poyser of Yoxall, Account Books, 1777–1804, M603.
Miscellaneous Autograph Letters, S. MS. 478.

Wirral Archives Service, Birkenhead

Birkenhead Improvement Commissioners, Minutes, 1833–59 B/001/1, 2.
Birkenhead Improvement Commissioners, Market Committee Minutes, 1835–51, B/013/1–3.
John Stafford (Macclesfield) Collection, MA/B.

Records in Private Hands

Eaton Estate Office, Eccleston, Grosvenor of Eaton, Eaton Household, List of Tradesmen's Bills from Chester, 1808–17, EV 376.
John Swanwick, Draper of Macclesfield, Invoices, Stock Books and Other Papers.
Lowe's of Chester, Day Books, 1792–5, 1810–11.

Printed Primary Sources

Books and Pamphlets

A Brief State of the Inland or Home Trade of England (London, 1730).
A Second Letter from a Hawker and Pedlar in the Country, to a Member of Parliament at London (London, 1731).
A Vindication of the Shop Tax (London, 1786).

Aikin, John, *A Description of the Country from Thirty to Forty Miles round Manchester* (London: John Stockdale, 1795).

An Alphabetical List of the Names of All the Freemen of the City of Chester who Polled at the General Election ... [in] *1747* (Chester, no date).

An Appeal to the Public on the Subject of Bazaars (London, 1816).

An Essay to Prove that Regarators, Engrossers, Forestallers, Hawkers and Jobbers of Corn, Cattle and Other Marketable Goods, Provisions and Merchandises are Destructive of Trade, Oppressors to the Poor, and a Common Nuisance to the Kingdom in General (London, 1718).

Arbuthnot, J.S., *An Inquiry into the Correlation between the Present Price of Provisions, and the Size of Farms* (London, 1773).

Aston, Joseph, *A Picture of Manchester* (Manchester, 1816).

Bagshaw, Samuel, *History, Gazetteer, and Directory of the County Palatine of Chester* (Sheffield, 1850).

Barbon, Nicholas, *A Discourse of Trade by N.B.M.D.* (London, 1690).

Barfoot, P. and Wilkes, J., *Universal British Directory* (4 vols, London, no date [1792–96]).

Batenham, George, *Panoramic Delineations of the Four Principal Streets of the City of Chester* (Chester: John Fletcher, 1816).

Bibliotheca Ratcliffiana: A Catalogue of the Elegant and Truly Valuable Library of John Ratcliffe, Esq; ... Which Will be Sold by Auction by Mr Christie ... (London, 1776).

Blome, Richard, *Britannia* (London, 1673).

Brontë, Charlotte, *Shirley: A Tale, by Currer Bell* (1849; Oxford World's Classics edn, Oxford: Oxford University Press, 2007).

Broster, Peter, *The Chester Guide* (Chester, 1781). Also edns for 1783, 1787 and 1797.

Chalmers, Thomas, *Discourses on the Application of Christianity to the Commercial and Ordinary Affairs of Life* (Edinburgh: Sutherland and Knox, 1848).

City of Manchester, Proceedings of the Council, November 1854 – November 1855.

Corry, John, *The History of Macclesfield* (London: J. Ferguson, 1817).

Defoe, Daniel, *The Fortunes and Misfortunes of the Famous Moll Flanders* (1721; Oxford World's Classics edn, Oxford: Oxford University Press, 2011).

Defoe, Daniel, *A Tour through the Whole Island of Great Britain* (1724–27; 2 vols, Everyman edn, London: J.M. Dent, 1962).

Defoe, Daniel, *The Complete English Tradesman* (London, 1727).

Dennis, John, *Vice and Luxury Publick Mischiefs: or, Remarks on a Book Intituled, The Fable of the Bees* (London, 1724).

Dibdin, Thomas Frognall, *The Bibliomania or Book Madness*, ed. Peter Danckwerts (1809, Richmond: Tiger of the Stripe, 2007).

Eliot, George, *The Mill on the Floss* (1860; Collins edn, London, 1952).

Elson, George, *The Last of the Climbing Boys: An Autobiography* (London: J. Long, 1900).

Exell, A.W. and Marshall, Norah M. (eds), *Autobiography of Richard Boswell Belcher of Banbury and Blockley, 1898; and, The Riot at Blockley in 1878* (Moreton-in-Marsh: Blockley Antiquarian Society, 1976).

Fawconer, S., *An Essay on Modern Luxury* (London, 1765).

Fiennes, Celia, *The Journeys of Celia Fiennes*, ed. and with an Introduction by Christopher Morris (London: Cresset Press, 1947).

Finney, Samuel, 'Survey of the Parish of Wilmslow', in T.W. Barlow (ed.), *The Cheshire and Lancashire Historical Collector* (2 vols, London: W. Kent & Co., 1853), vol. 1.

Forster, Nathaniel, *An Enquiry into the Causes of the Present High Price of Provisions* (London, 1767).

Girdler, J.S., *Observations on the Pernicious Consequences of Forestalling, Regrating, and Ingrossing* (London, 1800).

Glover, Stephen, *The History and Directory of the Borough of Derby* (Derby: H. Mozley and Sons, 1843).

Grylls, Richard G. (ed.), *A Cornish Shopkeepers's Diary 1843: The Diary of Henry Grylls Thomas, Draper and Grocer of St Just-in-Penwith, Cornwall* (Truro: Dyllansow Truran, 1997).

Hanson, Michael (ed.), *Ducal Estate Management in Georgian Nottinghamshire and Derbyshire: The Diary of William Gould 1783–1788*, Thoroton Society, Record Series, 44 (2006).

Hemingway, Joseph, *History of the City of Chester, from Its Foundation to the Present Time* (2 vols, Chester, 1831).

Herbert, George, *Shoemaker's Window: Recollections of a Midland Town before the Railway Age*, ed. Christiana S. Cheney (Oxford: B.H. Blackwell, 1948).

Hindley, Charles (ed.), *The Life and Adventures of a Cheap Jack by One of the Fraternity* (London: Tinsley Brothers, 1876).

Horner, Craig (ed.), *The Diary of Edmund Harrold, Wigmaker of Manchester, 1712–15* (Aldershot: Ashgate, 2008).

Houghton, J., *A Collection for Improvement of Husbandry and Trade* (London, 1690–1703).

Hughes, Thomas, *The Stranger's Handbook to Chester and Its Environs* (Chester: T. Catherall, 1856).

Jacob, Edward, *The History of the Town and Port of Faversham, in the County of Kent* (London, 1774).

Jones, Erasmus, *Luxury, Pride and Vanity, the Bane of the British Nation* (3rd edn, London, 1736).

Jowitt, Jane, *Memoirs of Jane Jowitt, the Poor Poetess, Aged 74 Years, Written by Herself* (Sheffield, 1844).

Law, William, *A Serious Call to a Devout and Holy Life*, in Janet Louth (ed.), *William Law, Selected Writings* (Manchester: Carcanet, 1990).

Mandeville, Bernard, *The Fable of the Bees*, ed. Philip Harth (Harmondsworth: Penguin, 1970).

Memoirs of the Late Thomas Holcroft Written by Himself, and Continued to the Time of His Death from His Diary, Notes, and Other Papers (3 vols, London, 1816).

Nightingale, Joseph, *The Bazaar, Its Origin, Nature, and Objects Explained, and Recommended as an Important Branch of Political Economy* (London, 1816).

Of the Interchangeable Course, or Variety of Things in the Whole World ... Written in French by Loys le Roy Called Regius: And Translated into English by R A. (London, printed by Charles Yetsweirt, 1594).

Oliver, Thomas, *The Topographical Conductor, or Descriptive Guide to Newcastle and Gateshead* (Newcastle-on-Tyne, 1851).

Owen, W., *An Authentic Account Published by the King's Authority of All the Fairs in England and Wales* (London, 1756).

Oxford in 1710 from the Travels of Zacharias Conrad von Uffenbach, ed. W.H. Quarrell and W.J.C. Quarrell (Oxford: Blackwell, 1928).

Paley, William, *Reasons for Contentment Addressed to the Labouring Part of the British Public* (1793).

Philemerus, J., *Of Luxury, More Particularly with Respect to Apparel* (London, 1736).

Pigot, I.M.B., *History of the City of Chester* (Chester, 1815).

Pigot, James & Co., *National Commercial Directory ... of Chester ...* (London, 1828 and 1834).

Reminiscences of an Old Draper (London, 1876).

Sentiments of a Corn-Factor, on the Present Situation of the Corn Trade (London, 1758).

Sibbit, Adam, *A Dissertation, Moral and Political, on the Influence of Luxury and Refinement on Nations, with Reflections on the Manners of the Age at the Close of the 18th Century* (London, 1800).

Silvester, Eusebius, *The Causes of the Present High Price of Corn and Grain* (London, 1757).

Smith, Charles, *Three Tracts on the Corn Trade* (London, 1767).

Smith, Mary, *The Autobiography of Mary Smith, Schoolmistress and Nonconformist* (London: Bemrose and Sons, 1892).

Smith, S.D. (ed.), *'An Exact and Industrious Tradesman': The Letter Book of Joseph Symson of Kendal 1711–1720* (Oxford: Oxford University Press, 2002).

The Art of Contentment: By the Author of 'The Whole Duty of Man' (Oxford, 1719).

The Case of the Fair-Trader (London, 1720?).

The Case of the Shopkeepers, Manufacturers and Fair Traders of England, against the Hawkers, Pedlars, and other Clandestine Traders (London, 1730).

The Commercial Directory for 1816–17 (Manchester, 1816).

The Court Leet Records of the Manor of Manchester from 1552 to 1686, and from 1731 to 1846 (12 vols, Manchester: Henry Blacklock, 1884–90).

The Noels and The Milbankes: Their Letters for Twenty-Five Years 1767–1792: Presented as a Narrative by Malcolm Elwin (London: Macdonald, 1967).

The Policy of the Tax upon Retailers Considered (London, 1786).

The Strangers' Guide through Birkenhead (Birkenhead: Law & Pinkney, 1847).

The Trade of England Revived (London, 1681), in J. Thirsk and J.P. Cooper (eds), *Seventeenth-Century Economic Documents* (Oxford: Clarendon Press, 1972).

The Tradesman's Director, or the London and Country Shopkeeper's Useful Companion (London, 1756).

The Whole Duty of Man (1704 edn, London).

Tucker, J., *A Brief Essay on the Advantages and Disadvantages which Respectively Attend France and Great Britain with Regard to Trade* (2nd edn, London, 1750).

Turner, Thomas, *The Diary of a Georgian Shopkeeper: A Selection by R.W. Blencowe and M.A. Lower*, ed. G.H. Jennings (Oxford: Oxford University Press, 1979).

UU, H., *Hints for Country Shopkeepers* (Moulton, 1847).

Vincent, David (ed.), *Testaments of Radicalism: Memoirs of Working Class Politicians 1790–1885* (London: Europa, 1977).

Webster, John, *The Duchess of Malfi*, IV, ii, 51–2 (1623; New Mermaid edn, London: A. & C. Black, 1993).

What is Luxury? ... by a Lay Observer (London, 1829).

White, Francis and Co., *History and General Directory of the Borough of Birmingham* (Sheffield, 1850).

White, Henry, *The Record of My Life: An Autobiography* (Cheltenham, 1889).

White, William, *Directory and Topography of Leeds, Bradford, Halifax, Huddersfield, Wakefield, and the Whole of the Clothing Districts of the West Riding of Yorkshire* (Sheffield: W. White, 1847).

White, William, *History, Gazetteer, and Directory of Leicestershire, and the Small County of Rutland* (Sheffield, 1846).

Whittemore, J., *Whittemore's Royal Brighton Guide* (Brighton, 1826).

Newspapers and Periodicals

Adam's Weekly Courant (subsequently *Chester Courant*)
Annals of Agriculture
Aris's Birmingham Gazette
Bradford Observer
Bury and Norwich Post and East Anglian
Cheshire Observer and General Advertizer
Chester Chronicle
Cheshire Sheaf
Derby Mercury
Illustrated London News
Keene's Bath Journal
Liverpool Mercury
London Gazette
Macclesfield Courier
Manchester Guardian

Manchester Magazine
Manchester Mercury
Manchester Times and Lancashire and Cheshire Examiner
Sheffield and Rotherham Independent
Sheffield Independent
Stockport Advertizer
Stockport Monthly Magazine and Journal
The Architectural Magazine and Journal

Acts of Parliament

An Act for Enlarging the Market Place, and Regulating the Markets, within the Town of Sheffield ... 27 Geo III c. 5.
An Act for Removing the Market between King Street and Castle Street in the Town of Sheffield ... 10 & 11 Victoria, cap. xlv.

Parliamentary Papers

A Copy of the Evidence Taken, and Report Made, by the Assistant Poor Law Commissioners Sent to Inquire into the State of the Population in Stockport, 1842, XXXV (158).
Journals of the House of Commons
Minutes of Evidence Taken before the Committee to Alter and Amend Two Acts ... as far as Relates to the Price and Assize of Bread, 1812–13, III (259).
Report from the Commissioners on Municipal Corporations in England and Wales, North-Western Circuit, 1835, XXVI (116), p. 497.
Report from the Select Committee on Manufactures, Commerce and Shipping, 1833, VI (H.C.690).
Reports of the Special Assistant Poor Law Commissioners on the Employment of Women and Children in Agriculture, 1843, XII, [510], p. 1.
Return of the Number of Hawkers Licensed in England, Scotland and Ireland, in Each of the Years, 1800, 1810, 1820, 1830, 1840 and 1843, 1844, XXXII (123), p. 377.

Secondary Sources

Adams, Suzanne, 'Purchasers from the Parsonage: Observations on Bath Dress and Reactive Shopping by the Penrose Family, 1766–67', *Costume*, 39 (2005): 79–90.
Adburgham, Alison, *Shops and Shopping 1800–1914: Where, and in What Manner the Well-dressed Englishwoman Bought Her Clothes* (London: George Allen & Unwin, 1981).

Alayrac-Fielding, Vanessa, "'Frailty, Thy Name is China": Women, Chinoiserie and the Threat of Low Culture in Eighteenth-Century England', *Women's History Review*, 18/4 (2009): 659–68.

Alexander, Andrew and Phillips, Simon, "'Fair Play for the Small Man": Perspectives on the Contribution of the Independent Shopkeeper 1939 – *c.*1945', *Business History*, 48/1 (2006): 69–89.

Alexander, David, *Retailing in England during the Industrial Revolution* (London: Athlone Press, 1970).

Alexander, Nicholas and Akehurst, Gary (eds), *The Emergence of Modern Retailing, 1750–1950* (London: Frank Cass, 1999).

Allen, R.C. and Weisdorf, J.L., 'Was there an "Industrious Revolution" before the Industrial Revolution? An Empirical Exercise for England, *c.*1300–1830', *Economic History Review*, 64/3 (2011): 715–29.

Ashmore, Sonia, 'Liberty and Lifestyle: Shopping for Art and Luxury in Nineteenth-Century London', in Hussey and Ponsonby (eds), *Buying for the Home*.

Astle, William (ed.), *'Stockport Advertizer' Centenary History of Stockport* (Stockport, 1922).

Bailey, Lucy A., 'Consumption and Status: Shopping for Clothes in a Nineteenth-Century Bedfordshire Gentry Household', *Midland History*, 36/1 (2011): 89–114.

Bal, Mieke, 'Telling Objects: A Narrative Perspective on Collecting', in Elsner and Cardinal (eds), *The Cultures of Collecting*.

Barker, Hannah, "'Smoke Cities": Northern Industrial Towns in Late Georgian England', *Urban History*, 31/2 (2004): 175–90.

Barker, Hannah, *The Business of Women: Female Enterprise and Urban Development in Northern England 1760–1830* (Oxford: Oxford University Press, 2006).

Barker, Hannah and Harvey, Karen, 'Women Entrepreneurs and Urban Expansion: Manchester 1760–1820', in Sweet and Lane (eds), *Women and Urban Life in Eighteenth-Century England*.

Batchelor, Robert, 'On the Movement of Porcelains', in Brewer and Trentmann (eds), *Consuming Cultures, Global Perspectives*.

Baudrillard, Jean, 'The System of Collecting', in Elsner and Cardinal (eds), *Cultures of Collecting*.

Bauman, Zygmunt, *Consuming Life* (Cambridge: Polity Press, 2007).

Benjamin, Walter, *The Arcades Project*, trans. Howard Eiland and Kevin McLaughlin (Cambridge, MA: Belknap Press, 1999).

Benson, John, *The Rise of Consumer Society in Britain 1880–1980* (London: Longman, 1994).

Benson, John and Shaw, Gareth (eds), *The Evolution of Retail Systems, c.1800–1914* (Leicester: Leicester University Press, 1992).

Benson, John and Ugolini, Laura (eds), *A Nation of Shopkeepers: Five Centuries of British Retailing* (London, 2003).

Berg, Maxine, *Luxury and Pleasure in Eighteenth-Century Britain* (Oxford: Oxford University Press, 2005).

Berg, Maxine and Clifford, Helen (eds), *Consumers and Luxury: Consumer Culture in Europe 1650–1850* (Manchester: Manchester University Press, 1999).

Berg, Maxine and Clifford, Helen, 'Selling Consumption in the Eighteenth Century: Advertising and the Trade Card in Britain and France', *Cultural and Social History*, 4/2 (2007): 145–70.

Berg, Maxine and Eger, Elizabeth (eds), *Luxury in the Eighteenth Century: Debates, Desires and Delectable Goods* (Basingstoke: Palgrave Macmillan, 2003).

Berg, Maxine and Eger, Elizabeth, 'The Rise and Fall of the Luxury Debates', in Berg and Eger (eds), *Luxury in the Eighteenth Century*.

Berry, Christopher J., 'Hume and Superfluous Value (or the Problem with Epictetus' Slippers) in Wennerlind and Schabas (eds), *David Hume's Political Economy*.

Berry, Helen, 'Polite Consumption: Shopping in Eighteenth-Century England', *Transactions of the Royal Historical Society*, 12 (2002): 375–94.

Bickham, Troy, 'Eating the Empire: Interactions of Food, Cookery and Imperialism in Eighteenth-Century Britain', *Past and Present*, 198 (2008): 71–109.

Blackman, Janet, 'The Food Supply of an Industrial Town: A Study of Sheffield's Public Markets 1780–1900', *Business History*, 5/2 (1963): 83–98.

Blondé, B. and van Damme, I, 'Retail Growth and Consumer Changes in a Declining Urban Economy: Antwerp (1650–1750)', *Economic History Review*, 63/3 (2010): 638–63.

Bohstedt, John, *The Politics of Provisions: Food Riots, Moral Economy and Market Transition in England, c.1550–1850* (Farnham: Ashgate, 2010).

Borsay, Peter, *The English Urban Renaissance: Culture and Society in the Provincial Town 1660–1770* (Oxford: Oxford University Press, 1989).

Borsay, Peter, *A History of Leisure* (Basingstoke: Palgrave Macmillan, 2006).

Bourdieu, Pierre, *Distinction: A Social Critique of the Judgement of Taste*, trans. Richard Nice (London: Routledge & Kegan Paul, 1984).

Brewer, John, *The Pleasures of the Imagination: English Culture in the Eighteenth Century* (London: HarperCollins, 1997).

Brewer, John and Porter, Roy (eds), *Consumption and the World of Goods* (London: Routledge, 1993).

Brewer, John and Trentmann, Frank (eds), *Consuming Cultures, Global Perspectives: Historical Trajectories, Transnational Exchanges* (Oxford: Berg, 2006).

Britnell, Richard, 'Urban Economic Regulation and Economic Morality in Medieval England', in Richard Britnell, *Markets, Trade and Economic Development in England and Europe, 1050–1550* (Farnham: Ashgate Variorum, 2009).

Brittain, Frederick, *The Corporation and the Markets* (Sheffield, 1876).

Brown, David, 'The Autobiography of a Pedlar: John Lomas of Hollinsclough, Staffordshire (1747–1823)', *Midland History*, 21 (1996): 156–66.

Brown, David, '"Persons of Infamous Character" or "An Honest, Industrious and Useful Description of People"? The Textile Pedlars of Alstonfield and the Role of Peddling in Industrialization', *Textile History*, 31/1 (2000): 1–26.

Campbell, Colin, *The Romantic Ethic and the Spirit of Modern Consumerism* (Oxford: Basil Blackwell, 1987).

Campbell, Colin, 'Understanding Traditional and Modern Patterns of Consumption in Eighteenth-Century England: A Character-Action Approach', in Brewer and Porter (eds), *Consumption and the World of Goods*.

Carnevali, Francesca, 'Luxury for the Masses: Jewellery and Jewellers in London and Birmingham in the 19th Century', *Enterprises et Histoires*, 46 (2007): 56–70.

Chartres, John (ed.), *Chapters from the Agrarian History of England and Wales, 1500–1750: Agricultural Markets and Trade 1500–1750* (Cambridge: Cambridge University Press, 1990).

Chartres, John, 'The Marketing of Agricultural Produce, 1640–1750', in Chartres (ed.), *Chapters from the Agrarian History of England and Wales*.

Chilton, C.W., '"The Universal British Directory" – A Warning', *Local Historian*, 15/3 (1982): 144–6.

Clark, J.C.D., *English Society 1688–1832* (Cambridge: Cambridge University Press, 1985).

Clery, E.J., *The Feminization Debate in Eighteenth-Century England: Literature, Commerce and Luxury* (Basingstoke: Palgrave Macmillan, 2004).

Cohen, Deborah, *Household Gods: The British and Their Possessions* (New Haven and London: Yale University Press, 2006).

Collinson, Barbara, *Kendals: One Hundred and Fifty Years 1836–1986* (Manchester, 1986).

Connell, Philip, 'Bibliomania: Book Collecting, Cultural Politics, and the Rise of Literary Heritage in Romantic Britain', *Representations*, 71 (Summer 2000): 24–47.

Corfield, Penelope J., 'Business Leaders and Town Gentry in Early Industrial Britain: Specialist Occupations and Shared Urbanism', *Urban History*, 39/1 (2012): 20–50.

Cox, Nancy, *The Complete Tradesman: A Study of Retailing in Early Modern England* (Aldershot: Ashgate, 2000).

Cox, Nancy and Dannehl, Karin, *Perceptions of Retailing in Early Modern England* (Aldershot: Ashgate, 2007).

Crossick, Geoffrey and Jaumain, Serge (eds), *Cathedrals of Consumption: The European Department Store, 1850–1939* (Aldershot: Ashgate, 1999).

Crossick, Geoffrey and Jaumain, Serge, 'The World of the Department Store: Distribution, Culture and Social Change', in Crossick and Jaumain (eds), *Cathedrals of Consumption*.

Crowley, John E., *The Invention of Comfort: Sensibilities and Design in Early Modern Britain and Early America* (Baltimore and London: Johns Hopkins University Press, 2001).

Cudworth, William, *Yorkshire Speyks and Bradfurth Dialect Sketches* (Bradford: W.H. Brocklehurst, 1906).

Cunningham, Andrew S., 'David Hume's Account of Luxury', *Journal of the History of Economic Thought*, 27/3 (2005): 231–50.

Dant, Tim, *Material Culture in the Social World* (Maidenhead: Open University Press, 2005).

Daunton, Martin, *State and Market in Victorian Britain: War, Welfare and Capitalism* (Woodbridge: Boydell Press, 2008).

Davis, Dorothy, *A History of Shopping* (London: Routledge & Kegan Paul, 1966).

Douglas, Mary, 'In Defence of Shopping', in Falk and Campbell (eds), *The Shopping Experience*.

Edwards, Clive, *Turning Houses into Homes: A History of the Retailing and Consumption of Domestic Furnishings* (Aldershot: Ashgate, 2005).

Edwards, Clive and Ponsonby, Margaret, 'Desirable Commodity or Practical Necessity? The Sale and Consumption of Second-Hand Furniture, 1750–1900', in Hussey and Ponsonby (eds), *Buying for the Home*.

Elliott, Paul, 'The Origins of the "Creative Class": Provincial Urban Society, Scientific Culture and Socio-Political Marginality in Britain in the Eighteenth and Nineteenth Centuries', *Social History*, 28/3 (2003): 361–87.

Elliott, Paul, 'Towards a Geography of English Scientific Culture: Provincial Identity and Literary and Philosophical Culture in the English County Town, 1750–1850', *Urban History*, 32/3 (2005): 391–412.

Ellis, Joyce M., *The Georgian Town 1680–1840* (Basingstoke: Palgrave, 2001).

Ellis, Markham (ed.), *Tea and the Tea-Table in Eighteenth-Century England* (4 vols, London: Pickering & Chatto, 2010).

Elsner, John and Cardinal, Roger (eds), *The Cultures of Collecting* (London: Reaktion, 1994).

Evensky, Jerry, *Adam Smith's Moral Philosophy: A Historical and Contemporary Perspective on Markets, Law, Ethics, and Culture* (Cambridge: Cambridge University Press, 2005).

Everitt, Alan, 'The Marketing of Agricultural Produce, 1500–1640', in Chartres (ed.), *Chapters from the Agrarian History of England and Wales*.

Falk, Pasi and Campbell, Colin (eds), *The Shopping Experience* (London: Sage, 1997).

Fawcett, Trevor, *Bath Commercialis'd: Shops, Trades and Market at the 18th-Century Spa* (Bath: Ruton, 2002).

Field, Clive D., 'Counting Religion in England and Wales: The Long Eighteenth Century, c.1680–1840', *Journal of Ecclesiastical History*, 63/4 (2012): 693–720.

Finn, Margot, *The Character of Credit: Personal Debt in English Culture, 1740–1914* (Cambridge: Cambridge University Press, 2003).

Fontaine, Laurence, *History of Pedlars in Europe* (Cambridge: Polity, 1996).

Foster, Charles F., *Seven Households: Life in Cheshire and Lancashire 1582–1774* (Northwich: Arley Hall Press, 2002).

Foster, Charles F., *Capital and Innovation: How Britain Became the First Industrial Nation* (Northwich: Arley Hall Press, 2004).

Fowler, Christina, 'Robert Mansbridge: A Rural Tailor and His Customers 1811–1815', *Textile History*, 28/1 (1997): 29–38.

Garon, Sheldon and Maclachan, Patricia L. (eds), *The Ambivalent Consumer: Questioning Consumption in East Asia and the West* (Ithaca and London: Cornell University Press, 2006).

Gauci, Perry (ed.), *Regulating the British Economy, 1660–1850* (Aldershot: Ashgate, 2011).

Gemmett, Robert J. (ed.), *The Consummate Collector: William Beckford's Letters to His Bookseller* (Norwich: Michael Russell, 2000).

Girouard, Mark, *Life in the English Country House: A Social and Architectural History* (New Haven and London: Yale University Press, 1978).

Glaisyer, Natasha, *The Culture of Commerce in England 1660–1720* (Woodbridge: Boydell Press for the Royal Historical Society, 2006).

Glen, Robert, *Urban Workers in the Early Industrial Revolution* (London: Croom Helm, 1983).

Grady, Kevin, 'Profit, Property Interests, and Public Spirit: The Provision of Markets and Commercial Amenities in Leeds, 1822–29', *Thoresby Society Publications*, 54/3 (1976): 165–95.

Gregory, Jeremy, '"For All Sorts and Conditions of Men": The Social Life of the Book of Common Prayer during the Long Eighteenth Century; or, Bringing the History of Religion and Social History Together', *Social History*, 34/1 (2009): 29–54.

Gregory, Jeremy, 'Transforming the "Age of Reason" into "an Age of Faiths"; or, Putting Religions and Beliefs (Back) into the Eighteenth Century', *Journal for Eighteenth-Century Studies*, 32/3, (2009): 287–305.

Gregson, Nicky and Crewe, Louise, *Second-Hand Cultures* (Oxford: Berg, 2003).

Greig, Hannah, 'Leading the Fashion: The Material Culture of London's *Beau Monde*', in Styles and Vickery (eds), *Gender, Taste, and Material Culture in Britain and North America* 1700–1830.

Griffin, Emma, 'Sports and Celebrations in English Market Towns, 1660–1750', *Historical Research*, 75 (2002):188–208.

Gurney, Peter J., '"The Sublime of the Bazaar": A Moment in the Making of a Consumer Culture in Mid-Nineteenth Century England', *Journal of Social History*, 40/2 (2006): 385–405.

Haggerty, Sheryllynne, 'Women, Work, and the Consumer Revolution: Liverpool in the Late Eighteenth Century', in Benson and Ugolini (eds), *A Nation of Shopkeepers*.

Hann, Andrew, 'Modernity and the Marketplace', in S. Pinches, M. Whalley and D. Postles (eds), *The Market Place and the Place of the Market* (Leicester: Friends of the Centre for English Local History, 2004).

Hann, Andrew, 'Industrialisation and the Service Economy', in Stobart and Raven (eds), *Towns, Regions and Industries*.

Hann, Andrew and Stobart, Jon, 'Sites of Consumption: The Display of Goods in Provincial Shops in Eighteenth-Century England', *Cultural and Social History*, 2/2 (2005): 165–87.

Harris, Bob, 'The Enlightenment, Towns and Urban Society in Scotland, *c.*1760–1820', *English Historical Review*, 126/522 (2011): 1097–1136.

Harvey, Karen, 'Men Making Home: Masculinity and Domesticity in Eighteenth-Century Britain', *Gender and History*, 21/3 (2009): 520–40.

Hay, Douglas, 'The State and the Market in 1800: Lord Kenyon and Mr Waddington', *Past and Present*, 162 (1999): 101–63.

Heller, Ben, 'The "Mene Peuple" and the Polite Spectator: The Individual in the Crowd at Eighteenth-Century London Fairs', *Past and Present*, 208 (2010): 131–57.

Hey, David, *Packmen, Carriers and Packhorse Roads: Trade and Communications in North Derbyshire and South Yorkshire* (Leicester: Leicester University Press, 1980).

Hill, Rosemary, *God's Architect: Pugin and the Building of Romantic Britain* (London: Allen Lane, 2008).

Hilton, Boyd, *The Age of Atonement: The Influence of Evangelicalism on Social and Economic Thought 1785–1865* (Oxford: Clarendon Press, 1988).

Hilton, Matthew, *Consumerism in Twentieth-Century Britain: The Search for a Historical Movement* (Cambridge: Cambridge University Press, 2003).

Hilton, Matthew, 'The Death of a Consumer Society', *Transactions of the Royal Historical Society*, 18 (2008): 211–36.

Hodson, Deborah, 'Civic Identity, Custom and Commerce: Victorian Market Halls in the Manchester Region', *Manchester Region History Review*, 12 (1998): 34–43.

Hodson, Deborah, '"The Municipal Store": Adaptation and Development in the Retail Markets of Nineteenth-Century Urban Lancashire', in Alexander and Akehurst (eds), *The Emergence of Modern Retailing*.

Humphries, Jane, *Childhood and Child Labour in the British Industrial Revolution* (Cambridge: Cambridge University Press, 2010).

Hunt, Margaret R., *The Middling Sort: Commerce, Gender, and the Family in England, 1680–1780* (Berkeley and London: University of California Press, 1996).

Hussey, David, 'Guns, Horses and Stylish Waistcoats? Male Consumer Activity and Domestic Shopping in Late-Eighteenth- and Early Nineteenth-Century England', in Hussey and Ponsonby (eds), *Buying for the Home*.

Hussey, David and Ponsonby, Margaret (eds), *Buying for the Home: Shopping for the Domestic from the Seventeenth Century to the Present* (Aldershot: Ashgate, 2008).

Hussey, David and Ponsonby, Margaret, *The Single Homemaker and Material Culture in the Long Eighteenth Century* (Farnham: Ashgate, 2012).

Hutchinson, Christopher, 'George Reynoldson, Upholsterer of York, fl. 1716–1764', *Furniture History*, 12 (1976): 29–33.

Isaac, Peter and McKay, Barry (eds), *The Reach of Print: Making, Selling and Using Books* (Winchester: St Paul's Bibliographies, 1998).

Isaac, Peter and McKay, Barry (eds), *The Human Face of the Book Trade* (Winchester: St Paul's Bibliographies, 1999).

Jefferys, James B., *Retail Trading in Britain 1850–1950* (Cambridge: Cambridge University Press, 1954).

Jensen, Kristian, *Revolution and the Antiquarian Book: Reshaping the Past, 1730–1815* (Cambridge: Cambridge University Press, 2011).

Johnson, James H. and Pooley, Colin G. (eds), *The Structure of Nineteenth Century Cities* (London: Croom Helm, 1982).

Karababa, Eminegül, 'Investigating Early Modern Ottoman Consumer Culture in the Light of Bursa Probate Inventories', *Economic History Review*, 65/1 (2012): 194–219.

Kelly, Ian, *Beau Brummell: The Ultimate Dandy* (London: Hodder & Stoughton, 2005).

Kowaleski-Wallace, Elizabeth, *Consuming Subjects: Women, Shopping and Business in the Eighteenth Century* (New York: Columbia University Press, 1997).

Lambert, Miles, '"Cast-off Wearing Apparell": The Consumption and Distribution of Second-Hand Clothing in Northern England during the Long Eighteenth Century', *Textile History*, 35/1 (2004): 1–26.

Lambert, Miles, '"Sent from Town": Commissioning Clothing in Britain during the Long Eighteenth Century', *Costume*, 43 (2009): 66–84.

Lambert, Miles, 'Bespoke versus Ready-Made: The Work of the Tailor in Eighteenth-Century Britain', *Costume*, 44 (2010): 56–65.

Lancaster, Bill, *The Department Store: A Social History* (Leicester: Leicester University Press, 1995).

Lee, Robert (ed.), *Commerce and Culture: Nineteenth-Century Business Elites* (Farnham: Ashgate, 2011).

Lee, Robert, 'Commerce and Culture: A Critical Assessment of the Role of Cultural Factors in Commerce and Trade from *c.*1750 to the Early Twentieth Century', in Lee (ed.), *Commerce and Culture*.

Lemire, Beverly, 'Consumerism in Preindustrial and Early Industrial England: The Trade in Secondhand Clothes', *Journal of British Studies*, 27/1 (1988): 1–24.

Lemire, Beverly, *Fashion's Favourite: The Cotton Trade and the Consumer in Britain, 1660–1800* (Oxford: Oxford University Press, 1991).

Lemire, Beverly, 'Second-hand Beaux and "Red-armed Belles": Conflict and the Creation of Fashion in England, *c.*1660–1800', *Continuity and Change*, 15/3 (2000): 391–417.

Lemire, Beverly (ed.), *The Force of Fashion in Politics and Society: Global Perspectives from Early Modern to Contemporary Times* (Farnham: Ashgate, 2010).

Lemire, Beverly, 'Fashion and the Practice of History: A Political Legacy', in Lemire (ed.), *The Force of Fashion*.

Louth, Janet, 'Introduction', in Janet Louth (ed.), *William Law, Selected Writings* (Manchester: Carcanet, 1990).

McCracken, Grant, *Culture and Consumption: New Approaches to the Symbolic Character of Consumer Goods and Activities* (Bloomington: Indiana University Press, 1988).

McCulloch Agnes, *The Headland with the Birches: A History of Birkenhead* (Birkenhead: Countywise, 1991).

MacKeith, Margaret, *The History and Conservation of Shopping Arcades* (London: Mansell, 1986).

McKendick, Neil, 'The Commercialization of Fashion', in McKendrick, Brewer and Plumb, *The Birth of a Consumer Society*.

McKendrick, Neil, Brewer, John and Plumb, J.H., *The Birth of a Consumer Society: The Commercialization of Eighteenth-Century England* (London: Hutchinson, 1982).

de Manchi, Neil, 'Adam Smith's Accommodation of "Altogether Endless" Desires', in Berg and Clifford (eds), *Consumers and Luxury*.

Mathias, Peter, 'Economic Growth and Robinson Crusoe', *European Review*, 15/1 (2007): 17–31.

Million, Ivor R., *A History of Didsbury* (Manchester: E.J. Morton, 1969).

Mitchell, Ian, 'The Book Trades in Cheshire 1680–1830', *Transactions of the Lancashire and Cheshire Antiquarian Society*, 95 (1999): 23–38.

Mitchell, Ian, 'The Changing Role of Fairs in the Long Eighteenth Century: Evidence from the North Midlands', *Economic History Review*, 60/3 (2007): 545–73.

Mitchell, Ian, 'Innovation in Non-Food Retailing in the Early Nineteenth Century: The Curious Case of the Bazaar', *Business History*, 52/6 (2010): 875–91.

Mitchell, Ian, '"Old books – New Bound"? Selling Second-Hand Books in England, c.1680–1850', in Stobart and van Damme (eds), *Modernity and the Second-Hand Trade*.

Mitchell, Ian, 'Retailing Innovation and Urban Markets c.1800–1850', *Journal of Historical Research in Marketing*, 2/3 (2010): 287–99.

Mitchell, Ian, 'Supplying the Masses: Retailing and Town Governance in Macclesfield, Stockport and Birkenhead, 1780–1860, *Urban History*, 38/2 (2011): 256–75.

Mitchell, S.I., 'Food Shortages and Public Order in Cheshire, 1757–1812', *Transactions of the Lancashire and Cheshire Antiquarian Society*, 81 (1982): 42–66.

Mokyr, Joel, *The Enlightened Economy: Britain and the Industrial Revolution 1700–1850* (London: Penguin, 2009).

Morrison, Kathryn A., *English Shops and Shopping: An Architectural History* (New Haven and London: Yale University Press, 2004).

Moss, Michael and Turton, Alison, *A Legend of Retailing: House of Fraser* (London: Weidenfeld & Nicolson, 1989).

Mui, Hoh-Cheung and Mui, Lorna H., *Shops and Shopkeeping in Eighteenth-Century England* (London: Routledge, 1989).

Muldrew, Craig, 'Interpreting the Market: The Ethics of Credit and Community Relations in Early Modern England', *Social History*, 18/2 (1993): 167–83.

Muldrew, Craig, *The Economy of Obligation: The Culture of Credit and Social Relations in Early Modern England* (Basingstoke: Macmillan, 1998).

de Munck, Bert, 'One Counter and Your Own Account: Redefining Illicit Labour in Early Modern Antwerp', *Urban History*, 37/1 (2010): 26–44.

Myers, Robin and Harris, Michael (eds), *Property of a Gentleman: The Formation, Organisation and Dispersal of the Private Library 1620–1920* (Winchester and Delaware: St Paul's Bibliographies, 1991).

Myers, Robin, Harris, Michael and Mandelbrote, Giles (eds), *Fairs, Markets and the Itinerant Book Trade* (New Castle: Oak Knoll and London: British Library, 2007).

National Trust, *Kedleston Hall* (London: The National Trust, 1988).

Offer, Avner, *The Challenge of Affluence: Self-Control and Well-Being in the United States and Britain since 1950* (Oxford: Oxford University Press, 2006).

Ogilvie, Sheilagh, *Institutions and European Trade: Merchant Guilds, 1000–1800* (Cambridge: Cambridge University Press, 2011).

Peck, Linda Levy, *Consuming Splendour: Society and Culture in Seventeenth-Century England* (Cambridge: Cambridge University Press, 2005).

Pennell, Sara, 'Consumption and Consumerism in Early Modern England', *Historical Journal*, 42/2 (1999): 549–64.

Pennell, Sara, '"All but the Kitchen Sink": Household Sales and the Circulation of Second-Hand Goods in Early Modern England', in Stobart and van Damme (eds), *Modernity and the Second-Hand Trade*.

Pevsner, Nikolaus, *The Buildings of England: Derbyshire* (Harmondsworth: Penguin, 1986).

Phillips, Martin, 'The Evolution of Markets and Shops in Britain', in Benson and Shaw (eds), *The Evolution of Retail Systems*.

Place, Geoffrey, 'The Quest for a Market Charter', *Cheshire History*, 5 (1980): 11–21.

Poole, William, 'The Duplicates of Sir Hans Sloane in the Bodleian Library: A Detective Story, with Some Comments on Library Organisation', *Bodleian Library Record*, 23/2 (2010): 192–213.

Poovey, Mary, *Genres of the Credit Economy: Mediating Value in Eighteenth and Nineteenth-Century Britain* (Chicago: University of Chicago Press, 2008).

Popp, Andrew, 'Building the Market: John Shaw of Wolverhampton and Commercial Travelling in Early Nineteenth-Century England', *Business History*, 49/3 (2007): 321–47.

Popp, Andrew, 'From Town to Town: How Commercial Travel Connected Manufacturers and Markets during the Industrial Revolution', *Journal of Historical Geography*, 35/4 (2009): 642–67.

Porter, Roy, 'Consumption: Disease of the Consumer Society', in Brewer and Porter (eds), *Consumption and the World of Goods*.

Porter, Roy, *Enlightenment: Britain and the Creation of the Modern World* (London: Allen Lane, 2001).

Porter, Roy, *Flesh in the Age of Reason* (London: Allen Lane, 2003).

Potvin, John and Myzelev, Alla (eds), *Material Cultures 1740–1920: The Meanings and Pleasures of Collecting* (Farnham: Ashgate, 2009).

Potvin, John and Myzelev, Alla, 'Introduction: The Material of Visual Cultures', in Potvin and Myzelev, *Material Cultures*.

Powell, Michael, 'Towards a History of Book-Ownership in Manchester', *Transactions of the Lancashire and Cheshire Antiquarian Society*, 97 (2001): 121–36.

Powell, Michael and Wyke, Terry, 'Penny Capitalism in the Manchester Book Trade: The Case of James Weatherley', in Isaac and McKay (eds), *The Reach of Print*.

Prickett, Stephen, *Narrative, Religion and Science: Fundamentalism versus Irony, 1700–1999* (Cambridge: Cambridge University Press, 2002).

Prochaska, F.K., 'Charity Bazaars in Nineteenth-Century England', *Journal of British Studies*, 16/2 (1977): 62–84.

Raven, James, *The Business of Books: Booksellers and the English Book Trade 1450–1850* (New Haven and London: Yale University Press, 2007).

Richmond, Wilfrid, *Christian Economics* (London, 1888).

Richmond, Wilfrid, *Economic Morals: Four Lectures* (London, 1890).

Riello, Giorgio, *A Foot in the Past: Consumers, Producers and Footwear in the Long Eighteenth Century* (Oxford: Oxford University Press, 2006).

Roche, Daniel, *A History of Everyday Things: The Birth of Consumption in France, 1600–1800* (Cambridge: Cambridge University Press, 2000).

Schmiechen, James and Carls, Kenneth, *The British Market Hall: A Social and Architectural History* (New Haven and London: Yale University Press, 1999).

Scola, Roger, 'Retailing in the Nineteenth-Century Town: Some Problems and Possibilities', in Johnson and Pooley (eds), *The Structure of Nineteenth Century Cities*.

Scola, Roger, *Feeding the Industrial City: The Food Supply of Manchester 1770–1870* (Manchester: Manchester University Press, 1992).

Scragg, Brenda J., 'William Ford, Manchester Bookseller', in Isaac and McKay (eds), *The Human Face of the Book Trade*.

Scruton, William, *Bradford Fifty Years Ago* (Bradford: G.F. Sewell, 1897).

Seigel, Jerrold, *Modernity and Bourgeois Life: Society, Politics, and Culture in England, France, and Germany since 1750* (Cambridge: Cambridge University Press, 2012).

Sekora, John, *Luxury: The Concept in Western Thought, Eden to Smollett* (Baltimore and London: Johns Hopkins University Press, 1977).

Shaw, Gareth, *British Directories as Sources in Historical Geography*, Historical Geography Research Series, No. 8 (Norwich, 1982).

Shaw, Gareth, 'The Study of Retail Development', in Benson and Shaw (eds), *The Evolution of Retail Systems*.

Shaw, Gareth and Wild, M.T., 'Retail Patterns in the Victorian City', *Transactions of the Institute of British Geographers*, New Series, 4 (1979): 278–91.

Sheldon, Richard, 'Practical Economics in Eighteenth-Century England: Charles Smith on the Grain Trade and the Corn Laws 1756–72', *Historical Research*, 81/214 (2008): 636–62.

Slater, Don, *Consumer Culture and Modernity* (Cambridge: Polity Press, 1997).

Slobada, Stacey, 'Porcelain Bodies: Gender, Acquisitiveness, and Taste in Eighteenth-Century England', in Potvin and Myzelev (eds), *Material Cultures*.

Smail, John, *Merchants, Markets and Manufacture: The English Wool Textile Industry in the Eighteenth Century* (Basingstoke: Macmillan, 1999).

Smith, Catherine, 'Urban Improvement in the Nottinghamshire Market Town, 1770–1840', *Midland History*, 25 (2000): 90–114.

Smith, Catherine A., *The Renaissance of the Nottinghamshire Market Town 1680–1840* (Chesterfield: Merton Priory Press, 2007).

Smith, Woodruff D., *Consumption and the Making of Respectability 1600–1800* (London: Routledge, 2002).

Spufford, Margaret, *Small Books and Pleasant Histories: Popular Fiction and Its Readership in Seventeenth-Century England* (London: Methuen, 1981).

Spufford, Margaret, *The Great Reclothing of Rural England: Petty Chapmen and Their Wares in the Seventeenth Century* (London: Hambledon, 1984).

Starkie, Andrew, 'William Law and *The Fable of the Bees*', *Journal for Eighteenth Century Studies*, 32/3 (2009): 307–19.

Stearns, Peter N., *Consumerism in World History: The Global Transformation of Desire* (London: Routledge, 2001).

Steedman, Carolyn, *Master and Servant: Love and Labour in the English Industrial Age* (Cambridge: Cambridge University Press, 2007).

Stobart, Jon, 'The Spatial Organization of a Regional Economy: Central Places in North-West England in the Early Eighteenth Century', *Journal of Historical Geography*, 22/2 (1996): 147–59.

Stobart, Jon, 'Shopping Streets as Social Space: Consumerism, Improvement and Leisure in an Eighteenth-Century County Town', *Urban History*, 25/1 (1998): 3–21.

Stobart, Jon, 'The Economic and Social Worlds of Rural Craftsmen-Retailers in Eighteenth-Century Cheshire', *Agricultural History Review*, 52/2 (2004): 141–60.

Stobart, Jon, *The First Industrial Region: North-West England c.1700–60* (Manchester: Manchester University Press, 2004).

Stobart, Jon, 'Selling (through) Politeness: Advertising Provincial Shops in Eighteenth-Century England', *Cultural and Social History*, 5/3 (2008): 309–28.

Stobart, Jon, *Spend, Spend, Spend: A History of Shopping* (Stroud: Tempus, 2008).

Stobart, Jon, 'A History of Shopping: The Missing Link between Retail and Consumer Revolutions', *Journal of Historical Research in Marketing*, 2/3 (2010): 342–9.

Stobart, Jon, 'Gentlemen and Shopkeepers: Supplying the Country House in Eighteenth-Century England', *Economic History Review*, 64/3 (2011): 885–904.

Stobart, Jon, *Sugar and Spice: Grocers and Groceries in Provincial England, 1650–1830* (Oxford: Oxford University Press, 2013).

Stobart, Jon and van Damme, Ilja (eds), *Modernity and the Second-Hand Trade: European Consumption Cultures and Practices, 1700–1900* (Basingstoke: Palgrave Macmillan, 2010).

Stobart, Jon and Hann, Andrew, 'Retailing Revolution in the Eighteenth Century? Evidence from North-West England', *Business History*, 46/2 (2004): 171–194.

Stobart, Jon, Hann, Andrew and Morgan, Victoria, *Spaces of Consumption: Leisure and Shopping in the English Town, c. 1680–1830* (London: Routledge, 2007).

Stobart, Jon and Raven, Neil (eds), *Towns, Regions and Industries: Urban and Industrial Change in the Midlands, c. 1700–1840* (Manchester: Manchester University Press, 2005).

Stoker, David, 'The Ill-Gotten Library of "Honest Tom" Martin', in Myers and Harris (eds), *Property of a Gentleman*.

Stoker, David, '"To All Booksellers, Country Chapmen, Hawkers and Others": How the Population of East Anglia Obtained Its Printed Materials', in Myers, Harris and Mandelbrote (eds), *Fairs, Markets and the Itinerant Book Trade*.

Styles, John, 'Product Innovation in Early Modern London', *Past and Present*, 168 (2000): 124–69.

Styles, John, *The Dress of the People: Everyday Fashion in Eighteenth-Century England* (New Haven and London: Yale University Press, 2007).

Styles, John and Vickery, Amanda (eds), *Gender, Taste, and Material Culture in Britain and North America* 1700–1830 (New Haven: Yale Centre for British Art, 2006).

Sweet, Rosemary and Lane, Penelope (eds), *Women and Urban Life in Eighteenth-Century England* (Aldershot: Ashgate, 2002).

The Bromuff Story: A Brief Chronicle of 150 Years of Progress 1814–1964 (Bradford: Brown, Muff, 1964).

Thomas, Keith, *The Ends of Life: Roads to Fulfilment in Early Modern England* (Oxford: Oxford University Press, 2009).

Thomas, Nicholas, 'Licensed Curiosity: Cook's Pacific Voyages', in Elsner and Cardinal (eds), *The Cultures of Collecting*.

Thompson, E.P., *The Making of the English Working Class* (Harmondsworth: Penguin, 1968).

Thompson, E.P., 'The Moral Economy of the English Crowd in the Eighteenth Century', *Past and Present*, 50 (1971): 76–136.

Tickell, Shelley, 'The Prevention of Shoplifting in Eighteenth-Century London', *Journal of Historical Research in Marketing*, 2/3 (2010): 300–13.

Toplis, Alison, 'A Stolen Garment or a Reasonable Purchase? The Male Consumer and the Illicit Clothing Market in the First Half of the Nineteenth Century', in Stobart and van Damme (eds), *Modernity and the Second-Hand Trade.*

Toplis, Alison, *The Clothing Trade in Provincial England, 1800–1850* (London: Pickering & Chatto, 2011).

Trentmann, Frank, 'The Evolution of the Consumer', in Garon and Maclachan (eds), *The Ambivalent Consumer.*

Trentmann, Frank (ed.), *The Making of the Consumer: Knowledge, Power and Identity in the Modern World* (Oxford: Berg, 2006).

Trentmann, Frank, 'The Modern Genealogy of the Consumer', in Brewer and Trentmann (eds), *Consuming Cultures, Global Perspectives.*

Trentmann, Frank and Taylor, Vanessa, 'From Users to Consumers: Water Politics in Nineteenth-Century London', in Trentmann (ed.), *The Making of the Consumer.*

Uglow, Jenny, *The Lunar Men: The Friends Who Made the Future 1730–1810* (London: Faber, 2002).

van Damme, Ilja, 'Middlemen and the Creation of a "Fashion Revolution": The Experience of Antwerp in the Late Seventeenth and Eighteenth Centuries', in Lemire (ed.), *Force of Fashion.*

van Leeuvan, Marco H.D., 'Guilds and Middle-Class Welfare, 1550–1800: Provision for Burial, Sickness, Old Age and Widowhood', *Economic History Review*, 65/1 (2012): 61–90.

Vickery, Amanda, 'Women and the World of Goods: A Lancashire Consumer and Her Possessions, 1751–81', in Brewer and Porter (eds), *Consumption and the World of Goods.*

Vickery, Amanda, *Behind Closed Doors: At Home in Georgian England* (New Haven and London: Yale University Press, 2009).

de Vries, Jan, *The Industrious Revolution: Consumer Behaviour and the Household Economy, 1650 to the Present* (Cambridge: Cambridge University Press, 2008).

Walsh, Claire, 'The Newness of the Department Store: A View from the Eighteenth Century', in Crossick and Jaumain (eds), *Cathedrals of Consumption.*

Walsh, Claire, 'Shops, Shopping, and the Art of Decision-Making in Eighteenth-Century England', in Styles and Vickery (eds), *Gender, Taste, and Material Culture.*

Walsh, Claire, 'Shopping at First Hand? Mistresses, Servants and Shopping for the Household in Early Modern England', in Hussey and Ponsonby (eds), *Buying for the Home.*

Webb, Sidney and Beatrice, 'The Assize of Bread', *Economic Journal*, 14 (1904): 196–218.

Wennerlind, Carl and Schabas, Margaret (eds), *David Hume's Political Economy* (Abingdon: Routledge, 2008).

White, Eryn M., 'The Material World, Moderation and Methodism in Eighteenth-Century Wales', *Welsh History Review*, 23/3 (2007): 44–64.

Whitlock, Tammy C., *Crime, Gender and Consumer Culture in Nineteenth-Century England*, (Aldershot: Ashgate, 2005).

Wigston Smith, Chloe, '"Calico Madams": Servants, Consumption and the Calico Crisis', *Eighteenth-Century Life*, 31/2 (2007): 29–55.

Wigston Smith, Chloe, 'Clothes without Bodies: Objects, Humans, and the Marketplace in Eighteenth-Century It-Narratives and Trade Cards', *Eighteenth-Century Fiction*, 23/2 (2010–11): 347–80.

Wild, M.T. and Shaw, Gareth, 'Locational Behaviour of Urban Retailing during the Nineteenth Century: The Example of Kingston upon Hull', *Transactions of the Institute of British Geographers*, 61 (1974): 101–18.

Wild, M.T. and Shaw, G., 'Population Distribution and Retail Provision: The Case of the Halifax-Calder Valley Area of West Yorkshire during the Second Half of the Nineteenth Century', *Journal of Historical Geography*, 1/2 (1975): 193–210.

Willcock, H.D. (ed.), *Browns and Chester: Portrait of a Shop 1780–1946* (London: Lindsay Drummond for Mass-Observation, 1947).

Williams, Raymond, *Keywords: A Vocabulary of Culture and Society* (London: Croom Helm, 1976).

Wilson, A.N., *The Victorians* (London: Hutchinson, 2002).

Wilson, Arline, *William Roscoe: Commerce and Culture* (Liverpool: Liverpool University Press, 2008).

Wilson, Ross J. '"The Mystical Character of Commodities": The Consumer Society in 18th-Century England', *Post-Medieval Archaeology*, 42/1 (2008): 144–56.

Windsor, J. 'Identity Parades', in Elsner and Cardinal, *Cultures of Collecting*.

Winstanley, Michael J., *The Shopkeeper's World 1830–1914* (Manchester: Manchester University Press, 1983).

Woodward, Donald, '"Swords into Ploughshares": Recycling in Pre-Industrial England', *Economic History Review*, 38/2 (1985): 175–91.

Worrall, T.H., *Reminiscences of Early Life Spent in My Native Town of Macclesfield* (Macclesfield, 1897).

Unpublished Theses

Collins, Diane, 'Fixed-Shop Retailing: Shrewsbury and Wolverhampton 1660–1900', unpublished PhD thesis, University of Wolverhampton, 2002.

Foster, David, 'Albion's Sisters: A Study of Trade Directories and Female Economic Participation in the Mid-Nineteenth Century', unpublished PhD thesis, University of Exeter, 2002.

Giles, P.M., 'The Economic and Social Development of Stockport', unpublished MA thesis, University of Manchester, 1950.

Willshaw, E.M., 'The Inns of Chester, 1775–1832: The Functions of Provincial Inns and Their Importance to the Local Community', unpublished MA thesis, University of Leicester, 1979.

Index

Adam, Robert 121
advertisements 10, 133, 151,
     see also shop advertisements under
     Chester, Derby and Stockport
  for employees 56
  and fashion 43, 58, 105, 112,
     125, 147, 185, 186
  and politeness 58, 104,
     105, 183
  and prices 57, 132
affluence 94, 177
Alexander, David 130
Allestree, Richard 87–8, 91, 97
Alstonefield (Derbyshire) 66
Anti-Corn Law League 171
apprentices 50, 56, 184
apprenticeship 46–7, 48, 51, 56,
     134, 146
arcades 129, 139, 140
Ashbourne 16, 110, 131
Ashover (Derbyshire) 80, 120
assize of bread 25, 39, 46
auctions 139–40, 142
Austen, Jane 104, 116

bakers 22, 24–5, 28, 38–40, 43, 46–7, 51,
     58
Balguy, John 15, 34–5
Banbury 43, 134
Barbon, Nicholas 85, 94
Barnsley 16, 45, 80
  Cordwainers' Society 47
Bath 42, 101, 108, 110, 114–15,
     140, 142, 145–6
Baudrillard, Jean 117
bazaars 1, 4, 11, 129, 137, 139,
     140–44, 151, 179,
  in Bath 142
  in Brighton 142
  charity 171

and department stores 144, 146
  in London 140–41
  in markets 156, 160, 164–5
  in Manchester 142
  in Norwich 142–4
  rules 141–2
Benjamin, Walter 116, 117, 124
bibliomania 122–3
Birkenhead 131, 158–9
  and Liverpool 175–6
  markets 156, 158–9, 163, 168–9
  market committee 163, 168–9
  trade depression 173–4
Birmingham 5, 134, 135–6, 137
  markets 155–6, 157
  and metal goods 45, 100, 173
  retail occupations at 38–9
Blackburn 50
  markets 30, 165–6
Bolton
  market 166
  retail occupations at 39
book collectors 110–11, 119–24
  Beckford, William 123
  Boothby, William 110, 119
  Dibdin, Thomas Frognall 120, 122–3
  Philips, John Leigh 123
  Ratcliffe, John 120–21
  Roscoe, William 123
  Spencer, 2nd Earl 122, 124
book trades
  itinerant 68–9
  second-hand 71–3
books
  collecting 119–24
  increased access to 104, 110
  increased number published 104
  and polite society 109, 110, 118,
     121–2, 124
  prices 120–21, 151, 165

For Product Safety Concerns and Information please contact our
EU representative GPSR@taylorandfrancis.com Taylor & Francis
Verlag GmbH, Kaufingerstraße 24, 80331 München, Germany